The Sphinx that Traveled to Philadelphia

After years of waiting, it was before me at last. The great face was so sad, so earnest, so longing, so patient. There was a dignity not of earth in its mien, and in its countenance a benignity such as never any thing human wore. It was stone, but it seemed sentient. If ever image of stone thought, it was thinking. It was looking toward the verge of the landscape, yet looking at nothing—nothing but distance and vacancy. It was looking over and beyond every thing of the present, and far into the past. It was gazing out over the ocean of Time . . .

— Mark Twain, *The Innocents Abroad (1869)*

The Sphinx that Traveled to Philadelphia

The Story of the Colossal Sphinx in the Penn Museum

By Josef Wegner & Jennifer Houser Wegner

Penn Museum
UNIVERSITY *of* PENNSYLVANIA MUSEUM
of ARCHAEOLOGY *and* ANTHROPOLOGY

Library of Congress Cataloging-in-Publication Data

Wegner, Josef W. (Josef William), author.

The sphinx that traveled to Philadelphia : the story of the colossal sphinx in the Penn Museum / Josef Wegner and Jennifer Houser Wegner.

  pages cm

Includes bibliographical references.

ISBN 978-1-934536-76-6 (hard cover : alk. paper)

1. University of Pennsylvania. University Museum—History. 2. Sphinxes (Mythology) 3. Excavations (Archaeology)—Egypt—Memphis (Extinct city) 4. Museums—Acquisitions—Pennsylvania—Philadelphia. 5. Memphis (Extinct city)—Antiquities. 6. Memphis (Extinct city)—Civilization. I. Wegner, Jennifer Houser, author. II. Title.

DT62.S7W44 2015

932—dc23

2015012597

Published for the University of Pennsylvania Museum of Archaeology and Anthropology by the University of Pennsylvania Press.

For Elizabeth Jean Walker,
Friend of Egyptology and the Penn Museum

TABLE OF CONTENTS

ACKNOWLEDGMENTS

This book on the Penn Museum's Sphinx of Ramses the Great began some years ago, but in a quite different form from what you now see. When we started thinking about writing a book on the Sphinx to mark its centenary in Philadelphia in 2013, it was our original intention to write a short history of the Sphinx geared towards children. However, once we began researching the Sphinx, we were amazed at the wealth of information on the discovery of the Sphinx, the Museum's early excavations in Egypt, and the fascinating ties of the Sphinx with Philadelphia history. We decided this was a story best told in full. The Sphinx has been a captivating object to research, and we are happy to be able to share its story. We would not have been able to do this without the help of many individuals and we are grateful for their interest and support of this project.

Several individuals deserve particular thanks in bringing the book to fruition. We would like to thank firstly Jennifer Quick, Senior Editor of Penn Museum Publications, who copyedited the manuscript and produced a layout of the book. Her careful eye, hard work, and calm demeanor were very much appreciated by us. She was a joy to work with. Anne Marie Kane of Imogen Design worked on the final design and we greatly appreciate her careful attention to the graphic layout. In the production of the book we are especially indebted to Jim Mathieu, Director of Publications, without whose efforts and expertise in publications, the Sphinx story would remain locked away in folders in our desk drawer. Also in bringing out this book, we wish to thank Julian Siggers, Williams Director of the Penn Museum, and Amanda Mitchell-Boyask, Director of Development, for their support of the publication. We hope that the book will help in a small way to further interest in the remarkable history and mission of this great Museum.

Assisting us at almost every step of the way in this undertaking was Alex Pezzati, the Penn Museum's Senior Archivist. It is not an exaggeration to say that without Alex's help, this project would not have come to fruition. Both Alex and Assistant Archivist Eric Schnittke spent many hours helping track down and reproduce the documents and images relating to the Sphinx. We are also grateful to Nancy R. Miller at the University of Pennsylvania Archives for assistance with locating additional archival information about the University's connection to the Penn Museum Sphinx. Francine Sarin and Jennifer Chiappardi of the Museum's Photo Studio took many of the photographs of Egyptian Section objects seen in this book, as well as scanned almost all of the original documents relating the Sphinx.

We would like to thank our friends and colleagues in the Egyptian Section, David P. Silverman and Steve Phillips, for their interest in this project. Jean Walker graciously read and commented on early versions of the book. Jean also took many of the photos of the Penn Museum objects in this book. Many other colleagues at the Penn Museum have assisted us throughout the course of this project. Katy Blanchard, Fowler-Van Santvoord Keeper of the Near East Section, and Lynn Makowsky, DeVries Keeper of the Mediterranean Section, both helped in locating objects with sphinx iconography in their collections.

As part of the 2013 centenary celebration of the Sphinx's arrival at the Penn Museum, the Museum's Exhibitions Department worked with us to set up a small display of sphinx-related "kitsch" from our personal collection, and that of the Curator-in-Charge of the Egyptian Section, David P. Silverman. We are grateful to Kate Quinn and her staff, Ben Neiditz, Courtney O'Brien, Tara Poag, Kevin Schott, and Yuan Yao, for their work on this special exhibition. The celebration also included a special "Hijinks with the Sphinx" day at the Penn Museum and we are grateful to Tena Thomason and Rachelle Kaspin of the Public Programs Department for their

ACKNOWLEDGMENTS

assistance in planning and executing this event. We are grateful to Pam Kosty and Tom Stanley of the Public Information Office for their enthusiasm for this project and for bringing in local news coverage for the event and highlighting the book-project. Jane Hickman graciously included an article about the Sphinx's arrival in Philadelphia in the Fall 2014 issue (Volume 56:2) of *Expedition* magazine.

Also among the Museum's staff we would like to express appreciation to Penn Museum docent Ben Ashcom for his interest in the Sphinx and his work with the seventh grade at the Henry C. Lea School in West Philadelphia to determine a more accurate weight of the Sphinx. Further work on determining the weight of the Sphinx was done by Paul Verhelst and Ross Davison who kindly analyzed the Lidar scanning data and produced a 3D model of the Sphinx.

We are grateful to the late Anne Sinkler Whaley LeClercq, who provided us with much information on the Coxe family, and whose wonderful book, Elizabeth Sinkler Coxe's *Tales from the Grand Tour 1890–1910*, provides a detailed and heartfelt portrait of the Coxe family. We are sorry she is not here to see the Sphinx book. We are also grateful to Jonathan Haupt, the Director of the University of South Carolina Press, for providing us with copies of some of Ms. LeClerq's images reproduced in this book. The staff at the Woodlands Cemetery in West Philadelphia answered our queries concerning the Coxe family graves there and assisted us in successfully relocating the burial place of Eckley Brinton Coxe.

Among the numerous other people who have given us time and attention we would like to thank the following individuals and institutions for providing us with images and information for use in this book: Alice Stevenson (The Petrie Museum); Tine Bagh (Ny Carlsberg Glyptotek, Copenhagen); The Metropolitan Museum of Art, NY; The British Museum, London; The British Royal Archives; John A. Larson and Kiersten Neumann (The Oriental Institute, Chicago); Emmanuelle Terrell (Musée des Beaux-Arts de Nice); Josue L. Hurtado (The George D. McDowell Philadelphia Evening Bulletin Collection at Temple University Library); Jefferson Moak (The National Archives, Philadelphia); The Library Company of Philadelphia; John Horne and Connie Robinson (The National Baseball Hall of Fame & Museum, Inc.); and Hakimah Abdul-Fattah (Eliot Elisofon Photographic Archives, National Museum of African Art, Smithsonian Institution) and Kirsten Taarnskov, Team leader & Project Manager, Carlsberg Archives. In addition, we are grateful to our friends and colleagues, Denise M. Doxey (Museum of Fine Arts, Boston) and Robert K. Ritner (University of Chicago) for their careful and insightful comments on the manuscript.

The following individuals have kindly provided permission to use their photographs in this publication, as well as in answering queries concerning the fascinating world of Egyptian sphinxes: Muriel Anssens, Robert Beck, Matteo Giovanni Colnago, Miguel Hermosos Cuesta, Giovanni Dall'Orto, Mike Gadd, Adam Groffman, Wally Gobetz, Jim Graham, Zoltán Horváth, Donald P. Houser, Chris Irie, Dennis Jarvis, Torben Jenk, Andrew M. Johnson, Emmanuel Keller, Heidi Kontkanen, Robert Korb, Jr., John and Linda McMackin, Steve Minnicola, Hans Ollermann, Bob Ousterhout, Steve Phillips, Ib Rasmussen, Danee Sarman, Hannelore Siegmeier, David P. Silverman, Tom Stanley, Darien Sutton, Dupy Tal and Moni Haramati, Michael Tinkler, Barry Welch, Berthold Werner, Andrew Zvonarev (Flickr.com/Russian Brothers), and Arian Zwegers. It is not hyperbole to say that the search for photographs was a world-wide endeavor.

We would also like to give a special thanks to our 11-year-old son, Alexander Wegner who has spent the last few years listening to his parents talk about the Sphinx "all the time." Alexander accompanied us on many of our Sphinx-related research visits and provided some of the artwork included in this publication.

PREFACE

Over one hundred years ago, on October 7, 1913, a German tramp steamer coming from Bombay via the Suez Canal sailed up the Delaware River. The ship docked at Christian Street on the Philadelphia waterfront, with an unusual cargo in its hold. Aboard the ship was a colossal granite sphinx of the Egyptian pharaoh Ramses II. Weighing over 12 tons, the Sphinx was destined for the recently built University Museum at the University of Pennsylvania. After dealing with the challenges presented by its size (and the timing of its arrival—in the midst of the 1913 World Series!), the Sphinx was unloaded and taken to the Museum. A month later, the statue was installed in the front garden of the Museum. After sitting outside for several years (and weathering a few impressive snowstorms!), the Sphinx was taken inside. Then, in 1926, the Sphinx was installed in the newly completed Coxe Egyptian Wing of the University Museum, and there it still resides. The Penn Museum Sphinx remains the largest Egyptian sphinx in America, and a favorite destination for generations of Museum-goers.

How did this colossal Sphinx come to Philadelphia? The story is a fascinating one of archaeological research and museum building in the days just before the First World War. It is a story of men and women who were passionate about the history of the world's great civilizations and what this history could tell us as citizens of the modern world. Part of this endeavor involved archaeological excavations that expanded our understanding of the distant past. Another part involved making the past tangible by bringing people face to face with artifacts and monuments from distant times and places. In that sense, the Sphinx is an emissary of the vanished civilization of the pharaohs. The story of the Penn Museum Sphinx is also very much a story about Philadelphia—the energetic, industrial-age city of a century ago.

The Philadelphia Sphinx is in many respects really the "quintessential sphinx." With its beautifully preserved lower body but timeworn, eroded face, the Sphinx captures the vast gulf of time between the modern world and that of ancient Egypt. Thirty-two hundred years ago would take us back to the days when the Sphinx guarded the temple of Ptah, god of Memphis, ancient capital city of the land of the pharaohs. Through the ages sphinxes have been renowned as creatures of mystery, and the Philadelphia Sphinx absolutely embodies that image. Its mysterious countenance— with just a hint of the eyes remaining—seems to gaze bemusedly upon our modern world. From the day of its arrival in Philadelphia, many people have projected onto this Sphinx suggestions about what it might think about us. What would Ramses the Great say if he could speak to us? In 1913, they wrote newspaper stories and poems about what the Sphinx might be thinking. In 2013, the Sphinx "tweeted" on Twitter in the guise of "Phil" the Sphinx!

The Sphinx has long been a treasured symbol of the Penn Museum but its story has never been fully told. Fascinating records of the Sphinx's discovery exist in the Archives of the Penn Museum, as well as in the newspapers of the time. As curators in the Egyptian Section, we are often asked questions about the Sphinx: How much does it weigh? Is it the biggest sphinx outside of Egypt? How did they move it? Why didn't they ever restore the Sphinx's head? What is a sphinx anyway? The occasion of the centennial of the Sphinx's arrival in Philadelphia was a perfect inspiration to tell that tale.

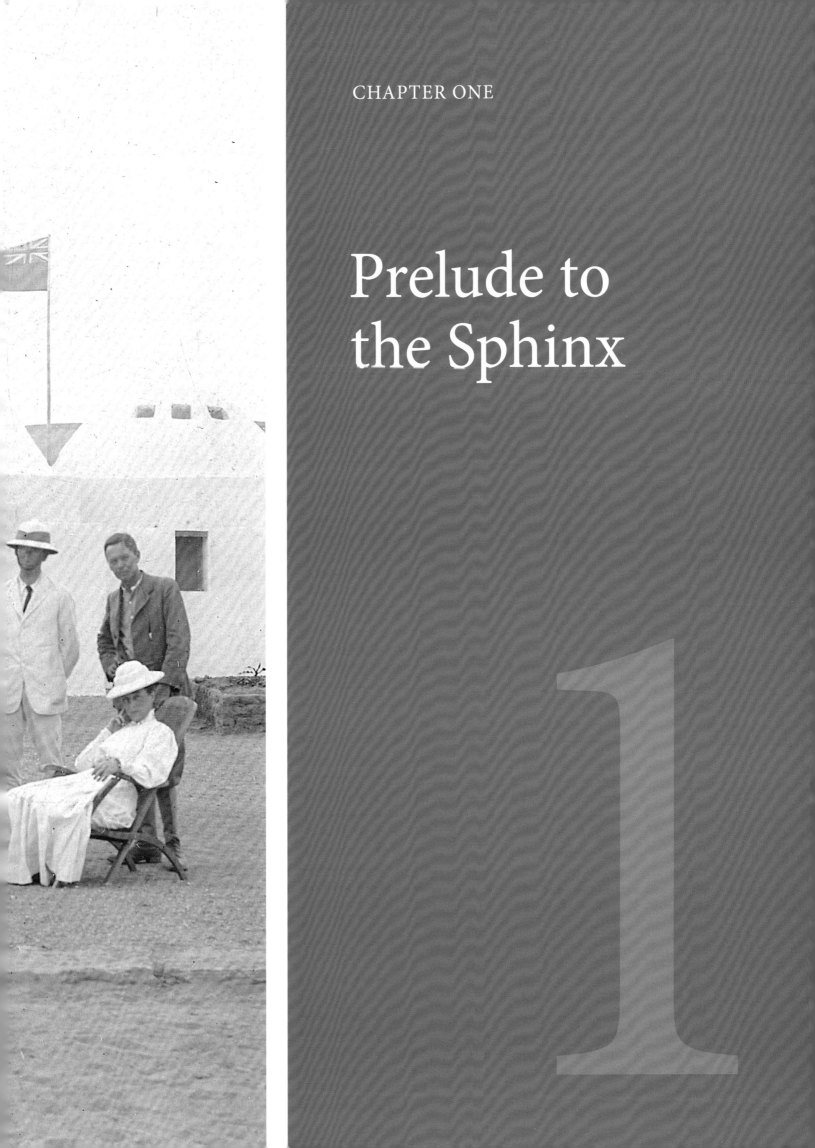

CHAPTER ONE

Prelude to the Sphinx

1

Building an Archaeological Collection

In October of 1913, a German tramp freighter, the *Schildturm*, steamed up the Delaware River and docked in Philadelphia. Onboard was a cargo of goatskins, cotton, and nuts from India, as well as a colossal Egyptian sphinx from Memphis, Egypt. Its destination was the University Museum of the University of Pennsylvania. The sphinx attracted considerable excitement, being at that time the second largest Egyptian monument to travel to America (after the Central Park obelisk which arrived in 1880 and was erected in 1881). Today, more than a century later, the Penn Museum sphinx remains the largest ancient Egyptian sphinx in the Western Hemisphere. How and why did this iconic object come to Philadelphia?

The University Museum, now the Penn Museum, is one of the great archaeological and anthropological research institutes in the world. Research in Egypt and the ancient Near East stands at the heart of the Museum. The Egyptian collection of the Museum, approximately 45,000 objects, is the result of a several different periods of activity that included both the Museum's sponsorship of excavations in Egypt, as well as the Museum's own excavations. At the time the sphinx arrived at the Museum in 1913, it joined an already sizeable Egyptological collection. Much of this material had come to the Museum through the efforts of an energetic woman, Sara Yorke Stevenson.

Sara Yorke was born to American parents in Paris in 1847. After growing up in France and later Mexico, she settled in Philadelphia in 1867 and married a lawyer, Cornelius Stevenson. Aside from efforts in the women's suffrage and education movement, Stevenson was a scholar (in 1894 she was awarded the first honorary doctorate to a woman at the University of Pennsylvania). From 1889–1905, as curator of Egyptian and Mediterranean archaeology, Stevenson ceaselessly advocated Penn's support of ongoing work in Egypt. Through financial assistance to the British Egypt Exploration Fund and a research organization she

1.1. Sara Yorke Stevenson (1847–1921) was the first curator of the Museum's Egyptian and Mediterranean section. [UPM image # 237288]

Museum of the University of Pennsylvania,
Philadelphia, Pa.

helped found, the American Exploration Society, Penn provided financial support excavations in Egypt from 1890–1905. A major incentive for the investment in excavations during that time was the policy of equitable division of finds between foreign archaeologists and the Egyptian Antiquities Service. Significant sets of archaeological material had come to Philadelphia beginning first in 1890.

At that time, the Museum did not yet physically exist and the University Library, now Furness Fine Arts Library, housed the collections. Stevenson endeavored throughout her career to bring on board a professional archaeologist in order for the Museum to sponsor fieldwork in Egypt directly. This was not successful during her tenure, but would occur after she left the Museum. In 1905, Stevenson resigned from the Museum over disagreements concerning Hermann Hilprecht, curator of the Babylonian Section. Her resignation, although unfortunate, was timely as it initiated a new phase of research and fieldwork in Egypt.

An important legacy of Sara Yorke Stevenson's tenure as curator of Egyptian and Mediterranean archaeology was a professional friendship she developed with one of the foremost excavators in Egypt: William Matthew Flinders Petrie. From the 1880s, Flinders Petrie (as he is usually known) had worked as one of the primary field excavators of the British research organization, the Egypt Exploration Fund. Division of finds from many of Petrie's excavations came to Philadelphia and at that point constituted the core of the Museum's Egyptian collection. Extensive correspondence between Stevenson and Petrie reflects his important role as an advisor to the Museum in its field activities and collection building.

Coincidentally, Petrie resigned from the Egypt Exploration Fund in 1905, the very same year Stevenson resigned from the University Museum. In 1906, he formed a separate organization, the British School of Archaeology in Egypt. Despite this break, Petrie's relationship with the Penn Museum remained close and constructive. He continued to advise the Museum in much of its field activities for several decades. As we shall see, one of his students, David Randall-MacIver, became the first curator of the Egyptian Section in 1907. Moreover, it was the Museum's ongoing support for Petrie's work now under the British School of Archaeology in Egypt that led to the discovery and transport of the sphinx to Philadelphia in 1913.

1.2. Postcard, ca. 1905, showing the original 1899 University Museum building as it would have appeared when the sphinx arrived (before the addition of the Rotunda and Coxe Wing, which later housed the Egyptian galleries).

1.3. William Matthew Flinders Petrie (1853–1942). [UPM image # 10546]

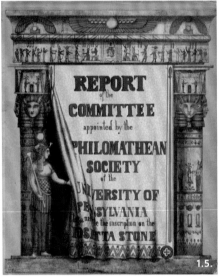

1.4. George Byron Gordon (1870–1927) was director of the University Museum for twenty years. This photograph shows him in Alaska in 1907. [UPM image # 11820]

1.5. Frontispiece of the Philomathean Society Report on the Rosetta Stone (1858). [Image courtesy of the University of Pennsylvania Archives]

In the years after 1905 the Museum entered a major phase of reorganization and expansion. In many ways, the completion of the first phase of the planned building designed by the architect Wilson Eyre spurred these changes. The 1899 building was only the first stage—the western wing—of a grand master plan envisioned for the growing institution, which would stretch all the way to the Schuylkill River (only some parts of which were completed over a thirty-year period from 1899–1929). Reflecting the establishment of its permanent building, the Museum was now engaged in a new phase of expanding its field activities around the world.

An important force in this new era was the recently hired curator of American Prehistoric Archaeology, George Byron Gordon. With the support of University Provost Charles Custis Harrison, Gordon quickly established himself as the Museum's de facto director; the Museum had no formal head administrator at that time. In 1910, Gordon officially became Director, a position he held until his death in 1927; before that point, however, Gordon was already involved in reshaping the direction of the Museum. Unlike the situation in Egyptology under Sara Yorke Stevenson, where the Museum supported excavations but did not undertake them directly, Gordon and others made a major push to initiate Penn's own excavations in Egypt. The Museum had already carried out a series of important and successful excavations in Mesopotamia at the site of Nippur, and it wished to make its mark in the growing field of Egyptian archaeology.

To this developing recipe, we may now add the critical ingredient: a person with money, passion, and interest in the archaeology of Egypt. At the same time that Sara Yorke Stevenson left and as George Byron Gordon stepped to the helm of the Museum, a University of Pennsylvania graduate, Eckley Brinton Coxe Jr., returned to Philadelphia from a lengthy trip up the Nile. This was not Coxe's first visit to Egypt but this trip had taken him all the way past the Sixth Cataract of the Nile to Khartoum. Coxe was fascinated and excited about the potential for archaeological work. Importantly, in 1895, he had inherited a significant fortune. In 1906, Coxe established the Eckley Coxe Junior Expedition to Nubia, the first direct Museum excavations in Egypt. Coxe's interest and support of the Museum were to have a lasting impact that continues to the present day. Coxe generously funded the first seasons of work in Nubia. Becoming Chairman of the Board of Managers in 1910, paralleling Gordon's own appointment as Director, Coxe personally paid for half of the day-to-day costs of running the Museum. His funds also paid for much of the Museum's additions to its original 1899 building. It is due to these three men—Flinders Petrie, George B. Gordon, and Eckley Brinton Coxe—that a colossal sphinx now resides in Philadelphia.

A Philadelphia Family with a Passion for Egypt

At the end of the 1850s, one of the undergraduates attending the University of Pennsylvania was Charles Brinton Coxe. Charles was the youngest of five brothers, all grandsons of an influential Pennsylvanian, Tench Coxe (1755–1854). During the late 18th and early 19th centuries, anticipating the coming importance of coal, Tench Coxe had purchased over a million acres of land in Pennsylvania's Schuylkill, Carbon, and Luzerne counties. In 1865, his five grandsons established Coxe Brothers and Company, an anthracite coal business, in Hazelton. Aside from being a member of a wealthy business family, Charles was also a scholar and had graduated with honors from the University of Pennsylvania in 1862. He attended the University at the same time as an interesting student project in Egyptology was published: *The Report of the Committee Appointed by the Philomathean Society of the University of Pennsylvania to Translate the Inscription on the Rosetta Stone.* The Frenchman Jean Francois Champollion had already deciphered Egyptian hieroglyphs in 1822. However, the Philomathean Society book was a serious restudy. This publication by several classmates at the University of Pennsylvania may have helped spark Charles' interest in Egypt. He worked separately on his own study of hieroglyphs and retranslated the Rosetta Stone.

In 1870, Charles married Elizabeth "Lizzie" Sinkler of Charleston, South Carolina. Lizzie was a woman with a fondness for travel. They gave birth to a boy, Eckley Brinton Coxe Jr. (named after Charles's older brother Eckley), in 1872. Just a year after Eckley's birth, his father Charles, only thirty years of age, died of tuberculosis in the midst of a trip to Cairo, Egypt. Lizzie returned her young husband's body to Philadelphia for burial at the Woodlands Cemetery in West Philadelphia. This early death of a father he never knew seems to have had an important and lasting influence on Eckley Coxe. Eckley himself developed a fascination for Egypt and archaeology as he grew up, perhaps a way to honor his father who had died too young.

Eckley Brinton Coxe Jr. followed in his father's footsteps and attended the University of Pennsylvania, graduating in the Class of 1893. Eckley, known as "Eck" by family and friends, had inherited considerable wealth from his father and uncle Eckley (Eckley Sr.) who died in 1895. For a period Eckley, who never

1.6. Eckley Brinton Coxe Jr. (1872–1916). This painting by Adolphe Borie shows him with the statuette of Merer discovered at Buhen in 1909. [UPM image # 174902]

1.7. Eckley Coxe and his mother, Mrs. Charles Brinton Coxe (Lizzie), at Windy Hill, Drifton. [Image courtesy of Annie Sinkler Whaley LeClerq]

1.8. The Coxe family residence at 1604 Locust Street near Rittenhouse Square in Philadelphia.

married, was called the wealthiest bachelor in Pennsylvania. After his graduation and with the considerable family fortune Eckley Brinton Coxe devoted much of his life to travel and the philanthropic use of his money. Coxe's foremost interest was archaeology and the work of the University Museum; it was here that he made his greatest mark, as we shall see. He was also dedicated to other causes including the work of the Children's Hospital of Philadelphia, then located at 18th and Bainbridge Streets. In 1915, Coxe used his money to buy the site for the new Children's Hospital in what is now University City. He might be pleased to know that a century later the Museum and Children's Hospital still sit across from each other in West Philadelphia!

The Coxe residence at 1604 Locust Street in Philadelphia was a family home shared with Lizzie Coxe's younger sister, Caroline Sinkler, and frequented by many other family and guests. Lizzie and Eckley also had a country house in Drifton, south of Wilkes-Barre, near the homes of many of the Coxe relatives. In 1895, following the death of Coxe's uncle, Eckley Brinton Coxe Sr., they built a grand 48-room country mansion named Windy Hill in Drifton. Eckley and Lizzie spent the rest of their lives shuttling between Windy Hill and Philadelphia. As we will see later, much of the correspondence concerning the sphinx and other archaeological matters were sent from Windy Hill.

During the winter months the Coxes frequently traveled abroad to Europe, the Mediterranean, and the Near East. Lizzie Coxe was a prolific writer and kept diaries in addition to writing essays and letters home to her relatives. Her writings reflect both her own and her son's deep fascination with the cultures, history, and archaeology of the Near East and Egypt. A collection of some of Lizzie's writings, recently published by Lizzie's great grandniece, Anne Sinkler Whaley LeClercq, provides insight into this adventurous Philadelphia family.

In 1895, the Coxes took a long trip up the Nile during which Eckley ventured as far south as the rock-cut temple of Ramses II at Abu Simbel in Nubia. Later on, in 1905, they made a more intrepid voyage that took them all the way to Khartoum. This was a remarkable journey and LeClerque discusses it in her book, *Elizabeth Sinkler Coxe's Tales from the Grand Tour 1890–1910*. Aside from being a fascinating account of travel in Egypt at the beginning of the 1900s, Lizzie's letters provide a glimpse of the interest in Egypt that runs through the Coxe family. It seems Eckley's own fascination was distilled through a long association that extended back to his father. But 1905 was a tipping point. It was upon returning from that trip that Eckley embarked on his long partnership with the University Museum.

The Eckley B. Coxe Nubian Expedition

Over the years of sponsoring the Egypt Exploration Fund, the University Museum had assembled a significant collection of archaeological finds from Egypt. This material had been given to the Egypt Exploration Fund by the Egyptian Antiquities Service, then secondarily divided among the various supporting institutions. The Penn collection was an important one containing

1.9. Windy Hill, in Drifton, Luzerne County, PA, was a 48-room mansion, which Eckley Coxe and his mother Elizabeth had built in 1895. It partially burned in a fire in 1938 but much of it is still intact and remains in the Coxe family today. [Image courtesy of Annie Sinkler Whaley LeClerq]

1.10. Eckley Coxe on camel in Cairo with cousins on a 1905 tour of Egypt. [Image courtesy of Annie Sinkler Whaley LeClerq]

1.11. David Randall-MacIver in Nubia, 1907. [UPM image # 175378]

1.12. The original dam on the Nile at Aswan was built in 1902. The raising of the dam's height between 1907 and 1912 threatened the archaeological sites that lay along the river's edge in Lower Nubia to the south of the First Cataract. This view on an old postcard dates ca. 1915 after the raising of the dam.

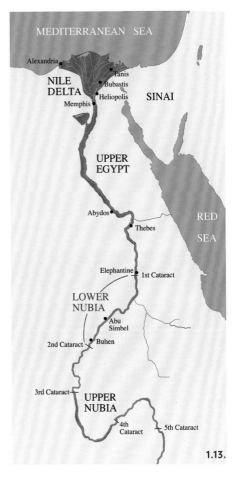

1.13.

1.13. Map showing the location of Lower Nubia.

a range of material from many time periods and parts of Egypt. Increasingly, however, it was felt that the Museum should be sponsoring its own excavations with direct control over publication and finds. In 1906 with the support of Eckley Brinton Coxe Jr., the Museum hired its first formal curator of the Egyptian Section. Acting on advice from Flinders Petrie, the Museum selected an Englishman, David Randall-MacIver. Randall-MacIver came with considerable experience in Egypt where he had worked with Flinders Petrie since 1899. In 1899, Randall-MacIver had discovered a temple of pharaoh Senwosret III at Abydos. (Over a century later, the Penn Museum's Egyptian Section is conducting extensive excavations of the Senwosret III tomb and temple at Abydos.) During his time working for the University Museum (1905–1911), he was field director of the Eckley Coxe Jr. Expedition to Nubia.

An important development that occurred in Egypt just as the Museum was establishing its program of field research was the raising of the Aswan dam (today called the Aswan Low Dam after the High Dam, its larger successor, was built in the 1960s). Built in 1902 at the First Cataract, just upstream from Aswan, the low dam was a mechanism for controlling the volume of the annual Nile inundation and establishing a reservoir of water to allow Egypt to manage periods of lower river volume. From 1907–12 a new project was underway to raise the height of the dam and increase the volume of the reservoir behind it. Archaeologists were concerned since this would cause a rise in the water levels behind the dam and potentially damage many of the still unexcavated sites known to exist in Lower Nubia (the region between the First and Second Cataracts). Consequently, the Egyptian Antiquities Service initiated the Archaeological Survey of Nubia, a comprehensive survey of sites in Lower Nubia. The University Museum itself chose to apply for permission to excavate sites in this interesting region, which Eckley Coxe had recently traveled through.

David Randall-MacIver proved to be an ideal field excavator. A physical anthropologist by training, he also had worked in southern Africa at the famous ruins of Great Zimbabwe (where he demonstrated the indigenous origins of the impressive Zimbabwe ruins), as well as in Algeria and Italy. Randall-MacIver had great ambition and plans for expanding the Museum's work in Egypt and the Mediterranean, which ultimately led to disagreements with Director Gordon. In Nubia, however, he worked with tremendous energy, as did assistant curator C. Leonard Woolley. Together, Randall-MacIver and Woolley conducted four active years of excavation in Lower Nubia, from 1907–10.

During the years of the Coxe Expedition to Nubia, Randall-MacIver and Woolley excavated five sites in the middle and southern part of Lower Nubia: Areika, Shablul, Aniba, Karanog, and Buhen. These sites spanned a range of time from the Middle Kingdom (ca. 2000–1700 BCE) through the New Kingdom (ca. 1500–1000 BCE) and the later Nubian Meroitic culture (ca. 300 BCE–300 CE). The Expedition's projects were among the first scientific work conducted in Lower Nubia and contributed significantly to our understanding of this region. Particularly important was the first systematic examination of the distinctive Meroitic culture (then called the Romano-Nubian period) of northern Nubia. The center of the far-flung Meroitic kingdom, which thrived ca. 300 BCE–300 CE, was at Meroe just north of modern Khartoum. The site of Karanog was a key northern administrative center of the kingdom. The Coxe Expedition also published a volume on Coptic churches of Nubia by Geoffrey

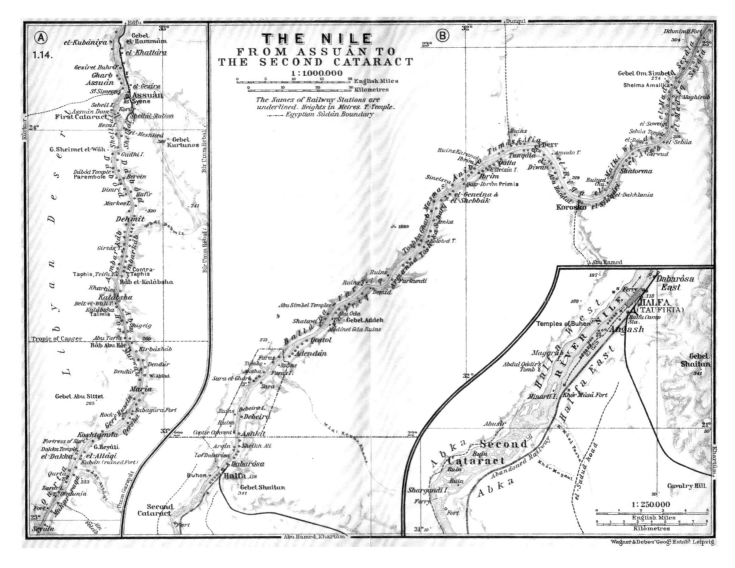

Mileham thus extending the range of time covered to over 3,000 years of history in Lower Nubia.

1.14. A 1914 map of Lower Nubia showing sites excavated by the Coxe Expedition, 1907–11. [After Baedecker's *Egypt*, 1914]

David Randall-MacIver was a productive field archaeologist and published results quickly. In collaboration with C. Leonard Woolley, eight volumes covering the Nubian excavations appeared promptly. The division of finds with the Egyptian Antiquities Service was generous and approximately 8,000 objects came into the Museum's collections from Lower Nubia. Today these form one of the world's major archaeological collections from Nubia.

1909: A Visit to Egypt and Nubia

In February of 1909, Eckley Coxe and the Museum's director, George Byron Gordon, boarded the Cunard Line steamer RMS *Caronia* bound for Alexandria, Egypt. Traveling with them were Coxe's mother, Lizzie, as well as Coxe's cousin Emily Sinkler. Their destination was the Museum's excavations in Nubia, then underway at Buhen where David Randall-MacIver was in the midst of completing the Pennsylvania excavation house.

1.15. In 1909 Eckley Coxe and George Byron Gordon sailed to Alexandria, Egypt, aboard the *Caronia* shown here on an old postcard. This is the same ship that, a few years later (April 14, 1912), sent an unheeded warning, "bergs, growlers and field ice," to another Cunard liner, the RMS *Titanic*.

1.16. Thomas Cook and Company's Nile Service paddle steamer, *Rameses the Great*; image from an old postcard.

The 1909 visit to Egypt was a very important one for the Museum's archaeological work in Egypt and one that, in fact, set the stage for the acquisition of the great granite sphinx from Memphis three years later. Traveling through Cairo and then up the Nile, Coxe and Gordon stopped to visit various archaeologists as well as to see the work going on. In Cairo they met Flinders Petrie who was then conducting his second season of excavation under his recently formed (1906) research organization: the British School of Archaeology in Egypt. Although the Museum was now engaged in its own fieldwork, the meeting with Petrie reaffirmed the Museum's long sponsorship of Petrie's research. Indeed, over the years of the Coxe Expedition to Nubia, the Museum continued financial support of Petrie's excavations. This ongoing financial commitment is ultimately what led to the sphinx of Ramses the Great coming to Philadelphia in 1913.

Coincidentally, in 1909 the Museum group set off upstream from Cairo journeying south to Aswan aboard the Cook and Co. Nile Service paddle steamer, *Rameses the Great*. At Aswan, Randall-MacIver met them and they continued upriver through the barren, but beautiful landscape of Lower Nubia. Now lost forever below the waters of Lake Nasser, Lower Nubia was then still pristine, a striking region with colorful sandstone hills flanking the delicate ribbon of greenery along the banks of the Nile. Here and there were archaeological ruins and stone temples, many built during the New Kingdom when the pharaohs had controlled Nubia as part of their empire. Buhen, at the Second Cataract, was one of these sites: a fortress built first during the Middle Kingdom and a series of temples added when the site was redeveloped by pharaohs of the New Kingdom. Most prominent was the still-standing temple of the female pharaoh Hatshepsut.

The visit to Nubia was a memorable one. Eckley Coxe's mother, Lizzie, kept a diary of the journey as she did on other trips. Her writing is full of insights into camp life in this remote region. The excavations were important and groundbreaking ones that were producing many significant finds. This affirmed Eckley's excitement about supporting substantial field research in Egypt. If Eckley ever harbored any doubts about supporting Egyptological work at the Museum this visit ended that: the results coming from the ground were so important, adding vital new information on the then largely unknown archaeology of Nubia, as well as the addition of many thousands of objects for the Museum's collection.

Although Coxe was widely traveled, the stay at the Buhen expedition house embodied the kind of new research he was interested in supporting. During his visit, he witnessed the discovery of artifacts that had not been seen for four thousand years. Randall-MacIver and Woolley were excavating the tombs of the

The camp and the wonderful mound of tombs were at the top of a high hill of copper coloured sand . . . Climbing up the hill you saw the three domes of the camp dazzling white against the deep blue sky and rising out of the red gold sand - from them flew the flags of England and America and in the middle the silver asp of Nubia. How proud and happy Eck was!

— Lizzie Coxe, from her journal from the Nubia trip of 1909

1.17. The University of Pennsylvania field house at Buhen. It was used only for the excavations of 1909 and 1910. [UPM image # 172539]

1.18. The 1909 team and visitors at Buhen. Eckley Coxe (seated, center); Lizzie Coxe (seated second from left); Caroline Sinkler (seated second from right); David Randall-MacIver (standing third from right); Leonard Woolley (standing far right). [UPM image # 172540]

1.19. Eckley Coxe standing in the courtyard of the Buhen field house in 1909, with the recently discovered statuette of the gardener, Merer. [UPM image # 35198]

1.20. The diorite statuette of the gardener Merer was Coxe's favorite object from the excavations in Nubia. He later had his portrait painted with the statuette (see page 5). [UPM object # E10751]

1.21. This faience plaque was found in 1909 on the shoulder of a body thought to be that of Merer. It has the throne name of pharaoh Neferhotep I of the 13th Dynasty, and may date Merer to that king's reign, ca. 1750 BCE. [UPM object # E10755]

1.22. The jewelry thought to belong to Merer. The objects were stolen from the Museum in 1911 and never recovered. [UPM image # 153909]

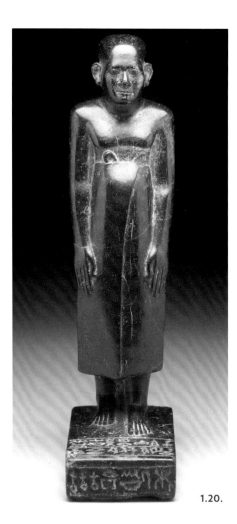

1.20.

1.21.

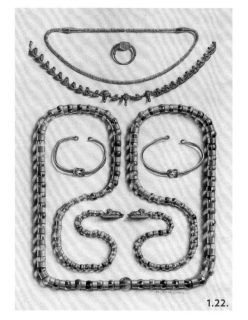

1.22.

Middle and New Kingdoms in and around the ruins of Buhen fortress. Although tomb robbers had plundered most of these in ancient times, many contained largely intact remnants of the original burials.

Coxe's favorite discovery—made in the midst of the 1909 visit—was the beautiful statuette of an official of the Middle Kingdom. The inscriptions on the statuette's base identify the man as Merer and his title as "gardener." Despite a lowly sounding title, Merer seems to have been an important official. Other objects in his tomb suggest he enjoyed royal honors. A rich set of gold jewelry came from Merer's tomb. Returned to the Museum in 1910 and placed on display, the golden jewelry was unfortunately stolen just a year later in 1911 when someone overturned the case in the Egyptian galleries. A group of rowdy Penn undergraduates were under suspicion by the police but no one was ever arrested. This remains one of the major unsolved thefts from the Penn Museum.

While Coxe and Gordon were visiting the excavations in Nubia, Flinders Petrie, who they had met in Cairo on their journey south, wrote a follow-up letter that reached them at Aswan. Petrie was working at Memphis. His letter has the address of Bedrasheyn, the modern town that lies just east of the ruins of Memphis. This is a pivotal letter because it resulted in the formal reestablishing of the Museum's support for Petrie's work, now under the auspices of the British School of Archaeology in Egypt. The main topic of Petrie's note was the long relationship that had previously existed during the tenure of Sara Yorke Stevenson from 1889–1905. Petrie expressed regret over the severing of this connection when Stevenson resigned in 1905. After his friend and associate David Randall-MacIver joined the Museum, there had been a request that Petrie no longer accept any financial contributions from Stevenson. Petrie's letter sought to end that constraint and to restore support and cooperation with the University Museum. He invited Coxe and Gordon to visit his excavations at Memphis and to see his exciting discovery of 1909: a stone palace belonging to pharaoh Apries (reigned ca. 589–570 BCE) during Egypt's 26th Dynasty.

Journeying back northwards from Nubia, Gordon and Coxe had a chance to visit Petrie's work at Memphis and see the impressive scale of the ruins there. Although the ongoing work in Nubia was incredibly important and producing numerous discoveries, Gordon was particularly interested in the possibility of acquiring some large-scale sculpture of the type that characterized the ruins of Memphis. From 1909 onwards, the Museum restored financial support to Petrie's research with the promise of receiving significant material from the division of finds.

Even as Gordon and Coxe reestablished the Museum's position as one of the financial backers of Petrie's British School of Archaeology in Egypt, they were moving forward with the Coxe Expedition to Nubia. After the 1909 visit, a further productive year of excavation was completed in 1910. Although spanning just five years in total, the work of Randall-MacIver and Woolley had produced a huge volume of finds for the Museum and material for publication.

During the years of the Coxe Expedition, the Museum made regular use of a travel and expediting company based in Cairo, J.W. Congdon and Company. At the end of the work at Buhen and Aniba, Congdon and Co. was engaged to handle the transport and shipping of the finds that the Egyptian Antiquities Service had granted to the University Museum. The export of these items was an official process and necessitated a consular invoice issued by the U.S. Consulate verifying the nature and legality of the material. The document on page 14 (Fig. 1.24) below is Congdon and Company's official export document for 1910 finds from Aniba and Buhen, stamped with the seal of the U.S. Consulate. The 44 cases of material shipped at the end of June 1910 comprised the main group of Nubian finds today

Bedrasheyn
17 March '09

Dear Dr. Gordon,

It was a great pleasure for me to meet Mr. Coxe and yourself; and as you write about affairs I must just give you an outline of all that I know about business with Philadelphia. Mrs. Stevenson had twenty years ago been energetically building up the Egyptian collection, and had usually sent over donations since then each year to my work, for which I had returned a share of antiquities.

When my friend Dr. MacIver became connected with Philadelphia I was informed expressly that it would make no difference to my relations with my old friend Mrs. Stevenson. But this last letter that I had about antiquities from him was a decision statement that I was not to accept anything more from Mrs. Stevenson.

I naturally wished to have heard somewhat about such a break of relations directly, rather than through a third party. I would not ignore an old friendship with one whom I greatly respected for her whole-hearted and unselfish devotion to the subject for so many years.

I received a second command to cease to apply to Mrs. Stevenson, a course that I had never adopted. And I could only reply that if any contribution came from the Museum, or anywhere else, it would receive due acknowledgement in division of objects as before.

I have heard nothing on the subject from Mrs. Stevenson. But you will now see how much in the dark I am, and how naturally my long-standing friendship has been in the foreground of this matter to me. I may thank Mr. Coxe for his kind letter, and believe me,

Sincerely yours,
W.M. Flinders Petrie

P.S. If by any chance you have time in Cairo on your return I should be most happy to show you the remains of the stone palace of Apries and other sites here.

1.23.

1.23. Transcription of a letter from Flinders Petrie to Gordon.

1.24. Consular form dated June 30, 1910, for material shipped from the Coxe Nubian Expedition. Note that the artifacts are verified as being the "professional production of the Workmen of Ancient Egypt."

1.24.

housed in the Museum's Egyptian collection. Here we see the signature of Edward Bell, Deputy Consul in Cairo, for export of the Coxe Nubian Expedition finds to Philadelphia.

J.W. Congdon and Co. had a long association with the Museum. As we shall see later, it would be the same company that was responsible for handling the complex process of moving the sphinx from Cairo to the Suez Canal. They were also involved in expediting shipments from other sites throughout Egypt in subsequent years of the Coxe Expedition's work.

A result of the Coxe Nubian Expedition was the addition of a huge assemblage of carefully excavated and documented archaeological material to the Museum's Egyptian Collection, forming, by far, the most important material in the Egyptian Section today. As noted above, the earlier period of support of Flinders Petrie and

the Egypt Exploration Fund helped the Museum form an important collection, but one that was assembled from the division of finds among many different supporting institutions. The Petrie objects are effectively samples of material from many sites and time periods of ancient Egypt. The Coxe Expedition material is different: other than artifacts that the Egyptian Antiquities Service chose to retain, the entirety of the finds came to Philadelphia since Penn—through Eckley Coxe's generosity—was the sole supporting institution. This would continue through the remaining years of the Coxe Expedition until 1925.

Despite the remarkable success of the Nubian Expedition, disagreements emerged and intensified between Museum Director Gordon and David Randall-MacIver about the scope and nature of the research. During the first year in Nubia, the Expedition had completed a survey of the Coptic churches of Lower Nubia which was published by Geoffrey Mileham. Randall-MacIver was interested in expanding that work to undertake a comprehensive survey and publication project devoted to documenting early Christian churches throughout the Eastern Mediterranean, thus a study of cultural interconnections rather than large-scale site excavations. "The Byzantine scheme" which Randall-MacIver advocated early on during the Coxe Expedition became a source of argument and Gordon was not

1.26.

1.26. Part of the vast holdings of the Nubian collection of approximately 8,000 objects in storage in the Penn Museum.

in favor of pursuing it. Gordon and Randall-MacIver were two strong personalities who did not see eye to eye. Randall-McIver's contract with the Museum continued through the end of 1911. However, because of the ongoing disagreements about the future direction of work he decided not to pursue reappointment.

When Randall-MacIver left the Museum his assistant C. Leonard Woolley also went on to other work. He continued to work in Nubia for University of Oxford in 1912 (he had been assistant curator there before taking the job with Penn). His career as a field archaeologist continued with work in Egypt, Syria, and Iraq during the 1910s and 20s. Woolley's association with the Penn Museum expanded significantly during his most famous work: twelve seasons of excavation at the city of Ur in Mesopotamia (1922–34). This work included the discovery of the famous royal tombs of Ur. Woolley's first major field experience under David-Randall MacIver and the years of the Coxe Expedition had contributed to the development of one of the great excavators in Near Eastern archaeology. His prior work for Penn during the Coxe Nubian Expedition also laid the groundwork for this later collaboration between the British Museum and the University Museum on the Ur excavations; but that is another story.

The resignation of David Randall-MacIver created an interlude in the Coxe Expeditions to Egypt. For two years, 1912–13, George Byron Gordon was busy searching for a new professional archaeologist to take the helm of the Egyptian Section. During those years, although not excavating, the Museum continued to contribute funds to both the Egypt Exploration Fund, as well as Petrie's British School of Archaeology in Egypt. It was during this brief hiatus in the Coxe Expeditions that the sphinx came to Philadelphia. Let us turn now to the next part of the story: the discovery of the sphinx and Flinders Petrie's excavations at the city of Memphis.

A – E10312

B – E10982

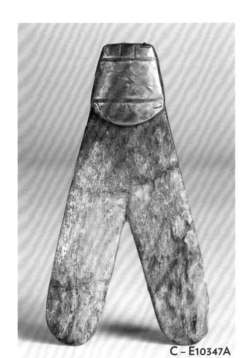

C – E10347A

D – E10898d

E – E8170

F – E7009

G – E7933
G – E7794
G – E7925

H – E8737

1.27A–H. Some examples from the major collection of artifacts recovered by the Coxe Expedition in Nubia during 1907–11. A-D objects from Buhen dating to the Egyptian Middle and New Kingdoms (ca. 2000–1000 BCE). E-H objects from Karanog, Meroitic culture, ca. 300 BCE 300 CE.

CHAPTER TWO

The Discovery of the Sphinx

The Work of the British School of Archaeology at Memphis

The University of Pennsylvania had been a longtime supporter of the excavations of Flinders Petrie through its contributions to the Egypt Exploration Fund. However, in 1906, following disagreements with the Fund's administrators, Petrie established a new organization, which he called the British School of Archaeology in Egypt (BSAE). To finance this venture, Petrie expanded an existing fund—the Egyptian Research Account (ERA)—that had been initially established to cover the costs of bringing students into the field. The ERA was reorganized to cover the costs of excavation and student assistants. Petrie assembled a committee of influential people and scholars to oversee the BSAE. He appealed to both private donors and institutions for support. The BSAE was based at University College London but unlike other British research schools abroad, such as the British Schools in Rome and Athens, there was no headquarters in Egypt itself. The goals of the BSAE were first and foremost conducting significant excavations in Egypt, publication of archaeological research, and the placement of important antiquities in the museums that had funded the work. After Museum Director Gordon and Eckley Coxe met Petrie in Egypt in 1909, they reaffirmed and increased support for the BSAE alongside the Museum's ongoing Coxe Expedition. The University of Pennsylvania's support for Petrie's research then going on at Memphis, just south of Cairo, would result in the impressive Sphinx of Ramses II coming to Philadelphia.

During its first two years, the BSAE conducted important excavations at Giza and several sites in Upper Egypt. Then, in 1908, Petrie turned his interest to what he considered to the most important site of ancient Egypt—Memphis. Memphis was ancient Egypt's original capital city, founded ca. 3000 BCE. The city, located on the western side of the Nile, had moved and evolved over thousands of years of

2.1. The area of the Temple of Ptah as it looked in 1908 during Petrie's first season at Memphis. [Image courtesy of The Petrie Museum of Egyptian Archaeology]

2.2. Pumping groundwater from an excavation area, 1908. [Image courtesy of The Petrie Museum of Egyptian Archaeology]

Egyptian history. Serving as capital city during the Pyramid Age of the Old Kingdom, as well as during most of Egypt's New Kingdom, the badly denuded ruins of this once great city had never been systematically investigated. Despite serious obstacles, the large scale, complexity, and importance of Memphis appealed to Petrie.

Known in modern times by the name of the nearby town, Mit Rahina, the ruins of Memphis were substantially covered by fields, groves of palm trees, as well as the modern houses of Mit Rahina and other villages surrounding it. Complicating the logistics of excavating, much of the site was covered in water during the months of the Nile inundation (September through November). Even when it was not inundated, excavating the ruins of Memphis was a daunting prospect because in many areas reaching down to the levels of the ancient city meant digging deeply into the alluvial plain of the Nile. The floodplain of the Nile has risen an average of 10 feet (3 meters) since the time of Ramses II, and something like 16 feet (5 meters) since the time of Memphis' foundation ca. 3000 BCE. Much of what once stood elevated above the Nile's floodplain now sits well below it.

Petrie and his assistants tackled the excavations of Memphis working on a large scale as was necessary for such a massive site. Over six years, 1908–13, he devoted attention to revealing different parts of the central ruins field. One of the major areas that attracted Petrie's interest was the ruins of the great Ptah Temple, part of the huge complex dedicated to Ptah, the primary god of Memphis. Petrie, like others before him, excavated in and around the destroyed gateways of the temple. During his initial season in 1908, he focused on the Western Gate and West Hall of Ramses II. In this area he found many votive stelae dedicated to Ptah. During his second and third seasons in 1909–10 he shifted his focus to another area north of the Ptah Temple where he discovered the ruins of a palace of pharaoh Apries of Egypt's Late Period (see postscript in letter from Petrie to Gordon in Chapter 1, Fig. 1.23). During the final three seasons he turned his attention back to the Ptah Temple enclosure. It was during the 1912 season that work on the North Gate of the temple enclosure exposed the granite Sphinx of Ramses II and related monuments.

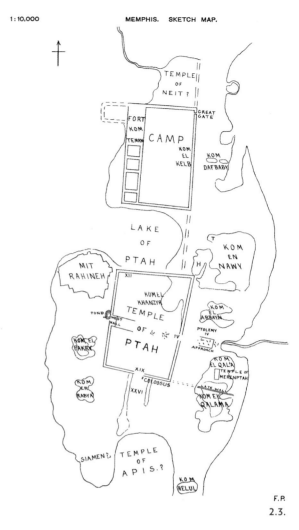

2.3. Petrie's initial plan of Memphis produced in 1908. This was the first overall archaeological plan of the major features of the ancient city. [After Petrie, *Memphis* I, pl. i]

2.4. Flooded area of the Temple of Ptah. [Image courtesy of The Petrie Museum of Egyptian Archaeology]

2.6a.

TREASURE-TROVE *of the* EGYPTIAN DESERT

THE GREAT ALABASTER SPHINX RECENTLY UNEARTHED AT MEMPHIS

2.6b.

One of the most interesting of the many discoveries made in Egypt during the past season is the huge alabaster sphinx, which was found at Memphis between the two great colossi of Rameses II. Beautifully sculptured, and not defaced in any way, this wonderful find is to be set up this summer, and will form one of the permanent attractions of Memphis. It is over 3000 years old, is 26ft. long by 14ft. high, and weighs about eighty tons. Picture by J. F. Cunningham.

EGYPTIAN SPHINX FOUND BY ITS TAIL

Ninety-Ton Monster, Carved Out of Alabaster, Unearthed Near Memphis.

LARGEST ONE EVER MOVED

Measures Over 14 Feet in Height and 26 Feet in Length and Petrie Says It Was Made in 1300 B. C.

CAIRO, Egypt, July 2.—A year ago on the marshy plains of Memphis, on the road to Sakkareh, a member of the British School in Egypt found a curiously carved object sticking out of a sand embankment. The season was so far advanced that nothing could then be done, but this year the excavators went to work, and the object was found to be the tail of a sphinx, weighing ninety tons and carved from a single piece of alabaster.

The monster measures some 14 feet in height and 26 feet in length. Alabaster being a rock foreign to the neighborhood, this sphinx ranks as the largest that has been transported. The figure bears no inscription, but is considered by Prof. Flinders Petrie, the Director of the British School in Egypt, to have been carved about 1300 B. C.

2.7.

2.5. Ruins of West Hall of Ramses II in the midst of palm groves. [Image courtesy of The Petrie Museum of Egyptian Archaeology]

2.6a, b. The Alabaster Sphinx shortly after its discovery in 1912. [Left after *The Graphic*, July 13, 1912, p. 63; above, photo courtesy of The Petrie Museum of Egyptian Archaeology]

2.7. Part of an article from *The New York Times*, July 14, 1912.

Another major challenge of working at Memphis was the dense stands of date palms that covered much of the site. Petrie labored long and hard with local villagers to lease the land and replant the trees after each year's excavations. This was a continual point of argument between Petrie and the officials of the Egyptian Antiquities Service who wished to appropriate the land from local villagers permanently. By 1913 Petrie had become somewhat disillusioned by these ongoing negotiations. Although he planned to continue work at Memphis in future years, 1913 was his last season there. The Penn Museum would play a crucial role in the end of Petrie's work at Memphis, as we shall see.

The Discovery of the Great Alabaster Sphinx

The Penn Museum Sphinx was not the only colossal sphinx discovered at Memphis in 1912. That very same year, Petrie and his assistants uncovered an even larger one lying on its side just inside the area of the South Gateway of the Ptah Temple: the great Alabaster Sphinx of Memphis. It is a true monster, an 80-ton colossus. With the exception of the Great Sphinx at Giza, it is the largest sphinx in existence. The Alabaster Sphinx is designated the largest "portable" sphinx, although due to its size (well over four times the weight of the Penn Museum Sphinx!) it is not very easily moved.

The Alabaster Sphinx was actually first found in 1911 when Petrie's assistant in Memphis, Ernest Mackay, noticed its tail protruding above the surface of the desert. In early summer of 1912, Mackay completed excavations around the fallen statue revealing its gargantuan size, and the story of the discovery immediately made headlines. News stories appeared around the world for several months afterwards, with travelers and writers photographing and publicizing this impressive find. However, Petrie himself said virtually nothing about its discovery in his publications. There are a variety of reasons for Petrie's reticence about the Alabaster Sphinx. A primary one is that it entirely lacks preserved inscriptions, so Egyptologists could not date it with certainty at the time. The published reports compared the sphinx's alabaster to that of the sarcophagus of Seti I (father of Ramses II) in the Soane Museum in London, and scholars speculated that the sphinx might belong to Seti I. The Alabaster Sphinx is also mentioned briefly in correspondence about the Penn Museum Sphinx as we shall see later.

2.8. *The Evening Record*, Greenville, Pennsylvania, October 19, 1912.

2.9. Postcard (ca. 1915) showing the Alabaster Sphinx at Memphis as it appeared shortly after Petrie's work. [Photograph by Lehnert and Landrock, Cairo]

2.10a.

2.10b.

2.10a, b. Hatshepsut's features can be seen on this sphinx (above) in The Metropolitan Museum of Art [31.3.166], Rogers Fund, 1931. [Image courtesy of The Metropolitan Museum of Art, www.metmuseum.org] The Alabaster Sphinx on display (right) at the museum in Memphis (modern Mit Rahina). [Image courtesy of Dennis Jarvis]

2.11. T.E. Lawrence (1888–1935) worked with Petrie in 1912, the year of the Sphinx's discovery. [UPM image # 100726]

In 1913 the Alabaster Sphinx was turned upright and levered onto stone blocks where it remained through the 1920s. Later it was moved slightly and a concrete base added. It became an anchor for the Open Air Museum in Mit Rahina where it remains today.

The Alabaster Sphinx remains something of a mystery since there are no inscriptions visible on the eroded base to provide the identity of the pharaoh (or pharaohs) whose buildings at Memphis it once watched over. Due to the style of its face, which is very well preserved, many Egyptologists believe the Alabaster Sphinx was originally carved to represent the female pharaoh Hatshepsut who reigned over a century before Ramses II during the 18th Dynasty of Egypt's New Kingdom. Later kings such as Ramses II may well have appropriated the Alabaster Sphinx to adorn their own additions to the Ptah Temple at Memphis.

It was while the Alabaster Sphinx was grabbing headlines in the summer of 1912 that the granite Sphinx of Ramses II emerged from the mud of Memphis. Of the two, one stayed in Memphis and the other traveled to Philadelphia. Let us look at the discovery of the Penn Museum's Sphinx and the man who excavated it.

The Sphinx and Discoveries at the North Gate

2.11

The red granite Sphinx in the Penn Museum is one of the many discoveries that resulted from the remarkable career of the great Egyptologist Flinders Petrie. As with all scientific disciplines, however, archaeology is never a single-handed effort. Archaeological research relies on collaborations of groups of people. Sometimes this includes very large teams of trained archaeologists, artists, architects, photographers, and other specialists. Petrie had established the British School of Archaeology in

Egypt partly as a way to bring promising new students into the field, providing them with a systematic introduction to the methodology of archaeology. In the years just before the First World War, therefore, he ran a kind of special archaeological "field school" where he personally chose a handpicked group of the best and brightest young archaeologists and helped to mentor their careers in archaeology.

Petrie was general director of the excavations but much of the actual excavation fell to these younger archaeologists who were often the ones working on-site alongside the workmen and keeping records of the material coming out of the ground. Many young scholars who went on to great achievements were associated with Petrie over the years of the BSAE. Certainly the most famous young scholar working with Petrie in 1912 was Thomas Edward Lawrence (1888–1935), best known today as "Lawrence of Arabia." During this time Lawrence worked at the cemetery site of Kafr Ammar, also known as Tarkhan. Located just south of Memphis, Kafr Ammar was a cemetery site that produced significant discoveries of Egypt's earliest periods.

Although the discovery of the Alabaster Sphinx was the most publicized find of the 1912 work at Memphis, the newspaper reports also mentioned work in other areas of Memphis. Due partially to a brief description of the Ptah Temple by the Greek writer Herodotus (5th century BCE) and other ancient writers, Flinders Petrie was drawn that year to continue the investigation of the gateways of the temple precinct. There were four major entrances into the temple facing the cardinal directions: north, south, east, and west. Petrie had worked on the West Hall and associated West Gate in 1908; the East Gate, which was largely destroyed, had already seen substantial work by other excavators in the 19th century. So in 1912 he devoted efforts to the Ptah Temple's North and South gates. The Alabaster Sphinx was found not far inside the location of the South Gate. What remained of considerable interest was the unlocated North Gate that Herodotus mentioned as being built originally by a king named "Moeris." The excavators started work along the north side of the enclosure wall searching for the exact location and remains of the North Gate.

Petrie was an industrious excavator and he combined the work at Memphis with excavations at other sites. In the early summer of 1912 Petrie himself was busy with work at another of Egypt's great ancient cities: Heliopolis, city of the sun god Re, just northeast of Cairo. He assigned work at Memphis to Ernest Mackay. Mackay was a recently married, 32-year old archaeologist who had already spent five years working with Petrie in Egypt. Petrie entrusted him with managing the significant work force needed to handle the deep and wet excavations in the Ptah Temple. In the brief report on the excavations at the North Gate contained in *Tarkhan I and Memphis V* (1912) and *Riqqeh and Memphis VI* (1913), we learn that Mackay was the one on site at the time of the Sphinx's discovery. So, it was Mackay who excavated both the Penn Museum Sphinx, as well as the great Alabaster Sphinx in 1912.

2.12. Ernest Mackay (1880–1943) was responsible for the excavations in the north end of the Ptah Temple. He discovered the Penn Museum's Sphinx. [Drawing from *Expedition* 52(1), p. 40]

2.13. This grainy photograph shows the quartzite gateway lintel of Amenemhat III found near the Sphinx in the area of the North Gate. The huge block measures 13 feet in length and 4 feet in height. Mackay left it in place and reburied it. [After Petrie, *Memphis* V, pl. lxxvii]

DISCOVERIES IN EGYPT.

WORK OF THE BRITISH SCHOOL.—II.

(FROM A CORRESPONDENT.)

The second half of the season's work, after that described in *The Times* of April 22, was devoted to the great city sites, Memphis, where the school has worked for four years already, and Heliopolis, where no British work* had hitherto been done. The need of working down 6ft. or more under water obliges these sites to be taken when the water-level is low, late in the season.

At Memphis, which was in the charge of Mr. Mackay, a gigantic sphinx of alabaster has been found, lying between the two well-known colossi. This is the largest sphinx that has ever been transported, being 26ft. long and 14ft. high, and weighing about 80 tons. Happily it has never been defaced, and except for some slight natural fissures, the face is as perfect as when carved. It does not bear any name, but belongs either to the XVIIIth dynasty, or the best work of the XIXth dynasty, about 1,300 B.C. It was thrown over on its side, anciently, but it will be set up again this summer, and will remain as one of the sights of Memphis, like the great colossus.

Further north, in the temple of Ptah, a fine group in red granite has been found, representing Rameses II. and the god Ptah, standing. Here, again, the faces are quite perfect, and only a small amount of weathering has occurred on the lower parts. The scale is life-size, with large crowns of feathers on the head, and the work is of the best class of the period. As the whole weighs about nine tons, it will be sent direct to the Ny Carlsberg Museum, Copenhagen. It is Denmark and not England that provides for the excavation of Memphis; but some day it is to be hoped that museums in England may have spirit for such work. A large figure of a scribe, covered with inscriptions, but headless, was also found near the group. These sculptures lay by the north gate of the temple enclosure, and here, deep down, was a lintel of Amenemhat III., showing that he had built this gateway. This is specially interesting as Herodotus ascribes the north gate to Moeris, the Greek name of this king. Thus it is seen that Herodotus had correct information about the builders, as he also correctly attributed the western pylon and colossi to Rameses.

2.14.

2.15.   2.16.

2.14. Part of an article from *The Times* (London), June 4, 1912.

2.15. Head of a priest found in Memphis near the Sphinx. Now in the Ny Carlsberg Glyptotek, Copenhagen (AEIN 1480). [After Petrie, *Memphis* V, pl. lxxvii]

2.16. A headless statue of a seated scribe named Amenhotep was also discovered in the area near the North Gate. In the Ashmolean Museum (1913.163). [After Petrie, *Memphis* V, pl. lxxvii]

At the north side of the Ptah Temple enclosure, Mackay put in a series of excavation squares to try to gain a picture of the original appearance of this area. It quickly became clear that there would be no intact gate, but by following the line of the brick enclosure wall, the excavators could gain some idea of the original position of the gateway. The most exciting result for Petrie was a huge quartzite slab, probably originally the lintel of a stone portal, inscribed with the name of pharaoh Amenemhat III of the 12th Dynasty (who reigned ca. 1831–1786 BCE). Moeris, the king associated with the North Gate in Herodotus' description of the Ptah Temple, is the Greek name for Amenemhat III. Consequently, for Petrie this was an exciting confirmation of the veracity of Herodotus' description of Memphis.

Other discoveries in the area of the North Gate were varied in size and time period. Everything that Mackay excavated in this area was toppled and much of it deeply buried. Finds included two partial statues of officials: a bald limestone head possibly depicting a priest, and a headless seated figure of a scribe named Amenhotep dating to the reign of Amenhotep III during the 18th Dynasty.

A series of colossal royal statues also emerged. One was a massive alabaster head, probably of Ramses II, which was too damaged for the excavators to remove from the ground. Two others were dyads (pair statues) of Ramses II standing alongside a god. One of these depicted the king with Osiris, god of the netherworld. This also was too badly damaged to move and was left in the ground. The other dyad, broken into three parts, was a magnificent over life-size figure in granite showing Ramses II standing hand-in-hand with the composite deity Ptah-Tatenen. The faces of king and god on this 8-ton figure were beautifully preserved and Petrie offered the statue to one of his major financial supporters, the Ny Carlsberg Glyptotek in Copenhagen, Denmark. This action was lamented in the report on the discoveries at the North Gate published in the *London Times,* which suggested that in the future British institutions should provide sufficient funding to allow such masterpieces to go to museums in the United Kingdom.

The other massive statue that Mackay found near the North Gate of the Ptah Temple was the over 12-ton granite Sphinx of Ramses II, which was acquired by the Penn Museum. The Sphinx was found sitting upright but evidently dislodged from its original location. It lay quite close to the dyad of Ramses II and Ptah-

2.17a, b. Two views of the Sphinx exposed during the 1912 excavations of Petrie at Memphis. Note the level of the groundwater. [Images courtesy of The Petrie Museum of Egyptian Archaeology]

2.17b.

2.18. The Ny Carlsberg Glyptotek (built 1897–1906) in Copenhagen was created to display the art collections of Carl Jacobsen. [Image courtesy of Ib Rasmussen]

2.19. Carl Jacobsen (1842–1914), Danish brewer and philanthropist, supported Petrie's excavations in Egypt. [Image courtesy of Kirsten Taarnskov, Carlsberg Archives]

2.20. This original photograph showing the back of the colossal dyad, was published in Petrie, *Memphis* V, pl. 77.

Tatenen. While the body of the Sphinx had been buried, its head had been exposed for a long period of time as indicated by the significant erosion. These two major finds at the North Gate, the pair figure of Ramses II with Ptah-Tatenen and the granite Sphinx, are closely linked. As we shall explore later in this book, the Sphinx appears to have once guarded the gateway to a special enclosure built by Ramses II and dedicated to Ptah in his special form, Ptah-Tatenen.

The Sphinx's Companion in Denmark

While the University Museum had the coal mining fortune of Eckley Coxe behind its growing Egyptian Section, Copenhagen benefited from the support of Carl Jacobsen, son of J.C. Jacobsen, the founder of the Carlsberg Breweries. Interested in augmenting the ancient Egyptian collection in Copenhagen, the

Glyptotek contributed substantial funds to many of Petrie's excavations. In 1913, they received the dyad statue of Ramses II and Ptah-Tatenen, which today forms the centerpiece of the Glyptotek's Egyptological collection, just as the Sphinx is an iconic artifact for the Penn Museum's Egyptian galleries.

Although Petrie and Mackay excavated other sculptures in the area of the North Gate in 1912, there is an especially close association between the Copenhagen dyad and Penn Museum Sphinx. The close similarity in the style of the inscriptions suggests both belong to the same set of monumental sculptures that adorned Ramses II's additions in the north part of the Ptah Temple enclosure. The texts on the back of the Copenhagen pair figure state the king to be "Ramses beloved of Ptah-Tatenen" and "Lord of feasts like his father Ptah-Tatenen." The Penn Sphinx does not explicitly name the god, but the carving of the king's name and other inscriptions suggest the same artisans carved both statues.

Although they are now separated, when we examine the Copenhagen dyad and the Penn Museum Sphinx together, one tells us a lot about the other. Since both statues belonged to Ramses II and were found in the same area of the Ptah Temple, the style of monumental sculpture was likely to be quite similar. Therefore, the face of Ramses II on the Copenhagen dyad provides an excellent indication of the original appearance of the eroded head on the Philadelphia Sphinx.

More important, however, is the association we see here of Ramses II

2.21. The Copenhagen pair statue of Ramses II and Ptah-Tatenen (AEIN 1483) was found in the same area of the Ptah Temple as the Penn Museum Sphinx. The statue is 11 feet (3.3 m) tall, 5 feet (1.5 m) wide, and weighs 8 tons. [Image courtesy of Tine Bagh]

2.22. Letter from Coxe to Gordon, December 30, 1912.

2.22.

with a form of Ptah called Ptah-Tatenen. In Egyptian, this means literally *Ptah-he-of-the-risen-ground*. This is a version of Ptah, the primary god of Memphis, unified in this case with another primal creator deity, Tatenen. Tatenen (*He-of-the-risen-ground*) signifies the concept of the first firm earth that rose from a watery nothingness at the beginning of the world. Tatenen grows to prominence at Memphis especially during the long reign of Ramses II, ca. 1279–1213 BCE. In this composite form, Ptah-Tatenen, we have a doubly potent version of Ptah as the ultimate creator of the universe. Ramses initiated major constructions at Memphis in honor of Ptah-Tatenen; the Copenhagen dyad and the Penn Museum's Sphinx both belong to these new structures built by Ramses II.

One could argue that the Ny Carlsberg Glyptotek received the preferable statue from Flinders Petrie's 1912 excavations at Memphis. Indeed, the Copenhagen statue is impressive with its pristine preservation of the faces of pharaoh and god. By comparison, the Penn Museum Sphinx is often described as "perfect, except for its head." Ultimately, though, which of these great statues you prefer is a bit of a personal aesthetic choice. The somewhat blocky style of Ramses II's figure on the Copenhagen dyad is not necessarily considered the height of ancient Egyptian sculpture. Of course, it would be wonderful if the Penn Museum Sphinx still had its head intact, but then it would no longer be a "quintessential sphinx" as Mark Twain said, "gazing out over the ocean of Time." And anyway, who would ever wish to trade a colossal sphinx for a pair statue?

Could Philadelphia Import the Alabaster Sphinx?

There is something else interesting in the Museum's correspondence with Flinders Petrie. Because Petrie's assistant Ernest Mackay discovered both the granite Sphinx of Ramses II and the Alabaster Sphinx during the same year, there was initially some confusion over which of the two was coming to the Museum.

Flinders Petrie wrote to Philadelphia at the end of November 1912 offering the red granite sphinx to the Museum for its support of the Memphis excavations (see below). However, newspaper reports had come out during the summer of 1912 about the discovery of the great Alabaster Sphinx. Which of the two sphinxes was Petrie offering to Penn? Might there even be a possibility of getting both of them?

In December of 1912, a few weeks after Petrie's initial letter offering the Sphinx to the Museum, Eckley Coxe wrote a note to Museum director George Byron Gordon telling him that he was in favor of accepting the Sphinx and that he would cover the costs of its transport to Philadelphia. Here, however, Coxe refers to it as "that large albaster [sic] Sphynx from Memphis." Clearly, Coxe who would have read about the Alabaster Sphinx in the newspapers was thinking at that early stage it was the great Alabaster Sphinx that would be coming to Philadelphia.

Unlike Coxe's initial confusion over the two massive sphinxes, Gordon did not think it was the Alabaster Sphinx that Petrie had offered to Penn. The letters from Petrie had made it quite clear that there was a granite sphinx that was different from the widely publicized Alabaster Sphinx. However, it apparently did occur to Gordon at some point that there might just be a possibility that the Egyptian Antiquities Service would not wish to retain the Alabaster Sphinx. If the granite sphinx could come to Philadelphia, what about the Alabaster Sphinx? What a wonderful addition to the growing collection of Egyptian archaeology at the University of Pennsylvania to have two of the largest sphinxes in existence! That seems to have been the impetus for several polite inquiries from Gordon regarding the status of the Alabaster Sphinx.

2.23. W. M. Flinders Petrie. [Image courtesy of The Petrie Museum of Egyptian Archaeology]

2.24. George Byron Gordon. [UPM image # 19134]

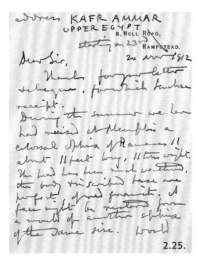

2.25.

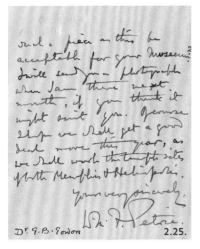

2.25.

address
Kafr Ammar
Upper Egypt
starting on 23rd
20 Nov. 1912

Dear Sir,

Thanks for your letter and cheque, for which I enclose receipt.

During the summer we have raised at Memphis a colossal sphinx of Rameses II about 11 feet long, 11 ton weight. The head has been much weathered, the body and inscribed base are perfect, of red granite. A face might be restored from a mould of another sphinx of the same size. Would such a piece as this be acceptable for your Museum! I will send you a photograph when I am there next month, if you think it might suit you. Of course, I hope we shall get a good deal more this year, as we shall work the temple sites of both Memphis and Heliopolis.

Yours very sincerely,
W.M. F. Petrie

2.25.

2.25. Letter from Flinders Petrie to Gordon, November 20, 1012, and (above) transcription of letter.

December 31, 1912

Dear Prof. Petrie:

I have your courteous favor of the 20th of November. I thank you for mentioning the colossal sphinx of Rameses II which you raised at Memphis during the summer. If you will kindly send me a photograph of this stone, I will let you know at once whether we will accept your offer of it.

Will you kindly also place a valuation on the object? It is probable, if we decide to take it, that we will make its purchase independent of our contribution already sent.

Very sincerely yours

Director

PROF. W. M. FLINDERS-PETRIE
Kafr Ammar
Upper Egypt

2.26.

2.26. Letter from Gordon to Petrie, December 31, 1912.

address P.O. Cairo
19 Jan. 1913

Dear Dr. Gordon,

I send you a print of a small photograph which a friend took of the granite sphinx; I hope to publish better ones this year. It is 11 feet long, and weighs about 11 tons. We would undertake its delivery at Alexandria free on the rail, to the care of any agent of yours, such as the U.S.A. Consul. Otherwise it would be left to the management of any shipping agency to collect from the rail.

I really cannot value it, as I know nothing of the cost of large monuments. If we are lucky this year or next we hope to send you some other good thing for your subscription besides this. Will that suit you?

Yours very sincerely,
W.M. Flinders Petrie

2.27.

2.27. Transcription of letter from Petrie to Gordon, January 19, 1913.

Just a few weeks after the granite Sphinx of Ramses the Great had arrived in Philadelphia and was installed in the Museum's courtyard, Gordon, on November 5, 1913, wrote to Petrie and inquired concerning the whereabouts of the Alabaster Sphinx. Apparently, Gordon was unsure what the plans were for it and thought it worth asking to see if there was any possibility it could follow the other sphinx to Philadelphia. Petrie responded that the other sphinx would remain at Memphis and become "one of the sights of Memphis." Imagine, however, if they had attempted to move the 80-ton alabaster monster from Memphis! The complaints that the Museum later received from the shippers about the weight of the smaller granite Sphinx would pale in comparison to those that would accompany the task of moving the great Alabaster Sphinx.

The fact that the Alabaster Sphinx was remaining in Memphis did not quell Gordon's interest in the possibility of Penn acquiring more monumental sphinxes. In one letter he even spoke about the possibility of a grand Egyptian sculpture gallery with its entrance guarded by a phalanx of sphinxes. This never happened although the Museum did eventually get a grand gallery of Memphite sculpture in a different way.

"We Have Raised at Memphis a Colossal Sphinx"

As mentioned, Petrie offered objects discovered to the institutions that supported his work through the British School of Archaeology, and they could then accept or refuse the objects. Over the years, Petrie had sent many objects to Philadelphia. Most of these were accepted into the Museum's Egyptian collection. Occasionally Museum staff decided they did not want the pieces and those they promptly shipped back! The Sphinx, however, was more than just a normal shipment of small artifacts. Special arrangements had to be made for its transportation from Memphis. Here we have the correspondence between Petrie and Gordon arranging for the delivery of the Sphinx to Philadelphia.

Petrie's first letter regarding the Sphinx dates to November 20, 1912. Over succeeding months, arrangements were made for its transportation. Altogether, it was just under a

year between Petrie's initial offer of the Sphinx and its arrival in Philadelphia on October 7, 1913. Petrie sent his handwritten letters mostly from the various sites where he was working in Egypt: the first comes from Kafr Ammar, just south of Memphis, where he started excavating immediately after his work at Memphis and Heliopolis.

Carbon copies of George Byron Gordon's letters to Petrie are preserved in the Archives of the Penn Museum. On December 31, 1912, Gordon wrote and asked to see a photograph of the statue. He also offered to make a separate contribution for the Sphinx apart from the normal funds given to the BSAE. This would ensure Petrie's continued goodwill towards the Penn Museum and the offer of further significant discoveries that were unwanted by the Egyptian antiquities authorities. We also learn from the December 31 letter that the dedicated Director was hard at work in his office on Near Year's Eve!

In a letter dated February 10, 1913, Gordon accepted Petrie's offer of the Sphinx and sent him information for organizing its shipment through J.W. Congdon and Co. in Cairo, the same company that the Museum worked with during the

2.28a, b. Field photos of the Sphinx taken in 1912. [Both images courtesy of The Petrie Museum]

February 10, 1913

Dear Prof. Petrie:

I thank you very much for your letter of the 19th of January enclosing photographs of the granite sphinx. Will you please have it shipped to the Museum? I notice that you will undertake its delivery at Alexandria, free on the rail and ask us to name an agent at that port to whose care it would be consigned. I do not happen to know any one who could act as our agent there and I am uncertain about the position of the U. S. Consul in such matters. The last things we had shipped from Egypt came through Congdon & Co., Sharia Kasr-el-Nil, Cairo, who acted as our agent. No doubt he has his forwarding agent in Alexandria and if this arrangement seems satisfactory to you, I would suggest that you take the matter up with Congdon and have him attend to the shipping for us and collect the charges here.

In an earlier letter you suggested that a cast might be made of the head of another sphinx of the same size, with a view to restoring this one. I would be very grateful to you indeed if you could have such a cast made and shipped to us.

Very sincerely yours

Director

DR. W. M. FLINDERS-PETRIE

2.29.

May 20, 1913

Dear Prof. Petrie:

Announcement has been made in American papers that your Egyptian collections are offered for sale. If this is the case, I would be very grateful to you if you would let me know what parts of your collections you are offering and at what price.

On February 10th I wrote you that we would accept your offer of the sphinx from Memphis and that you might ship it at your convenience. Since then I have had no word.

Ver sincerely yours

Director

PROF. W. M. FLINDERS-PETRIE
8 Well Road
Hampstead, N. W.,
England

2.30.

8, Well Road,
Hampstead, N.W.
28 May. 1913

Dear Dr. Gordon,

Your sphinx is being moved to Alexandria, where it will be taken over by Congdon for shipping. We could do nothing till about now as the ground must be clean of crops to get it across the fields.

As to my collection, it is by no means "for sale" in the usual sense. I offered it at cost price to University College 6 years ago, and the option to take it is nearly expired. My objective is to see it in a safe place where I can continue to work on it for the rest of my life, while not leaving it to any chances afterwards. If the College does not take it all, I wish to see a part in the next most available centre such as Oxford or Cambridge.

Yours very sincerely,
W.M. Flinders Petrie

2.31.

2.29. Letter from Gordon to Petrie, February 10, 1913.

2.30. Letter from Gordon to Petrie, May 20, 1913).

2.31. Transcription of a letter from Petrie to Gordon, May 28, 1913.

2.33.

Coxe Nubian Expedition. Three months went by and Gordon heard nothing. In a follow-up letter of May 20, Gordon inquired again. Petrie's reply a week later (May 28) came from his home in Hampstead, England, where he had returned for the summer. In the days before the benefits of refrigeration, most archaeologists worked in Egypt only during the winter months (October–March), since the chance of illness was very high during the heat of the summer (although Petrie sometimes worked during the summer because this was when ground water was at its lowest). In the May 20 letter Petrie informed Gordon that the transport of the Sphinx was underway and they had only been waiting for the winter crops to be cleared so the Sphinx could be moved across the fields surrounding Mit Rahina to the nearest rail station at Bedrashein.

In July, writing still from his home in Hampstead, Petrie reminded Gordon that, as he had requested, the Sphinx had been placed under care of the shippers, Congdon and Co., in Cairo. At this time, Petrie took the opportunity to request copies of various archaeological publications of the University of Pennsylvania. In Petrie's last letter before the Sphinx's arrival in Philadelphia, he thanked Gordon for the books but also mentions for the first time two other objects that he was sending in addition to the Sphinx. One was a fragmentary but striking bull-headed statue of the god Hapi with a human body. Although also from Memphis, this statue dates to an earlier era, Egypt's Middle Kingdom (ca. 2000–1700 BCE). Just three weeks after Petrie sent this letter the Sphinx arrived in Philadelphia.

One additional topic discussed in the letters between Petrie and Gordon is the substantial collection of artifacts that Petrie had assembled as a result of his work through the Egypt Exploration Fund and the British School of Archaeology in Egypt. Petrie was eager to see this assemblage form the core of a museum collection where he could continue to study and publish the material. He had offered it in 1908 to his institution, University College London, where he was then professor of Egyptology. Six years had elapsed without the university committing to accept this remarkable collection. In his letters regarding the Sphinx, Gordon took advantage of his good terms with Petrie to inquire about the fate of this

2.32. The Petrie Museum of Egyptian Archaeology, University College London; uploaded by Sidriel.13 on January 31, 2007 with a CC BY-SA 3.0 license; source is http://en.wikipedia.org/wiki/Petrie_Museum_of_Egyptian_Archaeology#mediaviewer/File:Petrie_Museum_of_Egyptian_Archaeology.jpg

2.33. This bull-headed Hapi statue was found at Memphis in 1912. [UPM object # E12327]

2.34a. Charles Custis Harrison was Provost of the University of Pennsylvania, and President of its Board of Managers between 1894 and 1929. He was instrumental in the establishment of the Penn Museum. [Image courtesy of the University of Pennsylvania Archives, #UARC20090218011]

2.34b. Harrison's statue, "Old Chuck," sits in the dormitory Quadrangle on Penn's campus.

collection. It is clear, however, that Petrie wished the material to remain in Britain where he could continue his research on it. In 1913, University College finally accepted the Petrie collection, which formed the core of what would then become the Petrie Museum, one of the world's great collections of Egyptian archaeology.

On October 4, 1913, Gordon wrote to the University of Pennsylvania's Provost, Dr. Charles Custis Harrison, informing him of the impending arrival of the Sphinx in Philadelphia. In the same letter he mentioned, somewhat ruefully, the fact that University College London had now purchased Petrie's extensive collection of excavated Egyptian artifacts. This was no doubt a disappointment to both Gordon and Harrison who viewed acquiring Petrie's collection as a way to form the world's foremost collection of scientifically documented Egyptian artifacts rapidly. At least the good news of the Sphinx's imminent arrival tempered this bad news.

The Petrie Museum at University College London represents, in many ways, a sister collection to the Penn Museum's Egyptian collection. The two are linked through having their early core collections established through the excavations of Flinders Petrie. Whereas the Penn Museum went on to fund many of its own later excavations that added to its collection, the Petrie Museum always retained Petrie's interest in the day-to-day life of ancient Egypt. Displays there exhibit the abundance of pottery, tools, weapons, and other artifacts of ancient Egypt collected through the extensive research of Flinders Petrie.

CHAPTER THREE

The Sphinx's Journey to America

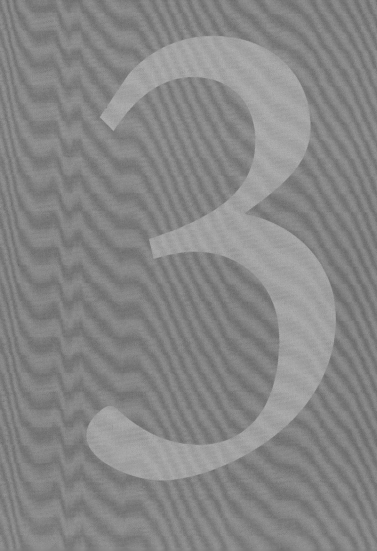

The Sphinx Visits Cairo

How did one transport an Egyptian sphinx weighing more than 12 tons 6,000 miles (9656 kms) across the Mediterranean Sea and Atlantic Ocean in 1913? Fortunately, technology had come a long way since the days when large Egyptian monuments like the Louvre sphinx (moved to Paris in 1828) or the St. Petersburg sphinxes (moved in 1832) were carried on sailing ships with considerable effort and risk. We will consider the story of those other great sphinxes that traveled outside Egypt later on. Nevertheless, moving a colossal sphinx such a distance still represented a considerable challenge.

It took a full year from the Sphinx's departure from Memphis to its arrival in Philadelphia. The Sphinx was hauled first from Mit Rahina to the nearby town of Bedrashein on the west side of the Nile. From Bedrashein it traveled by train to Cairo. During its previous work in Egypt, the Museum had dealt with Congdon and Co. for transporting objects to America. Arranging shipment of crates of artifacts was normally a straightforward business, but the transportation of the Sphinx was a special case. Letters between Director Gordon and Congdon and Co. tell us that Petrie had placed the Sphinx under the supervision of his assistant Reginald (Rex) Engelbach who was responsible for getting it to Congdon in Cairo for shipping.

Rex Engelbach was one of the younger associates working with Flinders Petrie as part of the excavations of the British School of Archaeology in Egypt (BSAE). In 1912 he had worked with Petrie at Heliopolis while Ernest Mackay excavated at Memphis. Engelbach later went on to an important career in Egyptology. He became Chief Inspector for Antiquities of Upper Egypt in 1920 and played an important role during the excavation of the tomb of Tutankhamun. In the 1920s and 1930s he became Curator in the Cairo Museum. Perhaps his brief time as supervisor of the Sphinx formed a unique experience in his career.

REGINALD ENGELBACH
Drawing by Mrs. Brunton.

3.1.

According to correspondence from Congdon and Co., after leaving Memphis the Sphinx was taken first to the Cairo Museum (or as it is more properly called, the Egyptian Museum; see sidebar, at right). The Cairo Museum is the repository for the most important material excavated in Egypt. Not only do the galleries and storerooms overflow with objects, but the gardens are also home to impressive sculptures, including a number of colossal sphinxes. The University Museum's Sphinx was briefly stored there, perhaps among its fellow sphinxes, before it was retrieved for the 6,000-mile voyage across the sea.

3.1. Rex Engelbach(1888–1946). [Drawing by Mrs. [Winifred] Brunton in *Annales du service des antiquités de l'Egypte* 48 (1948), pl. 1]

3.2a.

3.2a, b. Original letter, with transcription at right, from J. W. Congdon to Director Gordon, May 10, 1913.

CONGDON & CO.

Cairo, 10th May 1913

Dear Sir,

We have been informed by Mr. Rex Engelbach of the Egypt Exploration Exp, that you have instructed him to hand over to us, for transmission to you-a granite sphinx from Bedreshein.

This of course we shall be pleased to do- but as it is no small transaction, and involves much expense, for such a large and heavy piece of granite, weighing at least 11 tons, we must ask you to communicate with us direct, and send us a remittance of £150, to enable us to comply with your wishes-as we are not capitalists and cannot afford to make the outlay beforehand - of course, we will render you a full account afterwards, and remit any balance there may be, if we have over estimated.

The statue (or sphinx) is now ready for its first journey to Suez for shipment.

Awaiting your immediate reply.

The Director Museum
Philadelphia U.S.A.

We are Yours faithfully

J.W. CONGDON & CO.

3.2b.

THE CAIRO MUSEUM

Completed in 1902 (built in the same period as the original building of the University Museum in Philadelphia), the Cairo Museum was—and still is—the main museum of Egyptian antiquities in the world. Its collections include the celebrated treasures from the tomb of Tutankhamun. In 1913, the Cairo Museum stood a stone's throw from the Nile River, on the tree-lined downtown Maidan Qasr el-Nil Square. (Qasr el-Nil Square was renamed Tahrir [Liberation] Square after Egypt gained independence from Great Britain in 1952.) Electric tramways ran up the square along Mariette Pasha Street, named after August Mariette, the founder of the Egyptian Antiquities Service whose tomb sits in front of the Museum. In those days Cairo was a bustling and cosmopolitan city, but with under a million inhabitants it was still relatively small compared to the daunting mega-city of today.

To many eyes, the displays in the Cairo Museum have increasingly seemed crowded and out of date, as well as hard to get to through the throng of automobile traffic that incessantly swirls around Tahrir Square (long gone are the charming electric tram cars). The Egyptian authorities are in the process of building a new Grand Egyptian Museum near the pyramids at Giza where many of the treasures of the Cairo Museum will be displayed in new and improved surroundings. Still, it is hard to compete with the timeworn allure of the Cairo Museum, one of the world's grand archaeological museums.

3.3. Map showing the location of the Cairo Museum (Egyptian Museum). After Baedeker's *Egypt*, 1914.

3.3.

52   CAIRO. — *The Museum.* — LL.

3.4.

3.5.

3.4. Postcard ca. 1910 looking up Mariette Pasha Street, showing the Cairo Museum and gardens in front.

3.5. The Sphinx wrapped in burlap on a cart. This is the only known photograph of the Sphinx in transit in Egypt. [UPM image # 243700]

"The Sphinx Was Handed Over to Us Nude"

Congdon and Co. arranged for the transport of the Sphinx from Cairo to Suez by rail. At Suez the Sphinx was to be loaded aboard a freighter bound for Philadelphia. The letters between Congdon and Director Gordon reveal some of the difficulties involved in moving a colossal sphinx, even with the mechanized technology available in 1913. Congdon complained about the heavy weight of the statue, stating that photos "do not give an adequate view of its real size"; in fact they ended up charging extra for "exceptional freight." More problematic was finding a ship willing to take the statue. After sitting at the Suez docks for some time the Sphinx was finally loaded aboard a German freighter, the *Schildturm*. However, the *Schildturm*'s skipper, Captain Kloppenburg, was not entirely happy about having the stone monster on his vessel. He only agreed to take it under condition that he and his crew would have no responsibility for unloading it when they reached Philadelphia. Some of the reports from this time say that the Sphinx was "undesirable cargo"!

Regarding the preparations for shipping, Congdon also noted to Gordon that the Sphinx was handed over to them in a state unsuitable for a long sea voyage across the Mediterranean and Atlantic. In a letter of September 27, 1913, after the Sphinx had departed Egypt, Congdon writes, "The Sphinx was handed over to us nude and we had to pack it and protect it for the journey." At least we may be confident that Ramses II was modestly attired on his ocean voyage to Philadelphia.

In his letters to Gordon, Flinders Petrie had originally spoken about sending the Sphinx to Alexandria, Egypt's northern port city on the Mediterranean Sea. Although Alexandria was the main port of entry for passenger ships from Europe and America, it was not the best port for cargo coming from Cairo. Instead, we know from the communications between Gordon and Congdon that the Sphinx left Egypt by going first to Suez. Why? The Suez Canal provided the fastest and easiest way to get a sphinx onto a freighter bound for America.

CONGDON & CO.

Cairo, 27th Sept. 1913

Dear Sir,

We have much pleasure in informing, that the Sphinx has been safely shipped at Suez on the S.S. "Schildturm" for Philadelphia direct, and we hope to soon hear of its safe arrival.

Enclosed please find Bill of Lading and Insurance policy, together with our account of expenses connected with the shipment. This shews a balance to be returned to you of £70-6-0, for which please find cheque on London enclosed, which kindly acknowledge.

We did not pay the expenses of rail to Suez from Bedreschein, this we arranged should be paid by Mr. Flinders Petrie.

The Sphinx was handed over to us unde and we had to pack it and protect it for the journey.

We enclose two small photos of the Sphinx just leaving Cairo Museum but these do not give an adequate idea of its real size.

As this transaction is not an ordinary purchase one, we cannot send Consular Invoice – but we paid a nominal duty on £200 only.

We trust that you will be satisfied with our action in the matter, and we wait to hear from you upon arrival of the Sphinx, and hope it will be landed safely.

The Bill of Lading has been made out to the order of the University, so that you can arrange yourselves as to Clearance etc. by your own agent.

With every compliment

The Director
University Museum
Philadelphia U.S.A.

We are Yours very truly

J.W. CONGDON & CO.

3.6.

3.6. Transcription of letter from J.W. Congdon to Gordon, September 27, 1913.

3.7. Illustration of 'Progress' reaching Egypt with the opening of the Suez Canal (*Harpers Weekly*, December 18, 1869).

3.7.

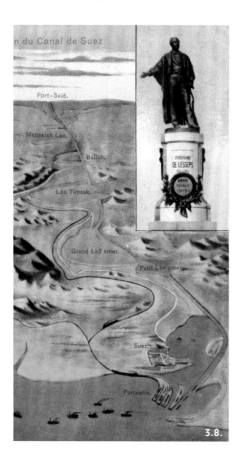

3.8. A 1912 postcard of the Suez Canal.

3.9. Port Said at the northern end of the Suez Canal in a postcard from ca. 1910. Note freighters almost identical to the *Schildturm* passing through the canal.

In 1913, the Suez Canal, running between the Mediterranean and the Red Sea, was the main artery of seaborne trade between Asia and Europe. It was built in 1859–69 by the Frenchman Ferdinand de Lesseps and the Suez Canal Company, and in the days of British rule, the canal used to be called the "Highway to India." Today, nearly 10% of the world's maritime trade still moves through the Suez Canal, generating more than five billion dollars a year for Egypt.

For Congdon and Co., Suez was the closest port by rail from Cairo and had the necessary facilities for loading the Sphinx onto one of the innumerable freighters that made use of the Canal. We do not have many details of this stage of the Sphinx's journey but we know it would have been taken on the rail line through Suez to reach Port Tewfiq, the main dockyard at the southern end of the Canal.

So, before the Sphinx could travel west it first had to travel east to the Suez Canal to be loaded aboard one of the many ships that passed through the Canal daily. In those days the railway to Suez skirted the scenic edge of the Nile Delta before heading eastwards through the Wadi Tumilat to Ismailia and then south along the edge of the Bitter Lakes. Had he been sentient, the Sphinx of Ramses the Great might have thought he was homeward bound to the great Ramesside capital city of Per-Ramses in the northeastern Delta, whereas he was headed out of Egypt entirely! Instead of northeast, the route took him south along the Sinai frontier, running straight through the town of Suez and out via a causeway to the shipping port, Port Tewfiq.

The Sphinx Boards the *Schildturm*

In 1913 large fleets of steamships plied the world's oceans, many of them making use of the Suez Canal. The problem was many of these ships already had set cargoes and destinations that would have prevented them from taking on a colossal stone sphinx going to America. At Suez, the Sphinx languished dockside for several months before the German freighter D/S *Schildturm,* coming westwards from Bombay and Karachi, loaded the Sphinx onboard. The *Schildturm* was a 5100-ton steam freighter operated by the Deutsche Dampfschifffahrts-Gesellschaft (DDG) "Hansa" of Bremen. The almost brand new (two-year-old) ship was mostly used for transport of dry goods and merchandise, so the prospect of carrying a colossal ancient Egyptian sphinx must have added a little bit of excitement to the crew's normal routine, even if Captain Kloppenburg considered it "undesirable cargo." What was the rest of the ship's cargo? Well, the port customs documents show the ship was filled with bales of goatskins, cotton, and myrobalan nuts from India used in making dyes for tanning.

Once loaded onboard the *Schildturm,* the Sphinx headed north to Port Said, the city on the northern end of the Suez Canal on the Mediterranean coast. From Port Said the *Schildturm* carried the Sphinx west through the Mediterranean

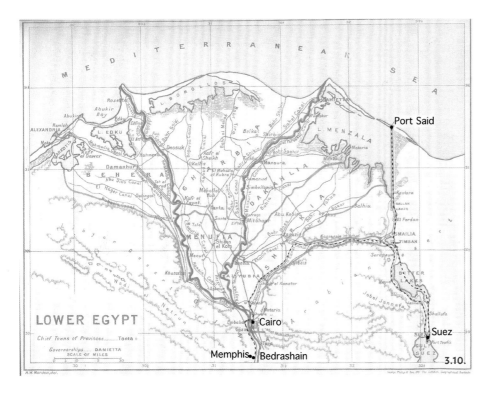

3.10. Map of the Sphinx's journey out of Egypt. The dotted red line indicates the train trip east to the Suez Canal, the blue, the trip by ship up to Port Said.

3.11. Suez's harbor, showing Port Tewfiq and the southern end of the Suez Canal. [After Baedeker's *Egypt* 1914]

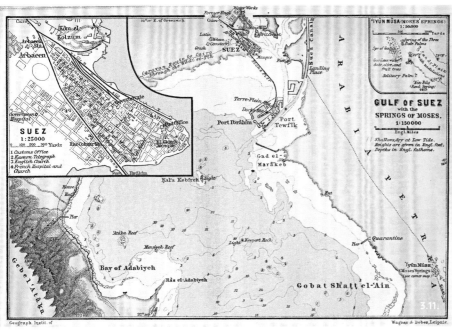

3.12. Train running through Suez station on the way to Port Tewfiq. The Sphinx would have passed the station on its way to the Suez Canal. Postcard from ca. 1915.

3.13. The docks at Port Tewfiq. Here the Sphinx waited three months for a ship willing to take it to Philadelphia.

3.14. The German freighter D/S *Schildturm* (ca. 1915). The Hansa shipping line, established in 1881, operated many ships over its 99-year history (the firm was closed in 1980).

with a stop in Algiers, and from there out into the Atlantic. Unfortunately for Captain Kloppenburg the timing of the ocean crossing to Philadelphia during late September and early October coincided with the Atlantic hurricane season.

Newspaper reports of 1913 in America tell us the *Schildturm* met with rough weather during its transit across much of the Atlantic, a concern for a mid-sized steamship. Unbeknown to Captain Kloppenburg, Egyptian monuments had been lost at sea before (most famously, the sarcophagus of king Menkaure from his pyramid at Giza which went down in 1838 on a ship in the middle of the Mediterranean Sea).

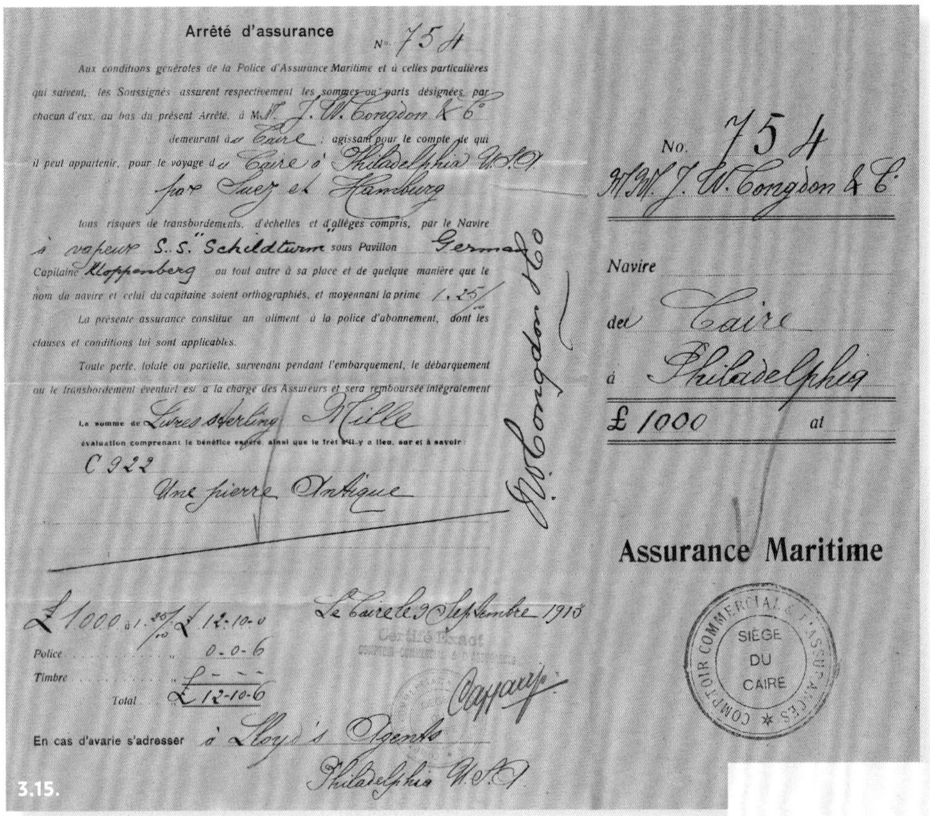

3.15. The Sphinx's traveling papers: maritime insurance certificate for the Sphinx on its voyage from Suez to Philadelphia.

3.16. Letter from Coxe to Gordon, September 19, 1913.

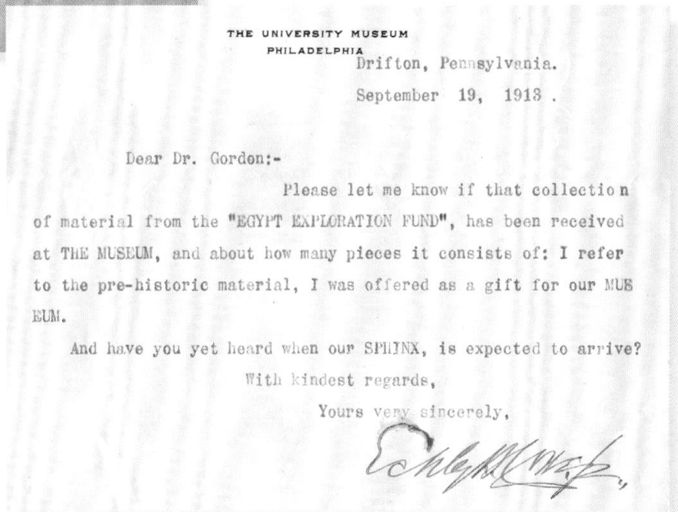

THE UNIVERSITY MUSEUM
PHILADELPHIA

Drifton, Pennsylvania.

September 19, 1913.

Dear Dr. Gordon:—

Please let me know if that collection of material from the "EGYPT EXPLORATION FUND", has been received at THE MUSEUM, and about how many pieces it consists of: I refer to the pre-historic material, I was offered as a gift for our MUSEUM.

And have you yet heard when our SPHINX, is expected to arrive?

With kindest regards,

Yours very sincerely,

3.16.

The Sphinx's Traveling Papers

So, what happened if the Sphinx was lost at sea? This was a real possibility to consider, especially given the time of year—Atlantic hurricane season—and there are plenty of examples of antiquities lost aboard ships that went down in the Mediterranean and Atlantic. Fortunately, as it turned out, the *Schildturm*'s crossing was merely slowed a little by the stormy autumn weather. Still, other disasters might be envisioned, such as the huge statue coming loose from its rigging and toppling into the murky depths of a harbor, never to be retrieved. Consequently, in Cairo Congdon and Co. took out a maritime insurance policy on the Sphinx in the amount of £1,000. For insurance purposes it was identified merely as "une pierre antique" (an ancient stone).

While the Sphinx was still on its 6,000-mile sea voyage, the Museum and its staff were, no doubt, filled with anticipation for the impending arrival of this colossal statue. They had only seen the Sphinx in the few photographs that Petrie and Congdon had forwarded to Gordon in Philadelphia. So, anticipating the day when the great granite figure would finally arrive in front of the Museum was an exciting prospect. It was, after all, the second largest ancient Egyptian object ever brought to America (after the Central Park Obelisk, which arrived in 1880). Eckley Coxe wrote to Gordon on September 19, 1913. It was a brief note containing a single line that barely conceals his anticipation, asking "have you yet heard when our SPHINX, is expected to arrive?"

3.17. Transcription of letter from Congdon to Gordon, November 3, 1913.

3.18. The *Schildturm* was renamed the *Flowergate* just prior to World War II.

CONGDON & CO.

Cairo, 3rd Nov., 1913

Dear Sir,

In response to your letter of 16th last, we enclose Consular Certificate as requested, and trust that all is in order, and that the Sphinx has duly reached Philadelphia safely, and that you are pleased with it.

Our telegram re additional freight was sent in consequence of the Shipping Co. having made an error in charging ordinary freight instead of exceptional, hence the increment although we do not agree with their methods, we had perforce to submit, hence our telegram.

Enclosed please find our small account for additional expenses, and hoping to have a line saying that Sphinx has safely reached you.

The Director   We remain yours very truly
University Museum
Philadelphia U.S.A.
                              J.W. CONGDON & CO.

3.17.

3.18.

3.19.

VESSEL BRINGS BIG SPHINX

Twelve-Ton Granite Image Will Be Placed in University Museum.

A 12-ton granite sphinx unearthed in Egypt by explorers from the University of Pennsylvania is on board the tramp steamer Schildturm, which arrived yesterday after a stormy two months' voyage from Bombay and anchored off the Girard Point piers. The sphinx, which is hewn from a single mass of red granite, the face being a likeness of Rameses II, is the largest and most important antiquity, next to Cleopatra's needle, ever brought to this country. It will be placed in the University Museum of Ethnology.

Some difficulty is expected in getting the image ashore because of its great bulk and weight. A special derrick probably will have to be erected and many horses brought into play to lift it from the vessel. It was dug up by the expedition under the direction of Professor Flinders Petrie.

The Schildturm stopped at Norfolk to land her Lascar seamen, who, under the terms of the shipping articles, cannot be taken north of the latitude of Hampton Roads, being of frail physique and unable to stand the cold of the North. The vessel on her return to the East will stop at Norfolk and reship the seamen.

3.20.

3.19. Article in *The Philadelphia Record*, October 7, 1913, announcing the arrival of the Sphinx.

3.20. A group of Lascar seamen, ca. 1915. [Image courtesy of the National Maritime Museum, Greenwich, London (http://collections.rmg.co.uk/collections/objects/552967.html)]

As we know, the passage of the Sphinx was a successful one and the Sphinx arrived in Philadelphia on October 7, 1913. No one had to collect on the maritime insurance. However, still to be resolved was the pesky issue of the Sphinx's weight. Nearly a month after the Sphinx arrived in Philadelphia, Gordon received a telegram and a letter from Congdon and Co. requesting additional charges for the transport of the Sphinx. The reason: it was "exceptional freight" and not "ordinary freight." Perhaps this "pierre antique" had caused Captain Kloppenburg and his crew a bit more trouble than they had bargained on. As we shall see, the companies who moved the Sphinx in Philadelphia would also charge extra for this unusual piece of cargo!

What happened to the ship that transported the Sphinx to Philadelphia? It continued to haul cargo for many years. Captured by the British during World War I, the *Schildturm* was sold to the shipping company Turnbull, Scott & Co. In 1918 it was renamed the *Flowergate* and operated until the Second World War. On June 6, 1944, the "sphinx-ship" was deliberately sunk off the French coast at Arromanches (Gold Beach) at Normandy. It and other old freighters were used to create artificial breakwaters, the "Mulberry Harbours," in order to allow the landing of the allied forces on D-Day. Surprisingly, the *Schildturm/Flowergate* was re-floated after Normandy, but in 1946 it was again deliberately sunk, for the final time, off the coast of Wales at Briton Ferry.

The Sphinx Crosses the Atlantic to…Virginia?

When Congdon and Co. arranged to transport the Sphinx, they had requested a ship that was sailing directly to Philadelphia. So, we might conclude that the Sphinx journeyed straight from Egypt to Philadelphia on the *Schildturm*—except that turns out not to be quite accurate. Strangely enough, before coming to Philadelphia the *Schildturm* and Sphinx took a 400-mile (644 km) detour south, docking first in Norfolk, Virginia. Here the story of the Penn Museum Sphinx touches on an interesting aspect of the history of shipping. The detour to Virginia had nothing at all to do with the ship's cargo but with the seamen that accompanied the Sphinx across the Atlantic.

Although the *Schildturm* was a German registered steamer, and Captain Kloppenburg was German, the ship was coming from India and many of the crew on the voyage were Lascars. The Lascars were Indian seamen, mostly from the southern part of the Indian subcontinent, who for centuries had served on European ships in southern Asia and the Indian Ocean. The Lascars had become

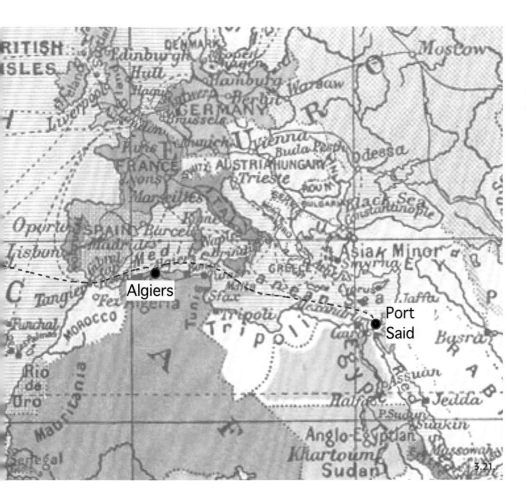

3.21. Map of the Sphinx's route across the Atlantic Ocean.

particularly important in the 19th century during the heyday of the British East India Company when that great trading conglomerate had relied on the Lascars to sail many of its ships. Lascars served especially as stokers in the coal-fired engine rooms of steam vessels like the *Schildturm.* As they were people who lived in the tropics, it was thought they were less susceptible to the heat and humidity of the engine room. Although the British East India Company was dissolved in 1874, the Lascars' role in shipping continued well into the 20th century.

The world of shipping in 1913 had lots of rules and regulations. One strange international policy was that Lascar seamen could not serve on ships in ports north of the 40th parallel of latitude. So Captain Kloppenburg stopped in Norfolk, Virginia, to drop off his Lascar seamen and take on another crew who then accompanied the *Schildturm* to Philadelphia. It is somewhat humorous to read the accounts of this in the newspaper reports. One of these, in the *Philadelphia Record,* states that the Lascars were unaccustomed to the "cold northern clime" of Pennsylvania and so had to be left in Virginia. It cannot have been that much warmer in Virginia in early October; and one suspects the able-bodied seamen would have had no problem surviving the weather in Philadelphia. In any event, in Virginia the Lascars bid farewell to the Sphinx as it continued on the final leg of its journey to Philadelphia.

CHAPTER FOUR

The Sphinx in Philadelphia

4

October 7, 1913:
The Sphinx Arrives

As the *Schildturm* steamed up the Delaware River on October 7, its Lascar crewmembers having disembarked in Virginia, the Sphinx was in sight of its final destination, but there were some additional hurdles to overcome. At that time Philadelphia was a burgeoning metropolis and one of America's most important inland seaports. The banks of its two rivers, the Delaware and Schuylkill, were lined with evidence of the city's industry and commerce. The Delaware waterfront was densely crowded with shipping piers. Stretching some 20 miles (32 km) from Port Richmond to South Philadelphia, the piers were dedicated to different shipping lines including both freight and passenger lines. The pier where the *Schildturm* first docked was Pier 47 in South Philadelphia; it belonged to the Hamburg-America Line, a larger affiliate of the Hansa Shipping Company which owned the *Schildturm*. Hamburg-America operated many passenger ships and the pier was suited only for passengers and light cargo, not heavy freight like the Sphinx.

News of the arrival of the Sphinx seems to have spread quickly. In 1913 Philadelphia boasted over a dozen daily newspapers, as well as a number of weeklies. Among the dailies were the *Philadelphia Daily Ledger, The North American, The Philadelphia Press,* the *Philadelphia Public Ledger,* the *Philadelphia Record, The Evening Bulletin,* the *Philadelphia Evening Ledger,* and the *Philadelphia Inquirer* (sadly, the only one of these papers remaining a century later). Reporters from the newspapers descended on Pier 47 for a glimpse of what was then the second largest Egyptian object ever to arrive in America. Stories appeared in all the daily papers and suggest quite a bit of excitement over the debarking of the Sphinx. However, at Pier 47 they quickly determined there was no machinery suited to unloading cargo as heavy as the Sphinx. In addition, from South Philadelphia the Sphinx would have to be hauled 4 miles through the busy city streets to reach the Museum. The decision was quickly made to move the *Schildturm* to another pier with the equipment needed to unload the Sphinx and with connections to rail lines that could be used to get the Sphinx across the city. After just a day in South Philadelphia the Sphinx headed north to Port Richmond.

4.1. Shipping pier of the Hamburg-America line in South Philadelphia where the Sphinx arrived on October 7, 1913. According to Director Gordon's letters it was apparently a gloomy, rainy October day much like this old postcard. The pier still stands today, one of a small number of Philadelphia's early 20th century docks that have been preserved nearly intact.

FIFTY MEN WILL MOVE BIG SPHINX

Twelve-Ton Specimen From Ancient Memphis Will Be Taken From Steamer Today

Half a hundred men will be necessary to remove the twelve ton Sphinx, bearing the face of Rameses II, from the steamship Schildturm at Christian street wharf this morning. The Sphinx, one of the largest archaeological specimens ever brought to this country, is consigned to the museum of the University of Pennsylvania, and arrived here Monday afternoon after a long trip from Suez.

It was necessary to install a large quantity of machinery at the wharf in order to insure the proper safety of the Sphinx. Officials of the museum will have to go through the usual formalities at the Custom House before the monument is allowed to enter. The men who will have charge of the unloading are all skilled mechanics. Transportation from the dock to the museum has been arranged for, but trouble is anticipated in getting the valuable relic into the court yard of the museum.

The monument comes here as part of the collection of Egyptian relics recovered during a recent expedition at Memphis, which was financed by the University and several British antiquarian associations. It is of red granite.

4.2.

Will Unload Sphinx Today.

Because there is no derrick on any centrally located wharf of sufficient strength to unload the 12-ton sphinx, just arrived for the University of Pennsylvania Museum, the steamer Schildstrum will today proceed to the Port Richmond ore piers where she will be relieved of her valuable burden. Once ashore the sphinx will be transferred to West Philadelphia as soon as the necessary Custom House formalities are concluded.

4.3.

LAND BIG SPHINX FOR U. OF P. TODAY

Being unable to get a crane powerful enough to lift from its hold the eleven-ton Rameses II sphinx, shipped here from Egypt for the University of Pennsylvania Museum, the steamship Shildatrum left Christian street wharf last night and steamed up to the Port Richmond coal wharves of the Reading Railway.

The sphinx will be lifted out at 10 o'clock this morning and started on its way to the university. A crane used for lifting locomotives will be utilized.

4.4.

4.2. *The Philadelphia Inquirer*, October 8, 1913.

4.3. *The Philadelphia Record*, October 8, 1913.

4.4. *The Evening Bulletin*, October 8, 1913.

4.5. *The North American*, October 8, 1913.

UNLOAD 11-TON SPHINX

Big Crane Makes Easy Job of Landing Egyptian Relic for U. of P.

The eleven-ton stone sphinx, brought here from Egypt for the University of Pennsylvania, was only a featherweight in the fifty-ton crane by which it was lifted from the hold of the steamship Schildturn at the Philadelphia and Reading Railway pier, below Allegheny ave., this afternoon.

The vessel had docked at Christian st. wharf, but there was no apparatus strong enough to handle the big relic. The crane at the Port Richmond piers is the largest in the city. It required only fifteen minutes to lift the sphinx from the hold of the vessel.

The usual custom house formalities must be complied with by the museum authorities, this being the first importation of the kind to come under the new tariff law at any port in the country. The figure was loaded directly onto a flat car and transported to the freight yards at 23d and Arch sts., from where it will be carted to the museum. One of the largest trucks to be found in the city, drawn by fourteen horses, and with fifty men to aid in the work, will be employed to carry the monstrosity from the yards.

The Sphinx is the largest specimen in the museum, and one of the largest Egyptian relics in this country. It was found recently in excavations at the site of ancient Memphis. It is the sphinx of Rameses II., and bears a likeness of the ancient ruler of the land of mystery.

4.5.

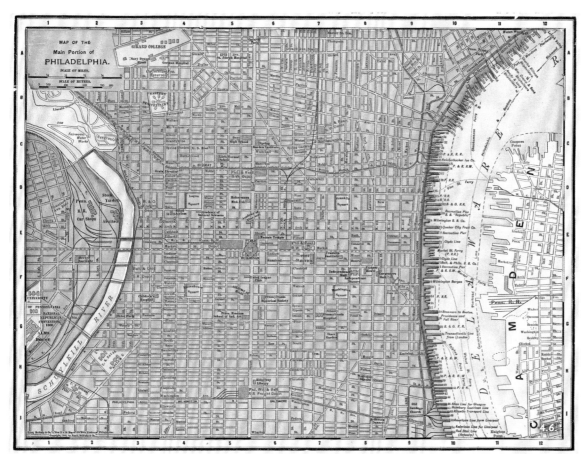

4.6. Pier 47 where the *Schildturm* docked is located at Christian Street, across from Old Swede Church in Queen Village. It was used by the Hamburg-America shipping line as we see in this 1913 map of central Philadelphia. (The Museum itself is not marked on this map; its location is instead labeled "National Republican Convention, 1900.")

PHILADELPHIA AND READING RAILWAY COMPANY'S TERMINAL, PORT RICHMOND,
PHILADELPHIA
4.7.

EXPORT PIER G, PORT RICHMOND, PHILADELPHIA, PHILADELPHIA AND READING
RAILWAY
4.8.

4.7. The massive river port of the Philadelphia and Reading Railway terminal at Port Richmond included piers for export of anthracite coal, as well as a host of other goods brought by PRR's rail network.

4.8. The 100-ton heavy lift crane at Export G. This crane lifted the Sphinx from the *Schildturm* onto a railroad car for the final leg of its journey across the city to the Museum.

4.9. The Philadelphia skyline of 1913, looking northwest over Center City. [Public domain image; source is http://commons.wikimedia.org/wiki/File:Downtown_Philadelphia_Pano_1913.jpg]

Philadelphia and Reading Railway's Giant Crane

Obviously what was needed to get the Sphinx out of the hold of the ship was a very large crane. The largest one then in operation on the Delaware waterfront was a 100-ton heavy cargo crane located at the freight terminal operated by the Philadelphia and Reading Railway Company at Allegheny Avenue in Port Richmond. Designed for lifting train engines in and out of ships, the crane at Export Pier G was perfect for the job. In addition, the freight terminal connected directly to The Reading's train tracks, which could be used to move the Sphinx to West Philadelphia some 10 miles away. By October 8 the *Schildturm* had moved north to Port Richmond and that same evening the giant crane had made short work of unloading the Sphinx. It took just 15 minutes to hoist the Sphinx out of the freighter and set it on the flatbed of a railway car for the final leg of its journey.

The Sphinx's arrival in Philadelphia owes much to the economic power of Pennsylvania anthracite coal. We have already noted that the business fortune of Eckley Coxe derived from coal mining. Similarly, the Philadelphia and Reading Railway, established in 1833, was a company with immense wealth that stemmed from the extraction and delivery of coal from the very same regions of eastern Pennsylvania. Although by 1913 governmental regulation had caused the company to diversify significantly, The Reading's facilities on the Delaware River where the Sphinx was unloaded were extensively used in the shipping of coal.

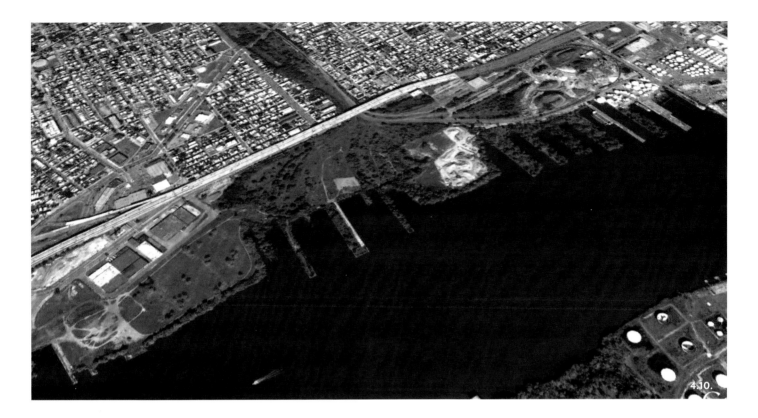

Bonds, Bills, and Consular Invoices

When the Sphinx arrived it wasn't possible to simply unload it and send it on its way to the Museum. Importing an Egyptian sphinx to America in 1913 was not just an issue of transportation and delivery. It was also a procedure that involved permissions, permits, and approvals at many levels. Like any cargo arriving in the Port of Philadelphia, the Sphinx had to have papers filed and fees paid. The arrival of merchandise had to be declared at Philadelphia's Custom House through filing of a shipping manifest.

The Museum fortunately had considerable experience with these procedures having brought many objects in by sea from distant lands. The Museum filed a Consular Invoice, an official document declaring the legality, value, and purpose of importing the Sphinx. This they sent through a custom's brokerage, E.H. Bailey

THE DEMISE OF THE PHILADELPHIA AND READING RAILWAY

In 1913 the Philadelphia and Reading Railway Company was at the height of its long and illustrious history. The company had by that time expanded well beyond coal and ran one of the largest and most modern passenger train systems in the United States. Whereas The Reading's freight lines ran to the Delaware River freight terminal in Port Richmond, passenger lines into the city converged on the magnificent Reading Terminal Headhouse on Market Street, still one of Philadelphia's great Gilded Age landmarks. Despite the diversification of the company, however, its fortunes were never far removed from its origins in the mining and transport of coal. By the time of the Second World War the reliance on coal for heating and energy was fading, and the company entered a long decline that ended with its sale to Conrail in 1976.

Today, the formerly bustling Philadelphia and Reading freight terminal at Port Richmond is one of the largest expanses of derelict land on the Delaware River waterfront. It is now cut off from the city by I-95, a highway that has isolated much of Philadelphia's waterfront. The river piers, now overgrown with vegetation, still stand, including Pier G where the giant crane unloaded the Sphinx. The city has had ongoing discussions about repurposing this area as well as the Philadelphia-Reading viaduct that runs westwards through the city.

4.11. The major reminder of the great Philadelphia and Reading Railway Company is the Reading Terminal Headhouse, which opened in 1893. Founded on its coal transport business, the company established an extensive and modern passenger train business. Postcard from ca. 1916.

4.12. The Custom House was located in the original Second Bank Building of the United States until it was moved in 1932. The "Old Custom House" is now preserved as part of Philadelphia's Independence National Park. Postcard dating to ca. 1910.

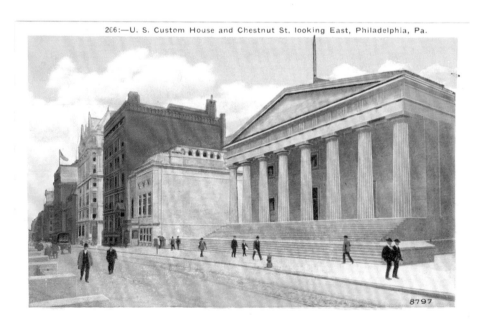

and Company. Also paid through these agents was the "bill of lading" for removal of the Sphinx from the *Schildturm*. All of this allowed the Sphinx to continue on the final leg of its journey to its new home in West Philadelphia and the Penn Museum.

Papers filed at the Philadelphia Custom House include, strangely, a shipping manifest listing the Sphinx on paper titled "Philippine Islands Foreign Manifest." Was this a mistake to do with the origin of the cargo? We know the ship had originated in Bombay and sailed via Karachi, Port Sudan, and Suez.

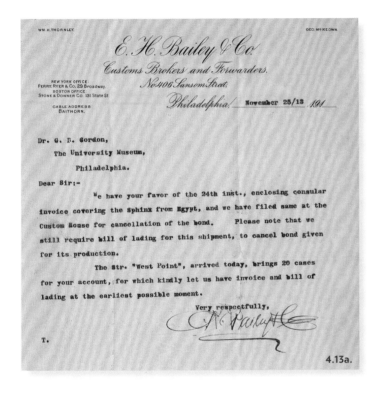

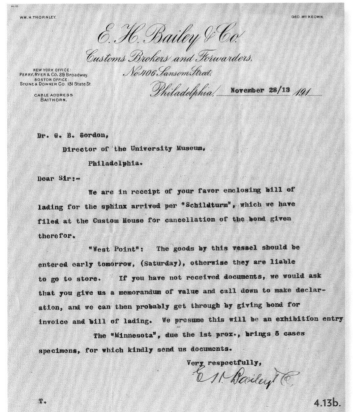

4.13a, b. Letters to Gordon from Customs Brokers E.H. Bailey and Company regarding the Sphinx's consular invoice and bill of lading.

4.14. Shipping manifest for the *Schildturm*. [Philadelphia Custom House records, courtesy of National Archives, Philadelphia]

4.15. List of the merchandise brought to Philadelphia aboard the *Schildturm*. [Philadelphia Custom House records, courtesy of National Archives, Philadelphia]

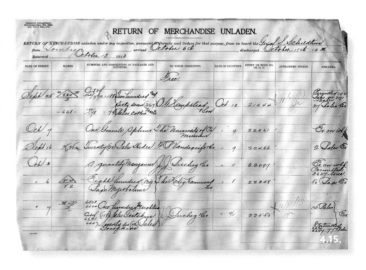

4.16. The Sphinx shares space with opening day of the World Series on the front page of *The Philadelphia Inquirer*, October 7, 1913. [Image courtesy of Dan Biddle and Jackie Rose]

4.17. Game program of the 1913 World Series (then called the World's Series).

The Sphinx Meets the 1913 World Series

Tuesday, October 7, 1913, was not just the day the Sphinx arrived in Philadelphia. It was also the opening day of the 1913 World Series between the Philadelphia Athletics and the New York Giants. The newspaper writers of that week were obsessed with baseball reports. Nevertheless, the story of the Sphinx's arrival managed to grab a front-page spot in *The Philadelphia Inquirer* (below a wry cartoon showing the World Series overshadowing the more pressing issues of the day—like women's suffrage, which was not achieved until 1920).

While the Sphinx sat at the dock on the Delaware, baseball was the topic of the day. The Athletics, coached by the famous Connie Mack, spent the week shuttling between the Polo Grounds in Manhattan and Shibe Park in Philadelphia. Although Philadelphia fared badly in game 2, the Athletics decisively defeated the Giants four games to one. Perhaps Ramses II had inadvertently brought good luck to the city with his timely arrival.

Such was the level of baseball fever in the city that several newspapers mention that after the Sphinx was unloaded in Port Richmond on October 8, it languished another week before the requisite workers could be gathered to offload it to a wagon for its final delivery to the Museum. If we are to judge from the photos of the 1913 World Series—crowds spilling out of Shibe Park and on nearby rooftops—it is easy to believe that most of the available workmen were watching baseball and not interested in moving a giant granite sphinx.

4.18. Shibe Park at 21st and Lehigh Avenue in North Philadelphia. Built in 1909, this was one of the finest baseball fields prior to the First World War, with a capacity for 25,000 fans. Later named Connie Mack Stadium, it was demolished in 1976. [Image courtesy of The Library of Congress Prints and Photographs Division, Image # LC-USZ62-79895]

4.19a, b. Fans sitting atop houses next to Shibe Park, 1913 World Series. [Image courtesy of The Library of Congress Prints and Photographs Division, Images # LC-B2- 2286-13 (P&P) and LC-DIG-ggbain-14493]

4.20. Although baseball might be construed to be a new and foreign custom to the Sphinx of Ramses II from Memphis, the Great Sphinx at Giza had already encountered this distinctively American sport with English origins. In 1887, a Spalding American baseball match between Chicago and All America occurred at the Sphinx's home. Here the teams pose with the Great Sphinx, which was only partially excavated at that time. [Image courtesy of The National Baseball Hall of Fame & Museum, Inc.]

The Sphinx's Brush with the Silver Screen

On the day the Sphinx docked in Philadelphia, Eckley Coxe wrote to Director Gordon suggesting—among other things—that someone should make a film (a "moving photograph") of the Sphinx being unloaded and transported to the Museum. Coxe proposed contacting the Lubin Manufacturing Company about making the film. If the Lubin Company showed the film, it would be a good way to attract attention to this exciting new addition to the Penn Museum. On October 9, Gordon wrote back to Coxe: "The Lubin Manufacturing Company called me up and said that they were going to try to get pictures of the unloading of the Sphinx by the Reading Railway crane at Port Richmond, and also of the journey to the Museum. The weather has been so dark, however, that I do not know what success they have met with." So, was a film of the Sphinx's arrival ever made?

4.21. Transcription of letter from Eckley Coxe to Director Gordon, October 7, 1913.

THE UNIVERSITY MUSEUM
PHILADELPHIA

October 7, 1913

Dear George:

I have just received your letter, telling me that our Sphinx has arrived safely, and that it came up the Delaware, on the steam-ship "Schildturm" from Suez.

After it has passed the custom house, and is ready for transport to our Museum, I am sure that it would be a very good idea to hire a motor-truck to move it, as it weighs eleven tons. If you can procure the motor-truck, I will be glad to pay for it, and the necessary men to move this wonderful Sphinx. It is the first Sphinx which has ever come to America, and we ought to feel very proud of it, I personally do. If you will give me Petrie's address, I will write and thank him for it, and also for the bust of the God of the Nile, Hapi; and for the part [of] a stone bull.

Please send me photographs of all of these objects.

I think soon it would be a good idea, to get Max Muller, to write a first class illustrated article for the newspapers, both in Philadelphia and New York about them, in especial our Sphinx, although of course it is not as old as The Sphinx at Gizeh.

I overlooked a few other photographs of some of the collection, we received from The Egypt Explordion Fund, I will soon send them.

How would do, to have a moving photograph taken of the transportation of our Sphinx from the unloading, transporting and receiving at Museum: I think that this could be arranged through Lewis M. Swaab 129 North 8th Street, or at least he could tell you who would do it. I would be very glad to have one for my own collection.

Or you might write direct to Lubin Manufacturing Company, 20th Indiana, Philadelphia, and see if they would take it, of course they would want to exhibit this film, and so it would be a good thing in every way.

With kindest regards,

Yours very sincerely,
Eckley B. Coxe Jr.

Here the story of the Sphinx touches on an often forgotten detail of early 20th century Philadelphia history. In the pre-Hollywood era of 1913, Philadelphia was home to one of the United States' most successful movie companies, the Lubin Manufacturing Company founded by Siegmund Lubin. Established in 1902, the company ran Lubin Studios, producing silent movies for public release. In 1910, the company built "Lubinville" at Indiana Avenue and 20th Street in North Philadelphia. Lubinville was the largest and most up-to-date motion picture studio in the United States. Between 1902 and 1916, the Lubin Company produced approximately one thousand silent films—primarily action and comedy—that were marketed to theaters on the East Coast.

Lubin was one of the early movie producers who realized the importance of mass marketing. After the first nickelodeon was built in Pittsburgh in 1905, Lubin built a small empire of these five-cent theaters up and down the East Coast

4.21.

4.22.

for marketing his films. These were popular venues and Eckley Coxe may have envisioned people getting their first glimpse of the Sphinx on a Lubin film.

Here references to the Sphinx film disappear in the Museum's correspondence, but letters in Archives seem to indicate that Lubin had taken footage of the Sphinx's unloading in Port Richmond. However, there is no copy of this footage in the Museum. Unfortunately, the celluloid film used by Lubin and others was highly flammable; in 1914 the main warehouse of the Lubin Studios caught fire, destroying the negatives of a number of his films. (It is estimated that 85 percent of the vast output of films produced before 1930 in the United States is now lost; corrosion of silver nitrate paired with its flammability took its toll on America's earliest movies.) What happened to Lubin's footage of the arrival of the Sphinx? We may never know. Perhaps the quality of the footage was poor due to the "dark weather." Perhaps the footage was discarded or destroyed in the 1914 inferno at Lubin Studios. However, just possibly, Lubin's "sphinx movie" is sitting yet to be found somewhere!

4.23.

4.24.

An Interview with the Sphinx

Among the numerous newspaper articles that covered the arrival of the Sphinx in Philadelphia there is one that stands out as being the most interesting and creative. On October 8, 1913, the writer H.T. Craven published a humorous interview with the Sphinx in *The North American.* Craven took advantage of the novelty of the situation to use the voice of the Sphinx to weigh in on various social issues of the day. In the "interview," the Sphinx seems unimpressed by the state of things. He comments on the baseball rivalry of the 1913 World Series (between the Philadelphia Athletics and the New York Giants), the glaring lack of pyramids, the odoriferous piggeries, and the apparent obsession with what he thinks is a god named "Dollar." (The "King Rudolph" to whom Ramses II refers is Rudolph Blankenburg, mayor of Philadelphia from 1911–16.) Finally the Sphinx decides to go back to sleep for a few thousand more years!

4.22. The "Lubinville" studio at Indiana and 20th Streets. [Photo courtesy the Library Company of Philadelphia]

4.23. A Lubin Nickelodeon on Chestnut Street, Philadelphia. Note the "¢5" in lights. Eckley Coxe thought that Lubin would show the film of the Sphinx in one of these popular theaters. [Photo courtesy the Library Company of Philadelphia]

4.24. Rudolph Blankenburg—the Sphinx's 'King Rudolph'—was mayor of Philadelphia in 1913. He was a highly influential politician known popularly as the "Old Dutch Cleanser" for his progressive reforms of city government. [Image from *The World's Work* (1914), p. 361]

4.25. H.T. Craven's "interview" with the Sphinx (published in *The North American*, Wednesday, October 8, 1913).

OUR ED'S PIGGERIES PUT JINX ON INTERVIEW WITH SPHINX

Old Rameses, Here for Penn, Gets a Whiff or Two and Then Wants to Go Back Home Again

By H. T. Craven

Long the interviewer pondered. Long he wondered what to say to the sphinx of old Rameses whom he called on yesterday. In his standard list of questions, not a single one would fit. He could

gabble with Carnegie, but he could not talk to "It." He had cornered politicians, floored them with his inside dope, but the sage of ancient Memphis robbed his thoughts of ev'ry hope. So they glared at one another in a silence grim and grave, till at last Rameses thundered: "Speak, abject and crawling slave. Must I lead the conversation; I, the king of countless lands; I, the potentate of Nilus; I, the ruler of the sands?" Still no answer till Rameses muttered, "Boy, I'll tell you what I'll do. I'm in search of information. I'll conduct the interview.

"First, where am I. Philadelphia? never heard its name before; is it many miles from Karnak; is it near to great Luxor? What are all these fragile buildings — not a pyramid I see. Where's the palace, where's the temple, where's a home for such as me? What is baseball, what's a 'series'? Do the Hittites war with us? What is all this silly pother; all this crude and childish fuss? Are there Giants in the country — never had 'em in my time. They were

only stuff for children down at Philae, the sublime. Do I like your native city? No, I cannot say I do. Why it doesn't seem half finished. Everything is cheap and new. Rudolph is the king, you tell me. Has he palaces and slaves? Has he tombs of noble mummies; where are his ancestral graves? What—he only rules the city. Who's the monarch of the land? He's installed by all the people? Isis, make me understand!

"Is there in this crazy empire any one whom I might know? Cleopatra dwells in Gotham! Take me to her, let me go to the luscious queen of Egypt, to that other sphynx I'd speak and I'd ask her, can you stand it living here week after week, where I hear that all is "Dollar," worshipped with a frantic greed?' Never back in smiling Memphis did I suffer any need of this god I find installed here, of the only king who's great in this shoddy land I've come to, he the only potentate. Home I never prayed for money. All the minions worked for me. I was just the sole contractor in the good old days B. C. Graft and muckrakes—nothing doing—in that age beyond recall. Then I was the only grafter Old Rameses had it all!"

As a subtle smile of triumph played upon that ancient face, lo an odor far from fragrant, permeated all the place. "By the thousand gods of Egypt is that piggeries I smell? Have you swineherds in the city? Look you, boy, and look you well, in the days of King Rameses we would run the place in style, and when hogs walked in the city, we would dump them in the Nile!

"Woe is me! Why have I awakened in an age so poor and mean? Let me sleep another eon and reflect on what I've seen."

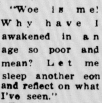

Then the life went from the image, which had dormant lain so long, and the interviewer wondered if perhaps he had been wrong and the thing had never spoken, never changed that stony gaze; that contemptuous stare of wisdom, born of Egypt's mighty days.

4.25.

Across the Schuylkill and Over the Wall

After traveling over 6,000 miles, the Sphinx was practically a stone's throw from its destination. Once Philadelphia and Reading's giant crane had lifted the Sphinx onto a rail car, the statue was moved over the train tracks to Philadelphia and Reading's freight yard at 23rd and Arch Streets. The Sphinx now had only to cross the Schuylkill River to reach its new home: the courtyard of the Museum at 33rd and South Streets. But traveling those final ten blocks was a challenge. One problem was that the rail tracks did not run all the way up to the front of the Museum, so the Sphinx had to be transferred from its rail car onto a special reinforced steel wagon. In addition, once it was in front of the Museum the Sphinx would have to be hoisted up and over the courtyard wall. All of this took some time. It was about a week before the Museum had made the full arrangements with Henderson and Co. of West Philadelphia to handle the rigging and installation of the Sphinx. Between October 8 and 18 the city's newspapers reported on the "homeless" Sphinx awaiting its move to the Museum.

Meanwhile, 50 University of Pennsylvania students, eager to see the Museum's new addition, offered to help bring the Sphinx across the Schuylkill River. The students' offer was welcome but in the end, 50 "brawny workmen" (who seem to have called it a "sphinnix") were enlisted for the job. The students instead organized a parade to welcome the Sphinx to the Museum.

SPHINX REMAINS ON RAILROAD CAR

Tackle Must Be Built to Get Unwieldy Art Treasure to University Museum.

Until special rigging is arranged, the eleven-ton sphinx intended for the University Museum must lie at West Philadelphia railroad station on a flat car.

Dr. Gordon, director of the Museum, does not see how it can be transferred without causing considerable damage to the wall and hedges of the court-yard. He thinks the specimen of Egyptian art will not be situated permanently until next week.

The Museum has never experienced difficulty in placing its treasures. Nor has it had anything which cost so much for transportation as this red granite figure of Ramesis II and the lion. The cost of bringing it from Suez, Egypt, where it lay for two months, was less than half the expense the Museum will incur through its removal from the steamer Schildturn, its transportation and placement.

The piece was undesirable freightage and the captain of the Schildturn was induced to take it only on condition he would not remove it at its destination.

Dr. Max Muller will begin work on the translation of the hieroglyphics on the pedestal as soon as it is placed. He expects interesting results. Professor Flinder Petrie, who found the sphinx, is said to have spent little time at the translation. 4.26.

TO MOVE SPHINX

Authorities of the University of Pennsylvania museums are hunting a contractor with the equipment necessary to move the eleven-ton sphinx of Rameses II from Twenty-third and Arch streets to the museum courtyard, at Thirty-third and Spruce streets.

The Philadelphia and Reading Railway yesterday transported the red granite monument to its Twenty-third street siding, the nearest point to the museum the railroad reaches. From there a reinforced steel wagon and a score of horses is necessary to move the sphinx through the streets. It is crated and will not be seen by the public until it is unveiled in the museum grounds. 4.27.

SPHINX STILL HOMELESS

No Contractor Yet Found Equal to Task of Removal.

The University Museum's twelve-ton sphinx the second largest piece of Egyptian art ever brought into this country, is spending its fourth day in the Reading freight yard at Twenty-third and Arch streets. No contractor has been found who has apparatus equal to the task of moving the mass of stone.

The work of removing the sphinx to the museum at Thirty-fourth and Spruce streets will not begin until Wednesday or later, Director Gordon said yesterday. 4.28.

STUDENTS OFFER AID IN REMOVING SPHINX

Fifty University of Pennsylvania students have volunteered to assist in the removal of the sphinx from the Reading freight yard, at Twenty-third and Arch Streets, to the Museum court-yard.

The Museum authorities are plainly puzzled over the problem of getting the huge piece of granite over the museum wall.

The students want to see the sphinx in the court-yard before a week has elapsed. 4.29.

4.26. *The Philadelphia Press*, October 10, 1913.

4.27. *The Philadelphia Press*, October 8, 1913.

4.28. *The Public Ledger*, October 11, 1913.

4.29. *The Philadelphia Press*, October 12, 1913.

427, BIRD'S EYE VIEW OF WEST PHILADELPHIA 4.30.

4.30. Early 20th century postcard view over the Market Street bridge and the Schuylkill River.

STUDENTS TO GREET SPHINX

Demonstration Expected to Follow Arrival at University.

The University of Pennsylvania, sometimes apathetic in regard to the archaeological specimens displayed in its museum, is becoming interested in the 12-ton Sphinx, which has lain for a week in a freight yard at 23d and Arch streets, defying efforts to transport it. Its arrival at the campus on Wednesday is awaited with curiosity, and the probability is that a student parade will form on Wednesday to accompany the aged monstrosity to the museum, at 33d and Spruce streets. The stone is 14 feet long, 6 feet high and 6 feet wide.

The Sphinx is to be moved to the museum courtyard. It will be swung onto a heavy iron-wheeled truck from its present perch on a flat car. Ten horses will be needed to haul it.

Fifty workmen will receive the Sphinx at the museum. There the mass of stone must be lifted over a coping ten feet high, up a flight of steps and upon its pedestal.

4.35.

NINE HORSES DRAW SPHINX

Ramases II., Eleven Tons of Sandstone, Rides in State from Freight Yard to Penn Museum

Rameses II. was hoisted off a box car by a steam crane to-day, deposited on a lumber truck, and then drawn in state by nine horses, to the University of Pennsylvania Museum, 33d and Spruce sts.

This Rameses the Second is a sphinx, and his sandstone form weighs eleven tons.

Nearly three weeks ago the old boy was brought to this port, and unloaded at the Port Richmond wharves. From there he was transported by rail to the Reading freight yard, 22d and Race sts.

The husky workmen who assembled there at 8 o'clock this morning, for the purpose of removing Rameses to his final resting place, betrayed little respect for the "sphinnix," as they called it. But they did handle Rameses with care, for the Egyptian gentleman is brittle.

A crowd of Penn students was on hand to greet the sphinx when it reached in the precincts of the University, and a special detail of police was present to prevent souvenir hunters from taking a hack at Rameses. The route taken on the way to the Museum was down 22d st. to Market, to 33d st., and thence to Spruce.

A large derrick had ben erected, and when the sphinx arrived at the Museum, block and tackle were attached, and Rameses was lifted over the wall into the garden.

A special track of heavy timbers ran from the wall, on th einside of the garden, to the spot where the sphinx was to rest. Rollers were placed under Rameses and he was rolled into place. 4.31.

Gets a 5,000-Year-Old Sphinx

A wonderful relic of Egyptian history, a sphinx figure of Rameses II, found a year ago in the ruins of ancient Memphis, has been taken to the University of Pennsylvania Museum, where it will be placed in the courtyard. The red granite carving shows the face of the king with the body of a lion. It was carved from a solid stone more than 5,000 years ago and is the first sphinx to be brought to this country. It weighs 11 tons and measures 12 feet across. Through its annual contribution to the British School in Egypt, the University of Pennsylvania has acquired title to the sphinx. 4.32.

If Rameses II could see his portrait sphinx hauled from a flat car to the University of Pennsylvania Museum on a stout dray by nine horses he would be impressed with the mechanical improvements that have been made since the age of pyramids and sphinxes and mummies. In his own days the sphinx would probably have been dragged by several thousand slaves. The most sweeping and fruitful change that has occurred since he sat on the throne of Egypt is the substitution of mechanical devices for human strength, and the most revolutionary social and economic change is that, whereas in his day human beings were exploited, it is now the forces and the treasures of nature that are exploited.

4.33.

12-TON SPHINX REACHES PHILADELPHIA ON WHEELS

Nine Horses Drag Stone Image to University Museum; Face Uncovered.

Special to The Free Press.

Philadelphia, October 18.—Reposing on a truck drawn by nine horses the 12-ton sphinx, which arrived some time ago from Egypt, was carted over the final stages of its journey to the University museum today.

The sphinx was removed from a flat car at Twenty-third and Arch streets, where it has been since its unloading from the steamship Schildtum several weeks ago.

When the sphinx arrived it was covered with burlap. For the journey today the covering had been removed from the great stone face and Philadelphians for the first time were permitted to gaze on the calm and majestic countenance of the stone Ptolemy which had lain buried for 32 centuries in the sands of Egypt. 4.34.

SPHINX IS FINALLY TAKEN TO MUSEUM

Eleven-ton Sculpture Escorted Westward by Fifty Workmen and Penn Students

With an escort of fifty brawny workmen and a crowd of Penn students, the eleven-ton sphinx representing Rameses II, which arrived here from Egypt a few weeks ago, was taken to the University Museum, Thirty-third and Spruce streets, yesterday afternoon.

The sphinx was hoisted from a box car in the Philadelphia and Reading freight yard, at Twenty-second and Arch streets, where it has been since its arrival, and deposited upon a truck, which was drawn by a team of nine horses to the museum. The procession, which went south on Twenty-second street to Market, west on Market to Thirty-third street and thence south to the museum, attracted the attention of many hundred passers-by, as this was the first time since its arrival that it had been uncovered.

It was lifted over the wall of the museum by a derrick and placed on a track of timbers that reached from the wall to the inside garden of the museum. A police guard was established to prevent souvenir seekers from chipping off pieces. 4.36.

4.31. *The Evening Bulletin*, October 18, 1913.

4.32. *The Dispatch* (Pittsburg, PA), October 18, 1913.

4.33. *The Philadelphia Record*, October 19, 1913.

4.34. *The Free Press* (Detroit, Michigan), October 19, 1913.

4.35. *The Public Ledger*, October 14, 1913.

4.36. *The Philadelphia Inquirer*, October 19, 1913.

4.37. *The North American*, October 19, 1913.

READY TO HOIST SPHINX OVER THE MUSEUM WALL

SPHINX'S FACE WORN OFF BY 12,000 YEARS OF WEATHER

RAMESES II ON WAY TO HIS NEW HOME HERE

Eleven horses and fifty men were required to move the 3000-year-old sphinx from Twenty-third and Arch streets to the University Museum, Thirty-third and Spruce streets. Darkness fell before the sphinx could be lifted over the museum wall, so work was delayed until tomorrow. The huge stone image, weighing eleven tons, rests today upon the pavement outside the museum, jacked up on heavy timbers.

RAMESES II SQUATS ON PHILA. SIDEWALK

Too Dark to Boost Him Over University Wall Last Night

GOES OVER TOMORROW

Darkness prevented workmen who superintended the hauling of the 3000-year-old sphinx of Rameses II from the freight yards to the University Museum, Thirty-third and Spruce streets, yesterday, from lifting the eleven-ton Pharaoh over the museum wall. As a result, old Rameses will occupy an undignified position on the pavement until Monday. A watchman is keeping a sharp eye upon him, to shoo off relic hunters.

The sphinx was hauled from the yards at Twenty-third and Arch streets, where it has been since unloaded from the German steamer Schildturm, which brought him from Egypt several weeks ago. A steamer crane made short work at the freight yard, and Rameses was placed on a big truck drawn by eleven horses. Alongside walked a solicitous crowd of workmen.

At the museum a derrick was erected, and a track of planks laid through the courtyard to the spot where Rameses is to remain. He will be boosted over the wall tomorrow.

Rameses' face shows his age, for it has completely disappeared, with the exception of his whiskers. He has a fine square bunch chopped off short. He wears no mustache. As for his body, it represents a lion, the entire statue being carved from hard red granite. About the base are inscriptions placed there by the great king's press agent.   4.37.

"Rameses' face shows his age, for it has completely disappeared, with the exception of his whiskers."

MANY NEW TREASURES AT UNIVERSITY MUSEUM

Greek and Roman Sculpture and Cretan Relics Soon to Be Placed on View.

GIANT SPHINX IS MOVED

Good Reports From Many Expeditions in Field During Summer.

With the opening of the scholastic year at the University of Pennsylvania the museum has rearranged a number of its exhibits and is preparing to have a series of exhibitions of the recent purchases which have not yet been shown to the public. In a short time there will be an exhibition in the west wing on the second floor of the museum of some fine specimens of Greek and Roman sculpture which never have been shown, while others just purchased are expected to arrive at the museum in time for the exhibit. There will be with these marbles exhibitions of Oriental art, which have been secured during the summer, including fine specimens of very ancient rugs, needlework, Chinese bronzes, porcelains and stoneware. The Cretan relics have been unpacked and will be shown to the public. The museum has by far the finest collection of Cretan relics in the country. There have been some recent additions to the Thomas H. Powers' memorial collection, consisting of specimens of Indian arts and crafts, while some additions to the Heye collection have been secured by the expedition of Professor Harrington to the Otoes.

Sphinx Is Removed.

The most recent important acquisition is the sphinx of Rameses II, which was moved yesterday to the courtyard of the museum. This will be the most spectacular exhibit in the institution and will be placed advantageously for public view. Reposing on an ordinary truck, drawn by nine horses, the final journey of the big carved stone was removed from a flat car at Twenty-third and Arch streets and carted through the streets. The route taken by the team drawing the sphinx was south on Twenty-third street to Market, west to Thirty-fourth and south on that thoroughfare to the museum. Here it was hoisted over the wall by a crane and deposited in a space designated for it in the institution. Fifty laborers were needed to unload it from the car to the truck yesterday morning. While the imposing figure sat in state, the men, like a guard of honor, in soiled working clothes, walked by the side of the vehicle during its journey to the museum.

When the sphinx arrived in Philadelphia it was covered with burlap. For the journey yesterday the covering had been removed from the great stone face and Philadelphians for the first time were permitted to gaze on the calm and majestic countenance of the stone Ptolemy which had lain buried for 32 centuries in the sands of Egypt. **4.38.**

Unloading Sphinx at University Museum

4.38.

RAMESES II TO ADORN MUSEUM WALL TO-DAY

Rameses II, nineteenth dynasty Pharaoh, will have his royal stone image permanently placed in the University of Pennsylvania Museum to-day, after having squatted on the concrete pavement all day Sunday, just like any ordinary person. Yesterday's rain soaked his burlap togment through.

A huge derrick will hoist the red granite figure over the Museum wall to-day. Then the sphinx will be assigned a permanent place in the Museum courtyard, and there will no longer be any necessity for the attendance of a watchman to prevent curio seekers from chipping off pieces of the stone body. There is little fear that the face can be more badly mutilated than it is. Thirty-two centuries have sufficed to erode Rameses' noble physiognomy until it bears little resemblance to a human face.

4.39.

4.38. *The Philadelphia Record*, October 21, 1913.

4.39. *The Philadelphia Press*, October 20, 1913.

On October 18, the Sphinx was loaded onto a big horse-drawn wagon and rolled to the Museum accompanied by the workmen, as well as the parade of University of Pennsylvania students. The short journey took the Sphinx up Market Street in what sounds like an impressive procession, drawing the attention of throngs of onlookers: "While the imposing figure sat in state, the men, like a guard of honor, in soiled working clothes, walked side by side of the vehicle during its journey to the museum" (*The Philadelphia Inquirer*, October 20).

The Sphinx of Ramses II spent nearly two whole days resting curbside on Spruce Street before it was set down in the Museum's courtyard, and many a passerby had a chance to get their first glimpse of the Penn Museum's new acquisition. In newspaper photographs we see the Sphinx on the wagon with just face and shoulders peeking out of its burlap covering. The University stationed special guards in case treasure-seekers attempted to break off bits of the statue as a memento. Some reports state that passersby started taking pieces of the burlap covering as souvenirs.

4.40.

The twelve-ton sphinx from Ancient Memphis, Egypt, sits on its stone haunches in the University Museum court yard after being safely hoisted over the troublesome brick wall. Hundreds of persons looked upon its uncovered figure for the first time yesterday. With the exception of the head, the 3200-year-old figure is in perfect condition. It is probably the most highly prized treasure in the museum.

The Sphinx

that was brought to the University of Pennsylvania last Saturday is supposed to have been cut out of stone in the days of the great Egyptian King Rameses II, 1300 years before the beginning of our era; yet at that early time across the Red Sea from Egypt stood Nineveh (where now stands Mossoul, a center of the Persian rug industry), and Nineveh was already then famous for its rugs, which went as prizes to the great kings of the East.

Many and many civilizations have risen and fallen and passed away since that day, but the glory and the splendor of the art of the Oriental rug has lasted through and survived them all.

4.41.

4.40. *The Philadelphia Press,* October 22, 1913.

4.41. Wanamaker's Department Store advertisement, October 1913.

On October 18 and 19 wooden tracks were laid down and a 50-foot wooden derrick was installed. By the evening of October 19 the workmen slid the Sphinx off the cart and slowly pushed it over two huge wooden beams up to the front of the courtyard wall. There it was attached to the hoist and on October 20, slowly, inch by inch, maneuvered up and over the wall and finally back down onto another wooden track over which it was slid to the back of the courtyard. Think of the relief of the workmen once they could just slide the Sphinx into place.

"The Most Highly Prized Treasure in the Museum"

Imagine the excitement during the week after the Sphinx first arrived. Here was the second largest Egyptian monument to arrive in America since New York's Central Park obelisk in 1880. Thousands of visitors thronged the courtyard to see the statue of Ramses II. For many this was undoubtedly the first Egyptian monument they had ever seen. Other than its size and the mystique imparted by the weathered head, many visitors were surprised by the delicate quality of carving on the Sphinx's lion body. One woman apparently rubbed her hands over the Sphinx's side and, astounded by the carefully chiseled ripples of the lion's ribs, reported her "discovery" to the Museum attendants. Actually these details are very important, as we discuss in another part of this book, so the woman was rightly impressed. People continued to project thoughts and opinions onto the Sphinx as in the "Interview with the Sphinx" in *The North American*. Some of these articles form an interesting commentary and critique on society in 1913.

It was not just Philadelphians who came to marvel. Within a few days, visitors reportedly arrived from up and down the East Coast to see the Sphinx. Even the city's merchants tried to drum up some business from the public interest in the new arrival. Wanamaker's Department Store in Philadelphia put out an advertisement claiming that their rugs for sale represented a tradition as ancient as the Sphinx itself…one wonders did the antiquity of the Sphinx motivate anyone to buy a rug from the store?

Two views of the Sphinx in its new surroundings (p. 71) were taken in 1915. Here we see the recently completed Rotunda behind the 1899 Museum building. The lotus flowers in the Museum's fishpond would be a familiar sight for an Egyptian sphinx, perhaps reminding him of his days on the Nile!

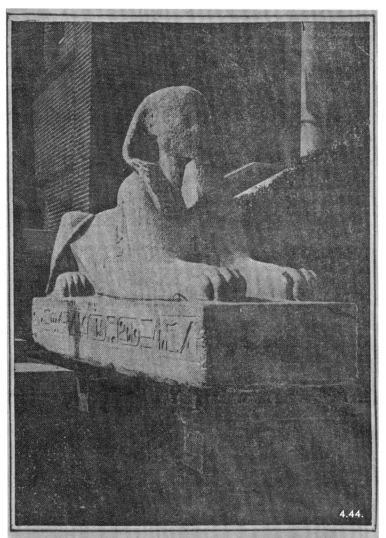

SPHINX OF RAMESES II, MIGHTIEST PHARAOH
This memento of Rameses II, known as the Pharaoh of the Oppression, now in the courtyard of the University Museum, is considered one of the best existing mementos of the famous monarch, with the possible exception of his colossal statue near the ruins of the sanctuary of Ptah. Thousands viewed the sphinx last week.

A Sphinx Visits Pennsylvania

AMERICA now has a Sphinx, supplied by the ruins of Memphis, Egypt, to the University of Pennsylvania. It is of red granite, chiseled out 3,100 years ago in honor of Rameses II. **4.43.**

4.42. *The Philadelphia Inquirer*, October 22, 1913.

4.43. *Colliers Weekly* (New York City), October 22, 1913.

4.44. *The Public Ledger*, October 26, 1913.

4.45.

4.45. A 1915 postcard of the University of Pennsylvania Museum.

4.46. The Sphinx to the left of the Museum's ivy-covered main entrance, ca. 1915.
[Image courtesy of the University of Pennsylvania Archives, #UARC20040315002]

4.46.

4.47. Franklin Field (left center) and the Museum (right) in 1915. The rotunda (far right) was completed after the Sphinx arrived, allowing the statue to be taken indoors in 1916. [Image courtesy of the University of Pennsylvania Archives, #UARC20030430007]

4.48. *The Public Ledger,* October 19, 1913.

Mr. Ramses Becomes a Football Fan

We know the Sphinx arrived in Philadelphia on opening day of the 1913 World Series. It was a fun exercise for people to speculate what the Sphinx would think of American sports. Might the Sphinx be a sports fan? Since his stone countenance was unable to answer, it was at least entertaining to envision what he might think. Of course, as an honorary Philadelphian it was obvious he had to be a supporter of Philadelphia teams!

The Museum sits directly opposite Franklin Field, the University of Pennsylvania's football stadium and main sports arena, and on October 18, preparations were underway for a game between the Penn Quakers and the Brown University Bears. In those days Franklin Field did not have the high tiers of seating that it does today (the stadium in its current form was not built until 1922). Instead it had lower, open stands. With the Sphinx set facing the stadium, it seemed natural to some that Ramses II's Sphinx might have some interest in the events going on across the way. The Quakers soundly beat the Bears 24–0. For

SPHINX ATTRACTS
CURIOUS THRONG

Rameses II Proves Rival o
Penn-Brown Football
Game.

A sphinx of Rameses II, 3000 years old
suspended by a 40-foot derrick in fron
of the University Museum yesterda
afternoon, proved a rival attraction t
the Pennsylvania-Brown fotball game
which was in progress on Franklin Field
just across the street.

SPHINX JOINS IN GRIEF AT OLD PENN

Students, Dismayed Over Defeat by Cornell, Go Home for Holiday.

Penn's grief-stricken students have gone home for the Thanksgiving vacation, carrying along much dismay and perplexity. The campus is hushed. No sound of scurrying feet disturbs the stillness of the classroom. The janitors and art relics at the University Museum alone remain to weep over the Cornell victory.

Rameses II, royal Egyptian sphinx, is unable to suppress his tears. His stone face streams with water. All night long he is said to have wailed and cried over the ignominious defeat. The gold fish, which make their home in the courtyard pool swim listlessly about their accustomed haunts, vainly seeking to hide their glittering bodies among the slimy weeds.

Hapi, god of the Nile, has lost his smile. Aeons of time had not been able to remove Hapi's grin, but the football result turned the trick and now the Billiken of the Egyptians has a face creased with the wrinkles of gloom. If Hapi is ever again to look like his old self, a sculptor will first have to chisel out the wrinkles.

Museum attendants optimistically declare it is a good thing Cornell victories come only one in twelve years. Otherwise incalcuable evil might result to the stone gods who take a Penn defeat so hard. Nevertheless some solace is found in the fact that the sphinx, although attached to the University for scarcely three weeks, is yet so imbued with the Penn spirit as to give way to grief over a football defeat.

4.49.

November 8, 1913

Expenses in connection with removal of sphinx from Memphis, Egypt.

Bill of Congdon & Co.	$391.00
Bill of Gailey,Davis & Co. Towing steamer from South St. Wharf to Port Richmond & labor	110.25
Bill of P. & R. Ry.Co.for crane service, labor, material in loading &c.	31.47
Bill of P. & R. Railway Transfer of sphinx from Port Richmond to 23rd & Arch Sts.	28.80
Bill of Henderson & Co. Hauling and setting up sphinx	225.00
Bill E. H. Bailey & Co. custom house charges	7.50
	$ 794.02

4.50.

superstitious sports fans the Sphinx seems to have brought Penn good luck on the day it arrived. Of course, despite the auspicious victory over Brown, the Quakers could not maintain their edge forever. A month later Penn suffered a crushing loss against Cornell, 21–0. On that rainy fall day, a writer for the *Philadelphia Press* suggested the water streaming down the Sphinx's face was actually tears shed at the Quakers' "ignominious defeat"!

4.49. *The Philadelphia Press*, October 29, 1913.

4.50. Part of a letter from Gordon to Eckley Coxe itemizing costs of moving the Sphinx.

How Much Did It Cost?

How much did it cost to transport a colossal sphinx over 6,000 miles from ancient Memphis to Philadelphia in 1913? Considering the Sphinx's size it was surprisingly cost-effective. Eckley B. Coxe, the Museum's main benefactor, paid the bill. Remember, he had agreed in 1912 to pay for transportation, even when he thought it might be the Alabaster Sphinx that was coming to Philadelphia.

On November 10, 1913, with the Sphinx comfortably positioned in the Museum's front courtyard, Director Gordon sent the final accounting to Mr. Coxe. A total of $391 was the charge by Congdon and Co. to cover the rail costs in Egypt and its shipping to Philadelphia from Suez on the *Schildturm*. A total of $403.02 covered the towing of the freighter to Port Richmond, the Sphinx's unloading using the large Philadelphia and Reading Railway's crane, and its transport from Port Richmond to the Museum. The grand total: $794.02.

Some of the newspapers at the time remarked on the high cost involved in moving the Sphinx. While $794.02 was certainly a hefty sum in 1913, converted to today's dollars the total bill appears to be relatively modest. Given the buying power of a dollar in 1913 this equals about $17,000 in today's dollars: surely a reasonable sum for a colossal sphinx for the University Museum. It would cost a lot more today to move such a big statue so far and so quickly. What is perhaps a little surprising is that it cost more to unload the Sphinx and transport it 12 miles (19 km) in Philadelphia than it did to haul it 6,000 miles across the Mediterranean and Atlantic!

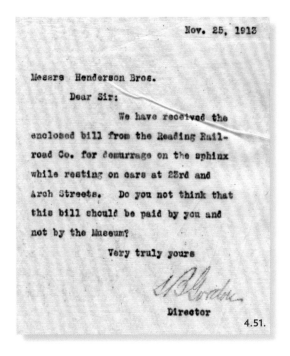

Nov. 25, 1913

Messrs Henderson Bros.

Dear Sir:

We have received the enclosed bill from the Reading Railroad Co. for demurrage on the sphinx while resting on cars at 23rd and Arch Streets. Do you not think that this bill should be paid by you and not by the Museum?

Very truly yours

Director

4.51.

June 15, 1914

Messrs Gailey, Davis & Co.,
316 Walnut St., Phila.

Dear Sir:

I have your letter of June 13th enclosing bill for $17.50 for extra labor in discharging the sphinx from the steamer Schildturm on October 10th last.

It was understood that your bill rendered on October 13, 1913, for which you received our remittance, covered all charges for which we were liable connected with the landing of the sphinx. If the bill now rendered was a legitimate charge, I fail to understand why it was not included in your bill of October and why nine months should have been allowed to elapse before any attempt was made to collect this amount.

Under the circumstances I cannot feel satisfied that we are liable for these charges.

Very truly yours,

Director 4.52.

July 2, 1914

Messrs Gailey, Davis & Co.,
316 Walnut St., Phila.

Dear Sir:

I have given the matter of the extra charges on the sphinx Ex S/S SCHILDTURM very careful attention. The conclusion to which I have arrived is that we cannot be held responsible for the charges indicated in your recent correspondence.

Very truly yours

Director 4.53.

So, by the middle of November, all the bills were paid up for transportation of the Sphinx…or so Director Gordon thought. Then, a series of requests began to arrive for extra expenses entailed in moving the statue in Philadelphia. Remember that Congdon and Company had billed the Museum extra on account of the Sphinx being "exceptional cargo." The companies that handled the Sphinx in Philadelphia did the same thing. First came the request from the Philadelphia and Reading Railway Company for the demurrage of the Sphinx on rail cars while it waited for ten days at 23rd and Arch Streets. This request Gordon simply forwarded on to Henderson Brothers whom the Museum had already paid for that stage of the Sphinx's transport.

Next, on June 13, 1914, exactly nine months after their original bill had been paid, an additional request came from Gailey, Davis and Co. This was the company who had worked with the Philadelphia and Reading Railway Company and managed the unloading of the Sphinx at Port Richmond. They considered the freight charge of $30/ton to be "in no way adequate to rates going on such cargo." They requested payment of an additional $17.50 for "extra labor involved in discharging the Sphinx ex this steamer in October last." Using a figure of 12 tons for the Sphinx's weight this would have totaled an additional $210. After several letters back and forth, Director Gordon politely declined to make payment. There the matter finally rested, as did the Sphinx in its new home.

The Sphinx Resides Outside

In October of 1913 the Sphinx was installed in the garden courtyard fronting the Museum. This location was never intended to be permanent but was necessary since construction of the Rotunda that now houses the Museum's Chinese collection was still going on behind the existing building. During this time the Sphinx sat on the left side of the main entrance propped on railroad ties. This location was oddly appropriate since this is the position the Sphinx would have assumed in ancient Memphis: guarding the north-facing gateway into the temple of Ptah.

During its three-year sojourn in the Museum's garden the Sphinx encountered something new: the cold and sometimes snowy winters of Pennsylvania. In December 1914 there was a sizeable

4.51. Letter from Gordon to Henderson Brothers, November 25, 1913.

4.52. Letter from Gordon to Bailey, Davis and Co., June 15, 1914.

4.53. Letter from Gordon to Henderson Brothers, July 2, 1914.

CHARLES SHEELER AND THE SPHINX

Following its arrival at the Museum, Director Gordon received numerous special requests to photograph the Sphinx. The Museum had photographs available for sale for 25 cents. but many people were interested in taking their own photographs. In 1915 the Philadelphia artist and photographer Charles Sheeler made a series of professional photographs of the Sphinx. These are some of the only remaining images from the Sphinx's three-year sojourn in the Museum garden. Sheeler later achieved fame as one of the most significant painters of American Modernism. Sheeler's art focused particularly on architecture and industrial structures, revealing his fascination with the 20th century industrial landscape. The juxtaposition of the ancient Sphinx against the backdrop of the Museum's brick facade appears to have appealed to his interest in materials and the built environment.

4.54. Charles Sheeler, 1883-1965. [Image after *Archives of American Art Journal* v. 5, no. 2, p. 3; v. 16, no. 4, p. 15]

4.54.

4.55. Photograph by Charles Sheeler of the Sphinx in the Museum courtyard, ca. 1915. [UPM image # 249486]

4.55.

October 22, 1915

My dear Prof. Petrie:

We have now received the sphinx and it has been placed in the courtyard of the Museum where it looks very well. At the present moment we are not able to put it indoors as the new building is not finished. The other objects which you have sent from London have arrived in New York, but are not yet cleared from the custom house.

I want to thank you for the trouble and interest that you have taken in behalf of our Museum.

We desire to renew our subscription to the British School of Archaeology in Egypt for the coming year and a draft for $1,500, equal to £308.6.6 will go forward in the next mail.

Very sincerely yours

Director

PROF. W. M. FLINDERS-PETRIE
University College
Gower Street, London, W.C.
England

4.56. Transcribed letter from Gordon to Petrie, Oct. 22, 1913.

4.56.

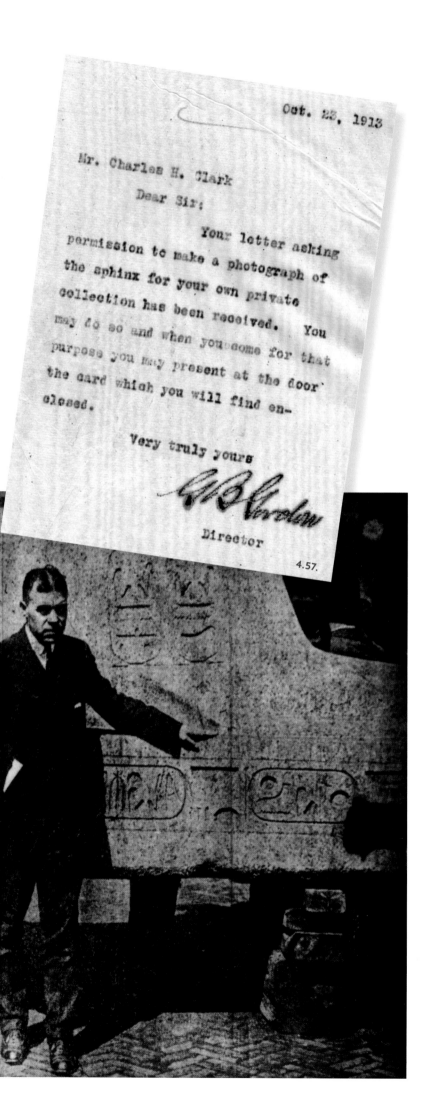

Oct. 23, 1913

Mr. Charles H. Clark

Dear Sir:

Your letter asking permission to make a photograph of the sphinx for your own private collection has been received. You may do so and when you come for that purpose you may present at the door the card which you will find enclosed.

Very truly yours

Director

4.57.

4.57. Request to photograph the Sphinx.

4.58. The Sphinx became a popular spot for outdoor photos. Here Assyriologist Stephen Langdon poses with the Sphinx. (*The Globe*, Bethlehem, PA, Oct. 10, 1916)

early winter snowstorm. A series of charming—and incongruous—photos taken of the Sphinx at this time show the statue from the sunny land of the Nile blanketed with snow. Snow is, after all, a substance for which the ancient Egyptians had to borrow a Semitic word, *srq*. A writer for the *Philadelphia Evening Ledger* put the Sphinx's imagined discomfort to verse claiming Ramses II was feeling bitterly cold and might even crack in two!—an unlikely outcome in reality.

Even though the idea that the Sphinx might crack in half seemed exaggerated, Museum officials were indeed worried about the long-term effects of weather on the statue. After the snowfall of December 1914 (and spurred by the *Evening Ledger* article and several others that followed), Eckley Coxe wrote to Director Gordon addressing his concerns about keeping the Sphinx outside. He even offered to pay for a wooden shelter to cover the Sphinx until the time it could be moved inside the Museum. It was decided that the wooden shelter was an unnecessary and ugly addition, but Coxe's worries about the potential damage of leaving it outside helped push the plans to move the Sphinx to a warmer, drier setting indoors.

PENN'S SPHINX SO COLD IT MAY BREAK IN TWO

But Is Too Big to Be Carried Through Doors of Museum.

The snappy end of an Arctic breeze that stings
    like the lash of a blacksnake whip,
Shrieked through the stark, denuded trees and
    into the face of the Sphinx did rip—
Who squats in granite grandeur glum,
In the yard of the U. P. Mu-se-um,
By age old disposition mum,
And longs for a foreign trip.

The Sphinx was cold as the frozen North, and
    he made his two-ton figure shake;
"Beware," at last he sputtered forth, "or my
    granite frame will freeze and break;
Once I was young and brae and bold,
But now, egad, I'm getting old;
And I wanna get out of the bitter cold
And go back home to bake."

Several blankets, ear muffs, pulse warm-ers and a large open fireplace are badly needed by the aged sphinx who sits in front of the University Museum at 34th and Spruce streets and defies the museum authorities to take him inside where it's warm. Officials have come to the con-clusion that if he stays outside much longer the cold will break him in half, but the only way of getting him inside is to break a hole in the wall, the door not being large enough.

The sphinx apparently is too old and "sot" in his ways to get acclimated. For several thousand years he had been ac-customed to a sun-baked residence in Egypt. He got so accustomed to the sun that he cannot get along without it. Professor Max Muller, noted Egyptologist, says that one year of this climate will do more to damage a sphinx than 5000 years of captivity in Egypt.

The full name of the sphinx at the museum is Rameses II. So far the mu-seum authorities have not decided what to do about him. He probably will have to stay cold for a time.

4.60.

4.60. *The Philadelphia Evening Ledger,* December 18, 1914.

The Sphinx Comes Indoors

In the autumn of 1916 Director Gordon made the final decision to move the Sphinx from the courtyard to inside the Museum's main entrance. Although a short journey, there were some worries about this move. One issue was whether the building's floor could support the over 12-ton Sphinx. Gordon consulted with the building's original architects—the architectural firm Cope and Stewardson—who confirmed that the Sphinx could be placed in front of the stairway leading down into the Museum's recently completed auditorium (now Harrison Auditorium). In a letter to the company who moved the Sphinx, Gordon was nevertheless concerned, stating, "we will relieve you from further responsibility in case the weight should prove too heavy for the strength of the floor."

Very fortunately, the architects' calculations were correct. The Sphinx did not crash through the floor of the main entrance and remained there until 1926. Only one known photograph currently exists in the Museum's archives showing the Sphinx regally welcoming visitors coming through the Museum's entrance.

Even though the Sphinx was moved inside the Museum, this location too was regarded as temporary. At that time the Egyptian galleries were located on the Museum's third floor in the "Fitler Pavilion." This space was not ideal for the scale of some of the objects and the Sphinx had to remain separated from the rest of the

4.61. Letter from Coxe to Gordon, December 18, 1914.

4.62. The Sphinx being moved in 1924 just prior to its installation in the almost-completed Coxe Wing. [Image courtesy of the George D. McDowell *Philadelphia Evening Bulletin* Collection at Temple University Library]

4.63. A view of the Sphinx being moved out of the Museum in 1924. The date on the photograph is August 9, 1924. [Image courtesy of the George D. McDowell *Philadelphia Evening Bulletin* Collection at Temple University Library]

4.64. Another view of the Sphinx "leaving" the Museum for the last time in 1924. [Image courtesy of the George D. McDowell *Philadelphia Evening Bulletin* Collection at Temple University Library]

Egyptological displays. Of developing concern was the fact that, at the time, huge architectural elements were being excavated in Memphis, Egypt, by the Museum's new Egyptian curator, Clarence Fisher (see the next chapter). The Museum hoped to receive some of these elements through the division of finds from the Egyptian Antiquities Service.

4.65. Letter from Gordon to Mrs. Charles Brinton Coxe (Eckley's mother), November 15, 1916.

November 15, 1916

Dear Mrs. Coxe:

I have your very agreeable letter of November 12th and I have also received a letter from Mr. Charles Sinkler, on behalf of the Executors of Mr. Coxe's Estate, which contains a statement relative to the Egyptian Expedition identical with the statement which you have so kindly written to me. The Egyptian work is one of the very greatest importance and it is very fortunate that provision has been made for carrying this work forward during the year 1917. The Museum is in every way to be congratulated on this circumstance.

The sphinx looks very well indeed in its now resting place just inside the entrance of the Museum at the head of the stairs which descend to the auditorium. Until the new part was finished he had to remain out of doors and I am glad to say he sustained no injury at all from the weather. This great sculpture looks much better indoors and it also improves the appearance of the entrance.

However, this cannot be regarded as its permanent resting place and I am heartily in accord with you that a large and impressive Egyptian Hall must be provided for all of our fine Egyptian collections. Such a Hall should be worthy both of the civilization of Ancient Egypt and of the noble and generous citizen through whose interest in that civilization so many fine things have come to Philadelphia.

It was a great disappointment to me not to have seen Eckley last summer and it has been a sorrow to me ever since. As you know, I never until this summer missed a visit to Drifton since I have been in Philadelphia and the days which I have spent there with yourself and Eckley were very pleasant ones to me.

I am glad to know that you are coming to Philadelphia soon and you may be sure that I am looking forward to the time when I shall be able to see you again.

Very sincerely yours

4.65.

The movement of the Sphinx inside corresponded with an unfortunate moment in the Museum's history. In the summer of 1916, Eckley Coxe, benefactor of the Museum's excavations and Chair of the Museum's Board, passed away unexpectedly. Gordon wrote to Coxe's mother Elizabeth (Lizzie) in November of that year with the idea of honoring Eckley Coxe with a grand "Egyptian Hall" to house the materials—including the Sphinx—from excavations he had sponsored in Egypt. This letter from Gordon to Mrs. Coxe is the first of many concerning the planning for what would become the Museum's Coxe Wing. The Wing, which opened in 1926, represents a new page in the Museum's interest in ancient Memphis. Just one year after the Sphinx arrived in Philadelphia the Museum was—surprisingly—awarded an excavation concession at the site of Memphis. With funds from Coxe, excavations commenced on a promising area southeast of the temple of Ptah and not far from where Petrie had unearthed the Sphinx in 1912.

Clarence Fisher discovered the well-preserved remains of a ceremonial palace of pharaoh Merenptah, the son and successor of Ramses II. Many large architectural elements from the Merenptah palace ended up coming to Philadelphia along with a host of other finds. Gordon's vision of an Egyptian Hall would be realized in a grander way than he originally thought. Most appropriately, the Sphinx of Ramses II would come to be reunited in Philadelphia with many other elements that also came from the grand Ramesside-era buildings of ancient Memphis. The Sphinx itself was the herald of a whole series of wonderful discoveries from Memphis that form the most unique components of the Penn Museum's Egyptian collections. In the next chapter we will examine what happened in the era after the sphinx's discovery, but importantly how the sphinx itself was a turning point, a fulcrum, in the history of the Museum's Egyptian collection.

4.66. The original Egyptian gallery of the Museum, ca. 1916, when it was located in the Fitler Pavilion. The Egyptian galleries, along with the Sphinx, were moved in 1926 upon completion of the Coxe wing. [UPM image # 237289]

4.67. View, ca. 1918, of the Sphinx sitting just inside the main entrance to the Museum. [UPM image # 237290]

CHAPTER FIVE

A Royal Setting for the Sphinx

Petrie Offers Penn the Treasure of a Princess

Following the arrival of the Sphinx in Philadelphia the Museum's relationship with Flinders Petrie could not have been better. The cordial letters between Director Gordon and Petrie show a professional respect between the two men. Petrie looked to the Penn Museum as a reliable source of financial support and as a promoter of the excavations of the British School of Archaeology in Egypt. At the same time, Gordon consulted Petrie for advice in the search for a new excavator to succeed David Randall-MacIver and the Museum's plan to continue the Coxe Egyptian Expedition.

On March 13, 1914, barely six months after the arrival of the Sphinx, a letter from Petrie addressed to Eckley Coxe arrived at the Museum. The letter contained a remarkable offer. Petrie had just discovered one of the most important groups of royal jewelry unearthed in Egypt in the days before Tutankhamun: the treasure of the 12th Dynasty princess Sit-Hathor-Iunet at the site of Lahun. The Antiquities Service had selected several of the objects to remain in the Cairo Museum. However, they granted the remainder of the treasure to Petrie who sought to place it in another museum. No doubt influenced by the recent positive experience of the Sphinx, Petrie offered this treasure to the Penn Museum. Today, however, the treasure of Sit-Hathor-Iunet may be seen in the Egyptian galleries of the Metropolitan Museum in New York, not in Philadelphia. What happened?

The Middle Kingdom (the 11th–13th Dynasties, ca. 2050–1750 BCE) dates half a millennium before the age of Ramses II. During the height of the Middle Kingdom, pharaohs built pyramids, many of these being located just south of Memphis and at the entrance to the Fayum region. The site of Lahun, about 50 miles (80 km.) south of Memphis, is the location of one of the royal pyramids from Egypt's Middle Kingdom. Here stands the pyramid of Senwosret II, fourth pharaoh of the 12th Dynasty. Surrounding it are other tombs including some belonging to other members of the royal family. When Petrie worked at Lahun in 1889–1890 he had uncovered the remains of a large town inhabited by the people who managed

5.1. Transcription of letter from Flinders Petrie to Eckley Coxe, Feb. 21, 1914.

> Strictly Private
>
> Lahun, Fayum
> Egypt
> 21 Feb. 1914
>
> My dear Sir
>
> I must ask you to keep this letter strictly private till the summer. So far as you may consult other persons, please do avoid ever mentioning or suggesting my name or this place. I am obliged to ask this for the sake of your personal safety, and that of our work.
>
> We have found a set of jewellery like that of Dahshur. I enclose rough prints to give you some idea of it. Maspero will certainly need the crown, and perhaps one pectoral, but there will be a large amount to go to some Museum and as Philadelphia has so long helped my work, I should give you the preference before any other American Museum.
>
> I cannot say without consultation what value should be put on such things; for nothing of this quality has ever been sold, the only parallel are the two great Dahshur finds now in Cairo. I should say the whole group would be worth somewhere between 50,000 $ and 100,000 $. My only question to you now is this: – If the half of this group is in the hands of the British School will you beat all in the running to secure it! I may say that the crown could be very well reproduced to go with the rest of the group.
>
> I shall be glad to hear whether we may regard you as a possible claimant for this, as soon as possible, as I shall have to settle the matter with Maspero at the end of March or early in April.
>
> Thanks for your letter. I am very glad that the Sphinx is acceptable. I fear we shall not be able to work Memphis this year, for various reasons.
>
> Yours sincerely,
> W.M.F. Petrie
>
> Eckley Coxe, Esq.

5.1.

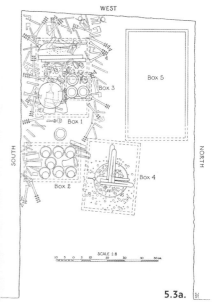

5.3a.

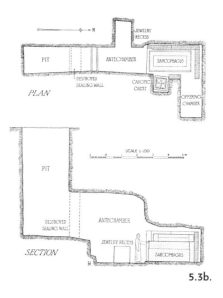

the mortuary temple of Senwosret II. In 1913 he returned again to conduct new excavations for the British School while continuing his work at Memphis. During his previous work he had discovered the interior of Senwosret II's pyramid but had not examined the area immediately around the tomb where burials of royal family members would be expected. The work mostly produced empty shafts leading to burial chambers plundered long ago. One of these robbed shafts, however, contained a mud-filled recess in the wall. When opened, this contained the treasure of princess Sit-Hathor-Iunet: a crown, two pectorals, necklaces, and caskets, one containing the princess's silver mirror and numerous other objects.

During the early 20th century the Antiquities Service operated on a system of division of finds. Normally, Egypt retained the better half of the finds—and any unique materials—for the Cairo Museum, where they were placed on display or kept in storage. Realistically, however, there were so many objects entering the Cairo Museum that they regularly sold off the less significant pieces in the

5.4.

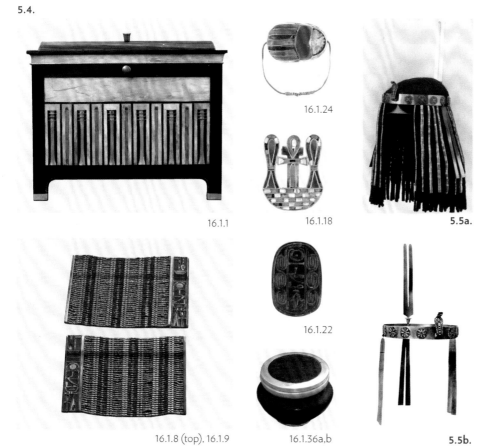

5.2. The pyramid of Senwosret II (12th Dynasty, ca. 1850 BCE) at Lahun. [Photo courtesy of Zoltán Horváth]

5.3a, b. The robbed tomb of princess Sit-Hathor-Iunet at Lahun contained a rich cache of her jewelry and burial goods that had escaped ancient tomb robbers. [After Winlock, *The Treasure of El Lāhūn*, (1935), fig. 2 (top), fig. 1 (bottom)]

5.4. Objects from the tomb of Sit-Hathor-Iunet now in the Metropolitan Museum of Art, New York: inlaid casket (16.1.1); bracelets with name of king Amenemhat III during whose reign she died (16.1.8, 16.1.9); jewelry (16.1.24, 16.1.18, 16.1.22), and a cosmetic jar (16.1.36a, b). [All objects are from the Rogers Fund and Henry Walters Gift, 1916. Images courtesy of The Metropolitan Museum of Art, www.metmuseum.org]

5.5a, b. The crown of Sit-Hathor-Iunet now in the Cairo Museum (JE 44919). [Images after Winlock, *The Treasure of El Lāhūn* (1934), pls. II and IV]

March 13, 1914

Dear Prof. Petrie:

Your letter dated February 21st and addressed to Mr. Eckley B. Coxe was received this morning. Mr. Coxe is at present in Cuba and will not be in reach of communication until about the first of April. Your letter will be treated with the strictest confidence, and I want to thank you for the courteous treatment which you have shown us in offering this museum the first opportunity of procuring the objects which you describe.

When Mr. Coxe returns I will take the matter up with him and, in the meantime, in order that I may be able to state the case to him as explicitly as possible, would you be good enough to follow up your present communication with another one either by cable or post, stating the result of your negotiations with Maspero? Perhaps you might be able to tell us by that time exactly the valuation placed upon the available objects.

I regret that I am not able to give you at the present time as satisfactory an answer as I feel your communication deserves.

Very sincerely yours

G. B. Gordon

Director

PROF. W. M. FLINDERS-PETRIE
Lahun, Fayum, Egypt

5.6.

Greenville, South Carolina

March 28, 1914

Dear Dr. Gordon:

I have received your letter enclosing a copy of a confidential from Prof. Petrie to me: as it was addressed to me. I am surprised that you opened it, or had a copy of it taken; in future please send all letters addressed to me unopened to me, or hold them for me at the Museum, unopened.

Of course you will not mention this letter in your report or to any person or persons at all; and upon no account to Mr. Rodgers for the press.

I expect to return to Philadelphia about April 8.

I hope you are well.

Yours sincerely

Eckley B. Coxe

5.7.

June 19, 1914

Dear Prof. Petrie:

I believe that I owe you apologies for more than one oversight. I find that I never acknowledged your letter of January 30th forwarded to me by Miss Murray referring to her proposed visit to this country. I have corresponded on Miss Murray's behalf with the people who have charge of the university extension lectures. The result has not been altogether encouraging for the reason that they seem to prefer men to lecture in their courses. However, I am writing to Miss Murray and will give her what advice I can with regard to her coming visit to America.

Your letter of April 2nd also remains unanswered for various reasons, the chief one being that our plans have remained in abeyance. I wish now to thank you for the trouble which you took to answer my letter and as soon as we have anything further to say on the subject I will take an opportunity of writing you again.

In the London TIMES I have read that your discovery of jewellery has now been divided between the Cairo Museum and the British School and the share of the latter being exhibited in London at the present time. I do not know, however, which pieces were retained at Cairo. Your private letter to Mr. Coxe on this subject was forwarded to him in South Carolina where he acknowledged its receipt on March 28th. As Mr. Coxe is travelling at present I am unable to discuss the matter with him, but I understand that he did not purchase any of the pieces.

I would be glad if you would tell me now whether a portion of the jewellery assigned to the School remains to be disposed of and whether this Museum might become a candidate for its acquisition in case it found itself in a position to do so. I would also be grateful if you would tell me how much money would be required for its acquisition.

Very sincerely yours

G. B. Gordon

Prof. W. M. Flinders-Petrie
University College, Gower St.,
London, England

5.8.

5.6. Letter from G.B. Gordon to Flinders Petrie, March 13, 1914.

5.7. Transcription of the letter from Coxe to Gordon, March 28, 1914.

5.8. Letter from G.B. Gordon to Flinders Petrie, June 19, 1914.

Museum's shop. This was a way of raising funds for the (chronically underfunded) Antiquities Service. In the division of the Lahun treasure Petrie benefited from his warm relationship with then director Gaston Maspero. The Antiquities officials chose to keep only three of the best objects for the Cairo Museum. What to do with the remainder of the Lahun treasure? Petrie was determined to see that the entire group was not further divided up but placed in a single public museum. He also wanted to use this sale to raise new funds for the fieldwork of the British School of Archaeology in Egypt. That is why he offered it to Coxe, knowing the Museum might be interested in the material for its growing collection.

The arrival of Petrie's remarkable offer precipitated a small misunderstanding between Director Gordon and Eckley Coxe. When the letter addressed to Coxe arrived he was traveling in Cuba. All of the prior correspondence with the Museum regarding the annual support for the British School of Archaeology had been between Petrie and Director Gordon. The recent matter of the transport of the Sphinx had also been handled directly between Petrie and Gordon. In view of Coxe's absence, Gordon opened the letter and replied to Petrie before Coxe's return. Eckley Coxe returned from Cuba, first visiting his mother's family home in South Carolina before returning to Philadelphia. Gordon sent a copy of Petrie's letter on to Coxe in South Carolina. Coxe's response is one of the rare

Imperial and Foreign Intelligence.

THE TREASURE OF LAHUN.

MYSTERY OF A PLUNDERED PYRAMID.

A FORGOTTEN HOARD.

HOW A PRINCESS'S JEWELS WERE DISCOVERED.

(By Professor Flinders Petrie.)

At the mouth of the Fayum, about 60 miles south of Cairo, stands the high, dark mass of the brick pyramid of Senusert II., built about 3400 B.C. The older custom of building pyramids of solid stone had given place in the 12th dynasty to the shorter method of building the bulk of black brick, and then covering it with a casing of large blocks of fine white limestone. A quarter of a century ago I found the entrance to this pyramid, and last winter I returned to it with the students and resources of the British School of Archæology in Egypt, in order to make a fuller clearance of the whole site.

This pyramid is better preserved than any other, in its surrounding works, owing to having been largely cut into a mass of rock. The rock features have not been plundered for stone, as has happened usually to buildings. The height of the permanent rock work has also caused sand and rubbish to accumulate, so that the worked faces were buried, in some parts as much as 15ft. in depth. It is therefore the most complete of the later pyramids, and also the most interesting in its architectural details. In order to make certain of finding all ancient entrances and structures, the whole surface far outside the pyramid has been completely bared, the rock scraped and brushed, and every fissure and crack examined; no site in Egypt has been so thoroughly searched.

PYRAMID OF SENUSERT II.

The pyramid casing was founded in a deep cutting in the rock, where a few blocks of it still remain. The sides probably varied two or three inches; the length was 350ft. So careful were the builders to preserve the soft marly foundation from damage by rain that a large trench filled with sand was cut round all sides of the pyramid. This trench varies from 11ft. wide on one side to 44ft. wide on another. It was about 3ft. deep, filled with very clean coarse sand, and covered with about 10in. of brown pebbles, which formed the immediate surrounding of the pyramid. The whole was enclosed with a panelled stone wall at least 12ft. high; where the rock stood high enough it was left as a core to this wall.

Around the enclosure wall were the tombs of the Royal family, of which 14 have been found. One of the most remarkable is a great tunnel descending by steps to 50ft. deep; after giving access to one tomb, it branched, and another long passage led to a second tomb 70ft. farther on. Another tomb had a stone trapdoor in the floor, which gave the largest access to the pyramid, and it must have been by this indirect way that the granite sarcophagus of Senusert was taken into the burial chamber, as the direct shaft into the pyramid was too narrow. Another of the tombs contained the Treasure, which is described below. Surrounding all the burials was the great brick wall of the temenos. This was 16ft. thick and about 30ft. high. It still remains to a height of 15ft., where it is protected by the rock cutting. A staircase of stone gave access to the top of the wall, for guards to keep watch over the Royal mausolea.

The great enclosure was graced on the lower sides by a line of trees around it, 42 along each side; these did not extend on the north and part of the west, where the rock rose around the sides. Fragments of the sculptured and painted shrines were found; these adjoined the pyramid on the east and the north sides. Many of the wooden mallets of the masons, and rollers for moving the stones, were found left behind on the rock foundations.

DISCOVERY OF THE TREASURE.

We now turn to the most surprising discovery of the Treasure, which is only paralleled by the results of De Morgan at Dahshur many years ago. One of the tombs of the Royal family had evidently been opened ages ago, and remained standing open, gradually filled up by dust and rain storms. On descending about 20ft. the burial chamber of a princess was found, containing a granite sarcophagus: this had been attacked, a hole broken in the lid, and everything abstracted. So far, nothing unusual appeared, and our workman was told to clear the hard mud out of a small recess, about 3ft. wide and 5ft. deep, in the side wall of the passage. This recess had stood open for many years, gradually filled with mud washed down and caked hard—nothing could look less promising. After a few cuts of the pick the man found some tubular beads of gold. He at once sent for one of the staff to return and after that the work was entirely done by English hands, nearly all of it by Mr. Guy Brunton. Five days were occupied and some evenings as well, February 10—15, in the gradual dissection of that cubic yard of mud. The final sifting of all the earth lasted much longer; a good deal of it needed to be completely washed away to extract the minute beads.

The first large object found after a pound weight of gold beads was the diadem. This is a band of burnished gold over an inch wide and large enough to surround the full wig. In front is an inlaid cobra, the Royal uræus, and around the band are attached 15 rosettes, each composed of four flowers and four leaves of openwork inlaid. It is thus of an entirely new pattern, most like that painted on the statue of Nofert. Behind the crown stood up high plumes of gold; at the back and sides, streamers of gold descended—the whole crown being over a foot and a half high. This is now in the Cairo Museum.

A pectoral of gold inlaid with lazuli and amazon-stone (green felspar) must have belonged to the girlhood of the princess; it has the cartouche of Senusert II., upheld by a kneeling man with palm branches, the emblem of millions of years. It is flanked by a hawk on each side, and is altogether 3½ inches wide. The back is exquisitely engraved in the gold. A second pectoral of similar design was a gift in the mature years of the wearer, as it has the cartouche of Amenemhat III. This also is in the Cairo Museum. The pectorals from Dahshur have square frames, but these outlined by the forms of the birds are more graceful in design. Collars of large gold cowries and of double lion-heads in gold, each over an inch

wide, are similar to those found at Dahshur. A third collar was of beads and pendants of gold, lazuli, amazon-stone, and carnelian.

A pair of armlets, over 3in. wide, are fastened by a broad sliding strip of gold inlaid with the titles and name of Amenemhat III. in carnelian. Each armlet has also six broad bars of gold to separate the rows of minute beads of gold, carnelian, and amazon-stone. A pair of bracelets of the same kind are 1½in. wide, with plain gold sliders. The mirror was of silver, with a head of Hat-hor of cast gold, and a handle of polished obsidian inlaid with plaited gold bands and leaves of carnelian and blue and white paste. This is now in the Cairo Museum. The toilet outfit also included three obsidian vases and a kohl-pot, all with gold mounting at top and base. Eight other vases of alabaster belonged to the funerary outfit.

The smaller objects comprised an amethyst necklace of very deep colour with lion-claw pendants of gold; five motto pendants of gold with inlaid carnelian signs; a necklace of rhombic beads of blue amazon-stone and carnelian; eight gold lions and nine knots from necklaces and bracelets; seven quadruple lion-heads; two inlaid scarabs; gold-handled razors; fragments of two caskets of ivory inlay, with gold emblems in the panels; and over 10,000 minute beads of gold, carnelian, and amazon-stone, belonging to the bracelets. Lastly, in a very massive limestone box, were found the four canopic jars of alabaster, with carved heads, giving the name of "the King's daughter, Sat-Hathor-ant."

MISSING THE OBVIOUS.

The extraordinary conditions of this discovery seem quite inexplicable. The tomb had been attacked; the long and heavy work of shifting the massive granite lid of the sarcophagus, and breaking it away, had been achieved; yet all the gold was left within arm's reach, in the recess of the passage, uninjured. The crown would have been bent in some part if it had been dragged out of the narrow opening of the sarcophagus, but it showed no signs of rough handling. The whole treasure seems to have been stacked in the recess at the time of the burial, and to have remained there, gradually dropping apart as the wooden caskets decayed in course of years, with repeated flooding of storm water and mud slowly washed in, down the pit. Had it been seen, or suspected, by those who so vigorously attacked the sarcophagus, it is impossible that they should have left it. No chance visitors in later years ever ransacked the pit, as it stood open, or they would soon have found the treasure. How such things should have escaped destruction under these conditions is an entire mystery. It cannot be that the whole was deliberately buried in mud to hide it from plunderers, as then the parts would have been in exact relation to each other. On the contrary, everything showed a long gradual decay and dropping apart, during which the wood and the threads were rotted by the wet, before they were bedded in the mud filling. The caskets had completely gone to pieces, and the ivory veneers had fallen about in every direction before they were covered over. Yet the whole was in an open recess, brushed past by every man who had worked at smashing into the sarcophagus. There never was a more astounding case of missing the obvious.

Such is the strange history of one of the greatest hoards of Egyptian jewelry that has survived. It is now necessarily divided, the Egyptian Government taking the larger objects, not yet represented in the Cairo Museum—the crown, the mirror, and one pectoral. The rest of this treasure is now safely arrived in England, and will be exhibited in July at University College.

5.9a–c. Flinders Petrie's article on the Lahun treasure in *The London Times*, May 20, 1914.

moments where we see his displeasure. He wrote a very pointed letter requesting that Gordon should never open his letters again.

Flinders Petrie, in the meantime, was busy publicizing the important discovery of the Lahun treasure through lectures and published newspaper pieces. This included a detailed article in the *London Times*. Gordon read the *Times* article and followed with some further questions to Petrie on the pieces and costs involved in acquiring the treasure.

Eckley Coxe considered the offer to the Museum, but despite the significant funds at his disposal he was not inclined to accept it. After much discussion between Gordon and Coxe after the latter's return to Philadelphia, they decided the acquisition of the Lahun treasure was not worth the financial investment and they declined Petrie's offer. For one thing, the Museum was beginning its next major building phase with the construction of the Rotunda behind the existing 1899 building. This and projected construction of additional elements of the original plan would absorb a good amount of Coxe's contributions to the Museum. A costly treasure excavated by someone else was not a priority.

So, the opportunity to bring the treasure of princess Sit-Hathor-Iunet to Philadelphia came at precisely the wrong time for the Museum. The widely publicized Lahun pieces were offered to other museums, and in the end it was the Metropolitan Museum in New York that acquired the treasure, now one of the highlights of their Egyptian collection. Herbert Winlock, curator of the Egyptian Department in the Metropolitan Museum, published a detailed volume on the treasure in 1935.

The Search for a New Excavator

At the same time as the letters were going back and forth concerning the treasure of princess Sit-Hathor-Iunet there was discussion of another matter: resuming the fieldwork of the Coxe Egyptian Expedition. When the Sphinx arrived in 1913 the Museum's excavations in Egypt were on hold after the departure of David Randall-MacIver in 1911. Gordon was now actively searching for a replacement and he and Coxe were corresponding with Petrie on the choice of the new archaeologist. He was, moreover, keen to locate new sites that would produce major sculpture of a type to complement the colossal Sphinx.

Petrie responded with some very detailed suggestions. He proposed various possible sites that might repay with significant new discoveries. Petrie even generously made the offer to accommodate the Museum's research within his ongoing work at Memphis. He also discussed the issue of finding a good archaeologist and spoke in glowing terms of an experienced American excavator, Mr. Clarence Fisher, a Philadelphian and University of Pennsylvania graduate.

Clarence Stanley Fisher (1876–1941) graduated in 1897 from the University of Pennsylvania with a degree in architecture. His involvement in archaeology began when he worked on the Museum's excavations at Nippur in Iraq from 1897–1900.

March 20, 1914

Dear Prof. Petrie:

There is some possibility that
this Museum may be sending an expedition to Egypt.
If this is done, we would desire a good site or
sites where there is a chance of good sculpture
being found.   I am therefore writing you to ask
whether you will be good enough to give me your
advice in this respect; that is to say, could you
give me a list of some of the sites which you could
recommend in case this Museum should find itself in
a position to send a properly equipped expedition for
excavating through a period of years? I do not spec-
ify whether the site should be early or late. If we
should be so fortunate as to secure a couple of sites
it would suit us to have different periods represented.

I would be glad if, for the present, you would
consider this letter quite confidential.

Very sincerely yours

G. B. Gordon
Director

PROF. W. M. FLINDERS-PETRIE
Lahun, Fayum, Egypt

5.10.

5.11.

Clarence S. Fisher

5.10. Letter from Gordon to Petrie, March 30, 1914.

5.11. Clarence Fisher (1876–1941). [UPM image # 140198]

5.12. Transcription of letter from Petrie to Gordon, April 2, 1914.

Lahun, Fayum, Egypt
2 April 1914

Dear Dr. Gordon,

In reply to your letter, the first consideration is how an expedition would be "fully equipped." As to material, that is easy; but as to men that is a serious matter. Unless a man has seen several sites dug over already, he can not interpret what he has before him, nor see then clues to further discoveries. This very year a great building is being quite misunderstood for lack of comparative knowledge. I hope you can secure the work of an experienced excavator; but otherwise you will need to find a fit man, and then have him trained in similar work, Merely digging holes to get plunder will not pass muster in Egypt, though it is unhappily done too often in other lands.

You need a great temple site for large sculptures. On such a site there is usually a complex of buildings, each of which requires to be separately traced out and planned. At Abydos I found ten different temple plans, one over the other. If you had Clarence Fisher on such a site he might succeed, but no one less capable could do so. It is a sad pity that his plans of Nippur are not yet published, as he was the only competent man engaged there. Granted your fit and trained man (whose ability must be already known to the Egyptian Department), the site would not be a difficulty. Delta sites possible are Benha, Thmuis, Ausim (Letopolis), and many others. In Upper Egypt, Oxyrhynchos, El Hibeh, Hemopolis, Cusae, Kom Esfaht, Kous and Erment. Most sites would yield sculpture of very varied periods.

Two temple sites are in my own permit, and I have private contracts with owners for some of the land – Memphis and Atfih. If you had a fit man I would be willing to give him some facilities to work on your behalf, provided he kept up our system of work in every way, and that we might publish the results within three years in our series on Memphis already in progress. You might also publish previously if you desired to do so.

Thanks for your reply to my private letter. I am sorry that I cannot hear anything decisive as to possibilities, in time before I have to settle here with Maspero.

Yours very sincerely,
W.M. Flinders Petrie

5.12.

5.13. George Reisner (1867–1942), with whom Fisher worked in Egypt. [UPM image # 238719]

5.14. Clarence Fisher excavating in the cemetery of Dendera, southern Egypt, 1916. [UPM image # 38942]

In Petrie's comments to Gordon he speaks of Fisher as the "only competent man engaged there." Fisher had gone on to work in Egypt where he furthered his experience in excavation under George Andrew Reisner, director of the Harvard-Boston Museum of Fine Arts Expedition to Egypt. Fisher and Reisner were both passionate field excavators who conducted excavation and documentation in a very systematic way, far ahead of many of their contemporaries. Fisher never managed to publish his ambitious excavations in a timely fashion, but this is not surprising given the pace and large scale of fieldwork that he pursued. Fisher was not an Egyptologist. He was, however, a capable and experienced archaeologist with an interest in architecture who fit with Gordon's priority to excavate large sites that would produce monumental pieces for the Museum's planned Egyptian wing.

Not long after Flinders Petrie's letter arrived with its positive review of Clarence Fisher, Fisher was hired as head curator of the Museum's Egyptian Section—such was the weight that Petrie's opinion evidently held with Director Gordon. Gordon sent the good news to Fisher on June 20, 1914, and made plans to meet with him by the middle of August to start discussing a return to Egypt.

Three weeks later World War I erupted in Europe but that did not put a damper on the Museum's plans. As long as the United States was not involved and Egypt was not directly in the theater of conflict, there was no reason not to proceed at full speed to resume work in Egypt.

Fisher Goes to Egypt in the Midst of War

Gordon and Coxe were very eager to get the University Museum back in the field in Egypt. Coxe had earmarked a significant sum for this purpose with the promise of more as needed. Director Gordon was in the process of planning for the next phases of expansion of the Museum. Already in the final planning stages for construction in 1915 was the western Rotunda (the first of three projected according to the Museum's original plan). Next would be the addition of a large

Egyptian wing. Gordon envisioned the Sphinx becoming part of a grand Egyptian gallery where the achievements of ancient Egypt would be exhibited in the form of "sculptured stone and hammered bronze."

Consequently, there was a push now not only to get back in the field, but also to acquire the kind of large and impressive objects, architecture, and statuary that would complement the Sphinx. This would be Fisher's primary objective: to get permission from the Egyptian Antiquities Service for the University Museum to excavate a major site. Fisher and Gordon discussed some of the large archaeological sites in the Nile Delta such as Tanis and Sais, which might produce major finds. In some cases other institutions had already laid claim to the sites of interest, but World War I presented a juncture during which Penn might get permission to explore sites formerly held by others.

Only ten days after hiring Clarence Fisher, Gordon sent the first of a series of letters to Gaston Maspero, then in his final year as Director of the Egyptian Antiquities Service, informing him that Fisher would soon be coming to Egypt as the Museum's representative. The letter to Maspero was the critical next step in securing a site for the Coxe Expedition to Egypt. Although the Museum had no current excavation permit, Gordon wanted to make it clear that Fisher was coming with the full backing of the Museum.

5.15.

5.15. Gaston Maspero (1846–1916) was head of the Egyptian Antiquities Service in 1914. By the time Fisher arrived, he had retired. His successor, Georges Daressy, did not get along with Flinders Petrie, which contributed to the awarding of the excavation site at Memphis to the Museum. [Photograph by Charles Reutlinger, image courtesy of Bibliothèque nationale de France, département Société de Géographie (http://gallica.bnf. fr/ark:/12148/btv1b8450965w/f1.item)]

5.16. Letter from Gordon to Gaston Maspero informing him of Fisher's hiring to excavate on behalf of the Museum, June 20, 1914.

June 30, 1914

Dear Sir Gaston Maspero:

I have your very courteous note of April 7th, together with a list of the sites which have already been assigned for excavation.

I thank you for this information and now write to say that we have some thought of applying to you during the coming autumn for the privilege of excavating some site which you might find it agreeable to assign to us.

My object in writing now is more particularly to advise you that Mr. Clarence S. Fisher, who has been associated with Dr. Reisner and who, I believe, is not unknown to you, has been appointed Curator of the Egyptian Section of this Museum. Mr. Fisher will be charged with our commission next autumn and will present our further communications to you in person.

Very sincerely yours

Director

SIR GASTON MASPERO
Director General
Service des Antiquites
Cairo, Egypt

5.16.

MUSEUM SENDS PARTY TO EGYPT

Despite the War, University Explorers Start for the Orient

Dr. Clarence S. Fisher, Leader of Expedition, Has Had Considerable Experience in Country

In pursuance of its purpose to enrich the University Museum with all possible contributions from archeology, the authorities on Saturday dispatched an exploring expedition to Egypt under the leadership of Dr. Clarence S. Fisher curator of the Egyptian section, to dig for antiquities. It will be known as the Eckley B. Coxe, Jr., expedition from the president of the Museum, who will finance it as he has other expeditions in the past.

This action was taken in spite of the war and on the strength of advices from Egypt that there would be no difficulty or danger in prosecuting the work. The University Museum authorities have the greatest confidence in the British authorities and hope to secure rich historical and artistic specimens for the institution as the British Government is very liberal to expeditions which at great expense dig things out of the buried past.

Dr. Fisher will go to London, where he will purchase his equipment and then push on to Cairo, where he will examine several sites and decide upon the best field of operations. The work of digging is expected to start early in January. Dr. Fisher had ten years' experience in excavations and knows many of the expert diggers and headmen among the Egyptians so that he will be able to get under way rapidly, although it is probable that the work this winter will be in large degree preliminary as to what is to follow, as it is intended to make this an important delving into the history of ancient Egypt.

Dr. Fisher a Philadelphian

Dr. Fisher was born in this city, graduated from the Department of Architecture, University of Pennsylvania, in 1897.

He was born in this city thirty-eight years ago, graduated from the Architectural Department of the University of Pennsylvania in 1897 and was research fellow in Babylonian architecture and went on one of the expeditions to Nippur. This trip changed the purpose of his life from practicing contemporary architecture to studying that of ancient civilization. He was architect of the Harvard Palestine Expedition, excavating for three seasons at Samaria. He also spent six years in Egypt excavating for the Harvard-Boston Museum expeditions.

Already the Museum has some of the finest Egyptian relics in this country, but it is desired to make this collection larger. The Museum sent four expeditions to Nubia—that portion of Egypt above the First Cataract at Assouan and the results were of the first importance as previously no careful scientific explorations had been undertaken in Nubia. All authorities recognize the great value of the results of these expeditions as throwing light on a hitherto unknown part of Egyptian history.

5.17.

U. OF P. PARTY GOES TO EXPLORE IN EGYPT

Expedition, Headed by Dr. C. S. Fisher Sure of Finding Treasures

WAR SPREAD NO TERROR

Notwithstanding the spread of the European war to the Egyptian zone, the University of Pennsylvania Museum has sent out another excavating expedition, which it is confident will discover great archeological and artistic treasures in the Nile country. The party left Saturday. It is financed by Eckley B. Coxe, Jr., president of the museum, and is headed by Dr. Clarence S. Fisher, curator of the Egyptian section.

Doctor Fisher will go direct to London, where he will purchase his equipment. Then he will proceed to Cairo, where he proposes to examine several sites and decide upon a field of operation.

Doctor Fisher has had ten years' experience in excavations and is acquainted with many of the expert diggers and headmen in Egypt. He expects to begin the work of digging early in January. While excavating in Egypt for the Harvard-Boston Museum expeditions a few years ago, Doctor Fisher uncovered the oldest known pyramid—that of Kha-be, a king of the third dynasty, at Zawietel Aryan.

The museum has some of the finest Egyptian relics in this country, but it is desired to make this collection larger. Four expeditions were sent by the museum to Nubia, and the results were of the utmost importance, as previously no careful scientific explorations had been undertaken in Nubia. Doctor Fisher will pay special attention to Egyptian architecture.

5.18.

5.17. *The Philadelphia Inquirer*, November 23, 1914.

5.18. *The Philadelphia Press*, November 23, 1914.

Nowadays when archaeologists depart for the field they normally do so knowing exactly where they will be working. It is, in fact, a difficult proposition to raise money without knowing what you are excavating and just how much funding might be required. It is equally hard to make plans for the size and organization of your team and the kinds of equipment you will need. Once you arrive and begin excavation it is normal to discover things you hadn't predicted, or for your research questions to change. *But,* you usually know your destination. That was not the case when, just four months after joining the staff of the Museum, Clarence Fisher was on a ship to Egypt.

In November 23, 1914, over a year had elapsed since the Sphinx had come to Philadelphia. The newspapers were once again filled with stories of the departure of the Museum's Coxe Expedition to Egypt headed by Clarence Fisher. The reports were optimistic at the likely success of the mission, despite the onset of World War I in July 1914. Tellingly, the newspapers say absolutely nothing about where in Egypt Fisher was going to work, mainly because the Museum had as yet no site concession or permission to work!

It must have been an exciting time for the 38-year-old Fisher. Here he was, now chief Curator of the Museum's Egyptian Section, with major financial backing from Eckley Coxe, and on his way to undertake groundbreaking new excavations. He went to Egypt by way of London where he stopped to purchase supplies and equipment needed for the planned large-scale excavations. From London, he went on via Port Said to Cairo where he arrived at the very end of 1914, a well-equipped and -funded archaeologist on the quest for a site.

Fisher could scarcely have guessed when he left Philadelphia that only two months later he would be digging at Memphis—the very site from which the colossal Sphinx of Ramses II had come the year before.

The Search for a New Site

On Christmas day, 1914, Clarence Fisher wrote a letter to Director Gordon from Cairo, telling him about the trip to Egypt. Much of the content of the letter has to do with various possibilities for securing an excavation permit. Fisher discusses several potential sites but favors the site of Tanis in the northeastern Nile Delta. Tanis is a great tell (a vast settlement mound) with remains of monumental temples at its center, and the site where several of the world's colossal sphinxes originated. Tanis was attractive for the promise of discovering large stone sculpture. Remember, Gordon was very interested in the possibility of adding additional sphinxes to the Museum's collection. Tanis could be the place to do that.

If the Museum were to start work at Tanis the best time to work in the Nile Delta would be during the spring and summer when the ground water reached its lowest level. Fisher therefore proposed that the Museum ask for two sites: a desert site, such as Giza, to be followed by work at Tanis during the optimal time of late spring and summer. Because he had worked extensively with George Reisner at Giza (and he was then staying at Harvard Camp), he was interested in working first at Giza and then continuing on to Tanis.

Both Giza and Tanis are large sites and each was divided into a number of different excavation areas. In 1914, the Austrians held permission to work on half of Tanis, and also the cemeteries to the east and south of the Great Pyramid at Giza. What Fisher was banking on was the impact of the war on archaeology in Egypt. Since Egypt was a British Protectorate, the beginning of the war meant that the Germans and Austrians were no longer allowed to work there. Fisher's understanding was that their excavation permits would be rescinded and granted to other institutions. After consultation with Gordon, Fisher submitted a request for work at Giza and Tanis.

Fisher did not have to wait long. Only five days after his request, Georges Daressy, the director of the Antiquities Service, replied rejecting the request. Contrary to Fisher's expectation, the Antiquities Service decided to hold the concessions of the Germans and Austrians until the end of wartime and the eventual return of archaeologists from those countries to Egypt.

5.19. Sections of a 3-page letter from Clarence Fisher to Gordon, December 25, 1914.

5.20.

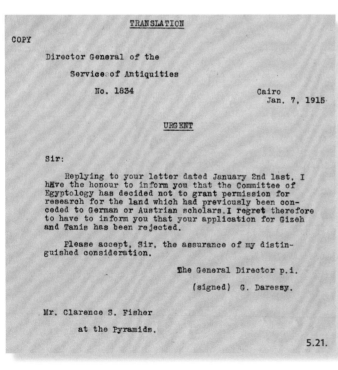

TRANSLATION

COPY

Director General of the

Service of Antiquities

No. 1834   Cairo
       Jan. 7, 1915

URGENT

Sir:

    Replying to your letter dated January 2nd last, I
have the honour to inform you that the Committee of
Egyptology has decided not to grant permission for
research for the land which had previously been conceded to German or Austrian scholars. I regret therefore
to have to inform you that your application for Gizeh
and Tanis has been rejected.

    Please accept, Sir, the assurance of my distin-
guished consideration.

              The General Director p.i.

                (signed) G. Daressy.

Mr. Clarence S. Fisher

    at the Pyramids.

5.21.

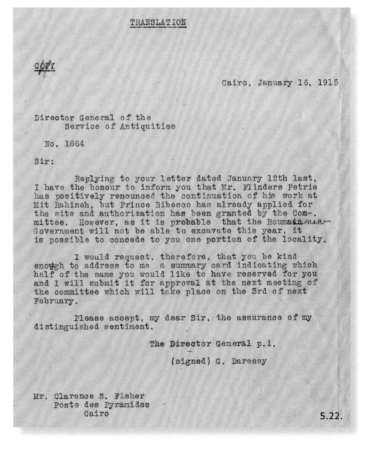

TRANSLATION

COPY

                  Cairo, January 16, 1915

Director General of the
    Service of Antiquities

  No. 1864

Sir:

    Replying to your letter dated January 12th last,
I have the honour to inform you that Mr. Flinders Petrie
has positively renounced the continuation of his work at
Mit Rahineh, but Prince Bibesco has already applied for
the site and authorization has been granted by the Com-.
mittee. However, as it is probable that the Roumanian
Government will not be able to excavate this year, it
is possible to concede to you one portion of the locality.

    I would request, therefore, that you be kind
enough to address to me a summary card indicating which
half of the same you would like to have reserved for you
and I will submit it for approval at the next meeting of
the committee which will take place on the 3rd of next
February.

    Please accept, my dear Sir, the assurance of my
distinguished sentiment.

              The Director General p.i.

                (signed) G. Daressy

Mr. Clarence S. Fisher
Poste des Pyramides
   Cairo

5.22.

5.20. The ruins of Tanis in the Nile Delta. The French held a permit for half of Tanis but Fisher hoped the permit for the other half, held by the Austrians, would be open. [Image courtesy of Heidi Kontkanen]

5.21. Translation of the letter from Daressy rejecting Fisher's application to work at Giza and Tanis, Jan. 7, 1915.

5.22. Translation of letter from Daressy to Fisher, Jan. 16, 1915, informing Fisher about the availability of Memphis for excavation, changing the direction of the Coxe Expedition and the Museum's Egyptian collection.

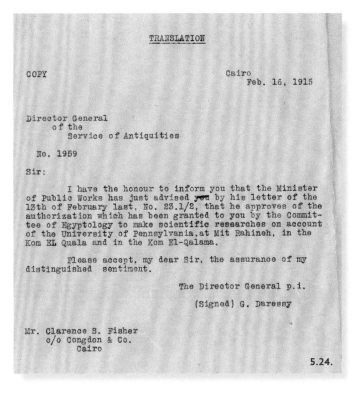

25 January, 1915

To M. Georg Daressy,
    Acting Director,
        Service des Antiquités,
            Cairo.

Sir:-

I beg leave to apply to the Department of Antiquités for permission to make archaeological excavations under the usual conditions, in that part of the site of Mit-Rahineh included under the names of Kom el Qal'a and Kom el Qalama. The area applied for is indicated on the accompanying map in red. This concession is asked for in the name of the Eckley B. Coxe Junior Egyptian Expedition of the University Museum, University of Pennsylvania, Philadelphia.. You have already in your hands my authorization to act for this institution.

I have the honor to remain,

Yours very respectfully,

(signed) C. S. Fisher,

Director.

5.23.

TRANSLATION

COPY

Cairo
Feb. 16, 1915

Director General
    of the
        Service of Antiquities

No. 1959

Sir:

I have the honour to inform you that the Minister of Public Works has just advised you by his letter of the 13th of February last, No. 23.1/2, that he approves of the authorization which has been granted to you by the Committee of Egyptology to make scientific researches on account of the University of Pennsylvania, at Mit Rahineh, in the Kom EL Quala and in the Kom El-Qalama.

Please accept, my dear Sir, the assurance of my distinguished sentiment.

The Director General p.i.

(Signed) G. Daressy

Mr. Clarence S. Fisher
    c/o Congdon & Co.
        Cairo

5.24.

5.23. Fisher's request for excavation permission at Memphis, Jan. 25, 1915.

5.24. Translation of approval of excavation request, Feb. 16, 1915.

Fisher was disappointed but he wrote back inquiring about other significant sites that might be open for Penn's Coxe Expedition.

A week later, Fisher received a letter from Daressy that would change the direction of Penn's work in Egypt and have a huge impact on the permanent Egyptian collection of the Penn Museum. Daressy informed Fisher that Flinders Petrie had renounced his work at Mit Rahina-Memphis. There had been a permit issued to a Romanian prince but, due to the war, he also would not be working that year. The Antiquities Service would grant Penn the permit to excavate at Memphis! Fisher responded quickly, defining the area of interest which centered on Kom el-Qal'a, a raised mound on the southeastern side of the Ptah Temple.

In February, Fisher received the good news; the Antiquities Service had approved and work could start immediately!

New Discoveries at Memphis

In an amazing turn of events, the Coxe Egyptian Expedition had now been granted permission to excavate one of the most promising parts of Memphis. The area of Kom el-Qal'a was formerly covered in the permit of Flinders Petrie and the British School of Archaeology in Egypt. However, Petrie had done very little work there as yet.

Kom el-Qal'a in Arabic means the "mound of the fortress"—an auspicious name for an excavation site. This tall, imposing hill lay adjacent to the southeast corner of the

5.25.

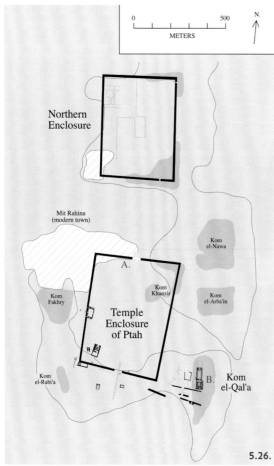

Ptah Temple. Petrie had found some interesting inscriptions relating to pharaoh Merenptah, son of Ramses II, in several soundings into the Kom el-Qal'a. More importantly Charles Edgar, chief inspector for the Antiquities Service, had reported in 1914 the presence of a large columned hall also belonging to Merenptah during rescue work he had conducted the previous year on the same mound. However, Kom el-Qal'a remained largely unexplored when Fisher began large-scale excavations there.

The work started with the upper levels which included the remains of houses dating to the Late Period (ca. 664–332 BCE) and Ptolemaic Period (ca. 323–30 BCE), relatively late in ancient Egyptian history. This first phase of work was itself significant: Fisher's excavations recorded the single largest expanse of the urban remains of Memphis ever examined. There are limitations to his work, but this still-unpublished excavation of the upper layers at Kom el-Qal'a was a promising start.

5.25. Excavations at Memphis, 1915. [UPM image # 38541]

5.26. Plan of central Memphis showing the Ptah Temple enclosure, location of the earlier 1912 discovery of the colossal Sphinx (A), and the Museum's 1915–20 excavations at Kom el-Qal'a (B).

5.26.

Most interesting for Fisher was what lay beneath the later occupational layers: material from the golden age of the New Kingdom. He was, however, a methodical excavator. He carefully documented all layers as he and his workmen gradually dug downwards from the surface.

The 1915 results at Memphis were promising and Fisher wrote to Gordon optimistically about discoveries to come. Even then, however, he did not realize the scope of the work and spoke about getting permission for another site such as Tanis. This would change significantly the following year with the discovery of the palace of pharaoh Merenptah. For five years the palace would dominate Fisher's efforts, although he also worked at other sites—Dendera and Thebes—in southern Egypt during the period of high groundwater at Memphis.

5.27.

5.27. Fisher discovered this magnificent quartzite head of an Amarna Period royal woman during his first season's work at Memphis. It is usually identified as Queen Nefertiti. The Antiquities Service chose to keep the piece and the head is in the Cairo Museum (JE 45547). [UPM image # 38325]

5.28. Satellite view of the Ptah Temple and its environs at Memphis, 2012. Today the Ptah Temple is almost entirely engulfed by the modern town of Mit Rahina. The area of the Merenptah Palace excavated by the Museum in 1915–20 is still unaffected and offers potential for new research building on the important discoveries of Fisher.

The Palace of Pharaoh Merenptah

One year later, in early summer of 1916, Fisher was back in Egypt continuing the Memphis excavations. Work during the second year proceeded to a considerable depth, in some areas ca. 15 feet (4.6 m) below the surface. Fisher now came to a full realization of what he was dealing with. Beneath Kom el-Qal'a was a huge palace complex dating to the reign of pharaoh Merenptah, the son of Ramses II. Through a wonderful coincidence, the palace dated to the same period of Egyptian history as the colossal Sphinx in the Museum (which itself has inscriptions of both Ramses II and Merenptah). Over the summer of 1916 the inner end of the palace emerged, exposing the remains of the beautifully decorated throne room containing the painted throne dais of Merenptah. Fisher wrote Gordon with the exciting news and spoke optimistically about the publications and objects for the Museum that would result from sustained work at Memphis.

5.28.

5.29. Portion of letter from Fisher to Gordon, May 2, 1916.

5.30. The throne room of the Merenptah palace, 1916. [UPM image # 34181]

number the direction in which the different photographs have been made, the number being the number of the photograph. This will make the plan more intelligible. The drawing is a tracing of the permanent field plan, on which are entered in colors the various walls. On the plan sent I have omitted the upper structures, so as not to confuse the drawing and make clear the plan of the palace itself. This is of course the principal building in any case.

I think this month's report will prove to you and Mr. Coxe that the Museum has one of the greatest sites in Egypt and one that ought to be carried to completion. The complete plan of this royal palace would be a piece of work, not only monumental but unique. As you will see, but little of the walls are missing in plan, and where breaks occur, the restoration is perfectly obvious. Nowhere in Egypt is such a royal palace preserved so perfect in plan. At El Amarna, pavements have been found but no connected plan of the entire building made. At Thebes the New York expedition have a royal palace with fine stucco but I do not know whether the plan is complete or not, as nothing has as yet been published. In any event, this building is of the greatest importance, because of its beautiful ornament, and the publication of it, with plans and colored plates will be one of the best things in the Museum series.

Now that we have the key to the situation and know what to expect and just where to excavate to complete the plan of the building, I would very much like to put to work double the amount of men we have, in order to clear the building as swiftly as possible. As you will remember the palace floor proper is about fifteen feet below the present surface, in some places even more, and this fifteen feet is hard packed debris. This means hard and tedious work. To double the force would cost nearly one thousand dollars a month more over a period of three months. I do not know whether the Museum would care to consider such an extra expense. **5.29.**

5.30.

Publicity around the discovery of Merenptah's palace caused a worldwide flurry of newspaper reports over the summer of 1916. The earliest reports focused on the information that fire had burned and sealed in much of the well-preserved throne room. However, when Fisher discovered that the throne room contained artifacts from a wide range of earlier periods, the reports became more sensational. The idea quickly emerged that Merenptah may have been a kind of antiquarian and his palace doubled as a museum where he collected objects from earlier times. How appropriate for the University Museum to have discovered an ancient example of a museum!

Another topic of interest to the public stemmed from the fact that Merenptah was a pharaoh often associated with the Exodus. If Merenptah was the Pharaoh of

5.31. Reconstruction of the throne room of the palace of Merenptah painted by Mary Louise Baker in 1919, based on Clarence Fisher's plans and drawings. [UPM image # 150556]

the Oppression, then the possibility emerged that the palace of Merenptah might be the very location where Moses and Aaron had pled with pharaoh on behalf of the children of Israel. This aspect of the palace discovery attracted the greatest amount of interest and was covered by many newspapers in cities large and small. The discovery of Merenptah had made a huge splash.

Towards the end of the summer of 1916 came another update to the story. As Fisher expanded his excavations outward from the throne room and into other areas, he realized this was no modest building. It was an enormous palace with dozens of columned halls, chambers, and passages in a mazelike configuration. To understand the palace and its actual functions and significance required a lot more work.

The excavations of the Merenptah Palace formed the main focus of Fisher's work through 1920 as he completed work on the building and also expanded investigation beyond the central structure. In this endeavor his excavations eventually lost steam. Fisher had excavated a grand royal palace at Memphis, but one for which the surrounding matrix of related structures is largely unknown. It is in all likelihood a ceremonial palace that linked Merenptah to Ptah. However, the exact relationships of the building's architecture and function are still unclear.

At the same time that Fisher was uncovering the throne room of Merenptah, his workers were excavating in another area just to the south of the palace. Here in 1915 Fisher uncovered the mysterious "South Portal"—a gateway with massive limestone jambs and columns set in a mud brick wall. The stonework has scenes, like the palace itself, showing pharaoh Merenptah interacting with the gods of Memphis. Fisher thought the South Portal would turn out to be one of the entrances into the palace, but as he continued work over the next several years he realized the South Portal was on a different orientation. The throne room, in fact, was on the south end of the palace and it faces northwards. Consequently, the main entrance

5.32. *The Washington Post*, July 10, 1916.

5.33. *The Cincinnati Enquirer*, July 10, 1916 (detail).

5.34. Schematic showing the Merenptah Palace and the South Portal that Fisher discovered in 1915.

FIND PHARAOH'S PALACE

American Archaeologists Make Great Discovery in Egypt.

CONTAINS RICH THRONE ROOM

Magnificent Building Also Housed a Museum of Relics of Stone Age and Sixth Dynasty, Collected by Meremptah, Son of Rameses the Great—Gold Ornaments Found.

Philadelphia, July 9.—The museum of the University of Pennsylvania tonight made public a report from Dr. Clarence S. Fisher, leader of the Eckley B. Coxe, Jr., expedition to Egypt, in which he tells of what appears to be the discovery that Meremptah had in his palace at Memphis an archeological museum something like those of the present day. Meremptah was the son of Rameses the Great, and by many is identified as the Pharaoh of the oppression as described in the Book of Exodus.

Was Destroyed by Fire.

The palace was discovered early in the present year, the report said. It was large and elaborately decorated, but at some time was destroyed by fire, traces of which are abundant. The palace was about 180 feet long and 100 feet wide and contained about twenty rooms.

The throne room was a magnificent chamber of about 60 by 40 feet. In describing this room, the museum announcement stated that "it is probable that this throne room, if not the same one, is similar to the one in which Moses and Aaron confronted the Pharaoh demanding that the people of Israel be permitted to go. * * * The authorities in Egypt admit that a great discovery has been made."

Gold Ornaments Found.

In the throne room were found gold ornaments, scarabs, vessels for various purposes and vases. The most interesting find, the report stated, was a collection of relics partly of the stone age and partly of the sixth dynasty (about 4500 B. C.) which indicated that Meremptah was a collector much like modern men or nations. The stone implements included knives, razors, sickles and arrowheads.

5.32

MUSEUM

Boasted By Meremptah

In His Egyptian Palace, 'Tis Disclosed By Expedition.

Son of Rameses the Great Was Collector Much Like Modern Men, American Says.

SPECIAL DISPATCH TO THE ENQUIRER.

Philadelphia, Penn., July 9.—The Museum of the University of Pennsylvania to-noght made public a report from Dr. Clarence S. Fisher, leader of the Eckley B. Coxe, Jr., expedition to Egypt, in which he tells of what appears to be the discovery that Meremptah had, in his palace at Memphis an archalological museum something like those of the present day. Meremptah was the son of Rameses the Great and by many is identified as the Pharaoh of the oppression as described in the Book of Exodus.

The palace was discovered early in the present year, the report said. It was large and elaborately decorated but at some time was destroyed by fire, traces of which are abundant.

The palace was about 180 feet long and 100 feet wide and contained about 20 room. The throne room was a magnificent chamber about 60 by 40 feet.

5.33

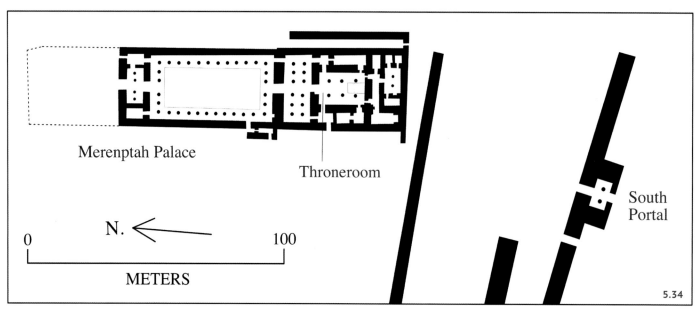

Merenptah Palace

Throneroom

South Portal

N. ⟵

0   100

METERS

5.34

5.35. Coxe Expedition excavations at the South Portal, palace of Merenptah, 1916. [UPM image # 33996]

5.36. The columns and gateway of the South Portal. These were granted to the Museum by the Egyptian Antiquities Service and are now on display in the Museum's Coxe Wing. [UPM image # 33944]

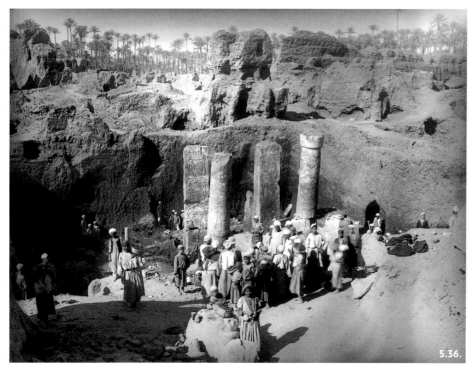

to the palace must have been from the north, not the south where the South Portal lay. Coming down to floor level, Fisher found many votive stelae and other objects suggesting the South Portal had some connection to a ritual building and may relate to an undiscovered temple that is associated with the palace.

The discovery of the South Portal illustrates some of the important, still unanswered questions about the Merenptah Palace. Fisher's excavations defined the main palace building, but not the entire area around it. The palace is certainly part of a complex of buildings that are linked together. Some further work in the area including Penn's continued excavations at Memphis in the 1950s attempted to provide more evidence but with only modest results. There is potential for expanding the work although, as in Fisher's day, the high water table presents a major obstacle at deep levels.

The Great Memphis Affair

Since the 1890s, the University Museum had maintained a close relationship with Flinders Petrie. This developed initially through Sara Yorke Stevenson and the Museum's sponsorship, up to 1905, of his work with the Egypt Exploration Fund. After 1906 when Petrie had established the British School of Archaeology in Egypt the Museum continued to be a supporter of Petrie's excavations. The Museum's support had been strengthened after Gordon and Coxe's 1909 visit to Egypt. The results of that partnership include the award to Philadelphia of the colossal Sphinx of Ramses II from Memphis. However, when news reached Petrie that the Antiquities Service in 1915 had granted permission to the University of Pennsylvania to excavate at Memphis, Petrie was surprised and angered. He came to the conclusion that he had been double-crossed by his long-time supporters in Philadelphia.

Since Petrie had planned to return to Memphis after the Great War, in 1915 he published a scathing statement in his popular journal, *Ancient Egypt,* calling into question the Museum's receipt of the excavation permit for Kom el-Qal'a at Memphis. Petrie regarded this as duplicitous treatment at the hands of the Egyptian Department of Antiquities and the University Museum. His note took on unfortunate political overtones.

Gordon was dismayed at Petrie's negative and public complaint about the Museum. He wrote, at first, a reply explaining the circumstances of the work at Memphis. When Petrie responded asking that Gordon correct statements printed in *The Museum Journal* that Petrie was no longer working at Memphis, Gordon met this head-on asking that Petrie rescind his comments in *Ancient Egypt.* No doubt both men lost some hours of sleep fretting over the issue.

Finally, on August 24, 1916, Gordon drafted a lengthy letter to Petrie explaining in detail the circumstances that had led to the Museum beginning excavations at Memphis. This letter furnishes an interesting glimpse into the politics of archaeology at the time of the First World War. Gordon reiterated to Petrie that

5.37. Petrie's journal, *Ancient Egypt,* from 1915.

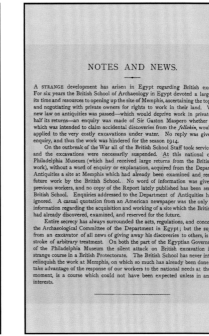

5.37.

BRITISH SCHOOL OF ARCHAEOLOGY IN EGYPT
AND EGYPTIAN ACCOUNT
UNIVERSITY COLLEGE, GOWER ST. LONDON

4 April 1916

Dear Dr. Gordon,

I am much obliged to you for your letter of 1 March, and for the June 1915 number of your museum journal on the subject, of which I had already received a copy five months after date.

After the close and friendly connections with Philadelphia extending over a quarter century, it seemed surprising that (during our enforced absence) no enquiry could be made before your taking over a site on which we had been working on a larger scale for six years. Our house is still standing, and a guard paid to keep it, on the ground close by, as much be well known to your expedition.

As to the Cairo Department, I was awaiting a reply to a business enquiry about our work, and that was the cause of my not working there six months before the war. But Sir Gaston Maspero always stated that if an excavation paused in work, he enquired whether they would resume it before granting the site to others.

The actual case is that the Temple you have worked was well known to us, we had cleared the inner end of it (Memphis I and II) and examined the columns which you have since cleared. We reserved it for work after the sebakhin had cleared the high ground over it. I think that in view of all this the statement in Ancient Egypt was to be expected.

However, I am very glad to have your assurance that you did not wish to take advantage of our enforced absence. I hope therefore that you will correct the statement in your Journal that our work at Memphis is brought to a close – it is only suspended for the war; and also that your expedition has taken up the excavation of the ancient capital – that I intend to resume.

Believe me,

Yours sincerely,

W.M. Flinders Petrie

5.38.

the Museum had not initially planned to work at Memphis but the Egyptian Antiquities Service offered it only after many other sites had been declined. He emphasized that Fisher had specifically inquired about Petrie's permit and the Antiquities Service confirmed that Petrie had renounced his permit. There was no planned "silent attack" on British excavations by the Egyptian government in collusion with the Penn Museum.

No doubt a major sticking point for Petrie was the ongoing publicity about the remarkable discovery of the Merenptah palace. Over the summer of 1916, Fisher was engaged on the first season of work on the throne room and, as we have seen, papers were coming out regularly with updates on the new discoveries at Memphis. With the exception of the Palace of Apries, Petrie's work at Memphis had never

5.39. Gordon's letter to Petrie explaining the events that led to the Museum's work at Memphis, August 24, 1916.

August 24, 1916

Dear Professor Petrie:

I received in due time your letter of April 4th replying to my communication of March 8th, in which I called your attention to certain statements printed in ANCIENT EGYPT (Part IV, 1915), upon which your name appears as editor.

Having in mind when I wrote you, the cordial relations which have in the past existed between yourself as Director of the British School in Egypt on the one hand and this Museum on the other, I cherished the thought that the appearance of the article in question was due to some unfortunate accident and that when your attention had been called to it, the error would be corrected and proper amends made.

It was, therefore, with pained surprise that I learned from your letter of April 4th that you not only assume full responsibility for the said article but that you undertake to show that certain statements which it contains and which have reference to this Museum, are justified or, to use your own words, "to be expected."

In order to call your attention once more to the seriousness of these statements and to the degree of responsibility which you assume in the matter, I reproduce two passages from the article referred to, in which the name of this Museum is used in a way which we cannot allow to pass unnoticed. The passages follow.

"On the outbreak of the War all of the British School Staff took service at once, and the excavations were necessarily suspended. At this national crisis, the Philadelphia Museum (which had received large returns from the British School work), without a

---

word of enquiry or explanation, acquired from the Department of Antiquities a site at Memphis which had already been examined and reserved for future work by the British School.........

"On both the part of the Egyptian Government and of the Philadelphia Museum the silent attack on British excavation is a very strange course in a British Protectorate. The British School has never intended to relinquish the work at Memphis, on which so much has already been done; and to take advantage of the response of our workers to the national needs at the present moment, is a course which could not have been expected unless in anti-British interests."

I have made a thorough investigation of the circumstances which attended the obtaining by the University Museum of its concession to excavate on the site of ancient Memphis. These circumstances, attested by the head of our expedition to Egypt and fully confirmed by the Directeur Général du Service des Antiquités, as well as by the Chief Inspector of Antiquities for Lower Egypt, are as follows.

The University Museum, through Mr. Clarence S. Fisher, who was at the time in Egypt, was negotiating early in 1915 for certain concessions with a view to conducting excavations in that country. These negotiations did not embrace Memphis, which was not even considered by the Museum until, our application for other sites having been refused, the Chief Inspector of Antiquities for Lower Egypt suggested to Mr. Fisher that he should make application for Memphis. Thereafter Mr. Fisher addressed inquiries to the Directeur Général du Service des Antiquités with a view to ascertaining the status

---

of Memphis respecting concessions and especially to learn what your own plans might be with regard to that site. The Directeur Général, in a letter dated January 16, 1915, replied to Mr. Fisher, stating that you had positively renounced the continuation of your work at Memphis. He stated moreover that after having been renounced by you, that site had been conceded to Prince Bibesco of Roumania on behalf of his government, which on account of the subsequent outbreak of the war, would not be in a position to hold its concession.

Upon receiving this definite and official assurance, Mr. Fisher made formal application for a portion of Memphis. Acting upon that application, the Service des Antiquités cancelled the concession already awarded to Prince Bibesco on the ground that the Roumanian Government, on account of the outbreak of the European war, would no longer be able to make this concession good by conducting excavations. The Service thereupon granted to Mr. Fisher on behalf of the University Museum that portion of Memphis for which he had applied.

This information is contained in the official records of which copies are in possession of this Museum. These records both directly and by implication convey the distinct impression that you had renounced entirely your concession at Memphis. That renunciation took place, not upon the outbreak of the European war, but before that event. Moreover, according to the same source of information, between the time when you had renounced the site and the outbreak of the war, Memphis had been conceded to Prince Bibesco, whose valid claims therefore antedated the war and intervened between your relinquished rights and Mr. Fisher's application.

It appears, therefore, that the statement that the British School never intended to relinquish the work at Memphis, is inconsistent with the

---

official information by which the Museum was guided in its negotiations for that site. I would be wanting in candor if I failed to call your attention also to the want of agreement between the facts of which we have positive knowledge and the statement in your letter of April 4th which reads as follows. "It seemed surprising that (during our enforced absence) no inquiry should be made before your taking over a site on which we had been working on a large scale for six years."

It is on record that Mr. Fisher did make inquiries and you will agree, I am sure, that these inquiries were directed to the proper authorities. Your great experience as an excavator in Egypt and your intimate knowledge of the laws and regulations governing excavations in that country will not admit of any doubt on your part that Mr. Fisher as representative in Egypt of this Museum was correct in addressing his official inquiries to the Service des Antiquités.

It has been the consistent policy of this Museum to co-operate with other organizations carrying on investigations for the benefit of science and scrupulously to avoid even the appearance of competition and rivalry which we hold to be derogatory to those liberal interests for which the University Museum stands in common with all scientific bodies. In requiring official assurance that you had concluded your work at Memphis before making application for that site, Mr. Fisher was acting in strict conformity with that policy.

I notice with satisfaction your reference in your letter of April 4th to the close and friendly relations which have existed between yourself and this Museum for over a quarter of a century. The University Museum has ever been happily mindful of these relations and has lost no opportunity of promoting this mutual good will. If it were necessary to confirm this statement, my letters to yourself

---

during the last six years and the official records of the Museum and of the British School will furnish such confirmation. I regret that your recollection of these close and friendly relations did not cause you to make some inquiries before publishing a statement calculated to impair the credit of this Museum in the minds of right thinking people everywhere.

Your great reputation, the debt which the scholarly world owes to you and the acknowledged accuracy of your work, combine to give any public utterance for which you stand responsible, a special weight and significance. Speaking as you do with the authority of one who enjoys the public confidence, your words may be expected to carry conviction to all who read them. Your responsibility in this respect is therefore a very large and a very serious one.

The unwarranted statements which you caused to be published have subjected and are still subjecting this Museum to undeserved injury and injustice. To one of your intelligence it is not necessary for me to explain the seriousness of an accusation which would put this Museum in the false position before the public of obtaining valuable concessions by irregular and reprehensible methods in order to serve anti-British interests in Egypt.

Relying upon your well known respect for justice and fair play, I trust that I may now with confidence depend upon you to publish in ANCIENT EGYPT a complete retraction of the unwarranted statements concerning this Museum to which I have called your attention and which appeared in the pages of that journal.

In order that no part of your letter of April 4th shall remain unanswered, I feel it to be incumbent upon me to say that we see no reason why we should accede to any request that calls

---

for the qualification of statements that we have already published. It seems scarcely necessary to add that your interests in Memphis and your future activities there do not wait upon this Museum. No one knows better than yourself that all plans of this kind are dependent upon the constituted authorities at Cairo.

Believe me to be

Very faithfully yours

Gordon

Director

PROF. W. M. FLINDERS PETRIE
University College
Gower Street
London, W.C., England

uncovered anything so well preserved and of such scale. Perhaps galling to him was that he had personally recommended Fisher to Director Gordon, as well as provided the Museum with suggestions as to which sites might be most fruitful. Petrie had even invited the Museum to participate as part of his future work at Memphis.

Petrie noted that he and his assistants had been aware of the Merenptah building through their soundings (although Petrie thought it was a temple rather than a palace). Moreover, the chief inspector of Lower Egypt, Charles Edgar, had already observed the presence of the Merenptah throne room when he had stopped locals who were digging *sebakh* (fertilizer) out of Kom el-Qal'a in 1914 (before Fisher's arrival). Petrie emphasized that he planned to resume his work at Memphis after the World War. It was certainly in Petrie's mind that he should be the one excavating the Merenptah Palace.

The great "Memphis Affair" introduced a sour note to the Museum's long friendship with Flinders Petrie. In the end, Gordon and Petrie came to terms and principal blame was directed to Georges Daressy and the Antiquities Service. Petrie stated that he would correct his statements in his journal *Ancient Egypt* so long as Gordon corrected the statements in *The Museum Journal* that Petrie had given up work at Memphis. In fact, despite the energetic debate, Petrie in the end conducted no further work at Memphis.

5.40. Transcription of letter from Petrie to Gordon, September 13, 1916.

BRITISH SCHOOL OF ARCHAEOLOGY IN EGYPT
AND EGYPTIAN ACCOUNT
UNIVERSITY COLLEGE, GOWER ST. LONDON

13 Sept 1916

Dear Dr. Gordon,

I ought to thank you for your letter of 24 Aug received today and for the enquiry which you have made as to the Memphis affair.

The conduct of the Department of Antiquities is inexplicable. After I had addressed a letter to the late Director, and was awaiting a reply, the site was granted successively to Rumania and Philadelphia, without one word on the subject to me, either from the Director or the Inspector. This was entirely contrary to the professed conduct of the Director in case concessions were not continued, that an enquiry would be made as to their abandonment before granting them to others. So far from abandoning it, I was, on the contrary - waiting for a reply as to my conditions of work being continued.

You write of my "renunciation" being before the war. I never renounced the site, either before or during the war. I still think it surprising - as I have said in my letter 4 April - that no enquiry was made of me after I had been working there for six years, and still had a house there (shown in your views) and maintained a guardian there.

However, your position is legally correct, owing to the incorrect statements of the Department of Antiquities as to my giving up the site, while I was still waiting their answer to my enquiries.

I shall gladly state in Ancient Egypt that the action of the Philadelphia Museum was based entirely on the official statements of the Department of Antiquities, and was quite in order on that ground; though unfortunately without any reference to myself or the excavation of the site.

How the Department came to ignore my letter about the site, and to treat it as unoccupied, was not within the cognizance of the agency of Philadelphia at that time.

I may say that I have received assurances from the present Director that he recognizes that my work at Memphis will be resumed, and is only interrupted by the war. " Nous ne considérons rieus à Mit Rahineh avant votre reponse (6 Nov 1915). I trust therefore that, although you state that you "see no reason... for the qualification of statements that we have already published," you will correct the remarks in your journal that I have given up the site, and that it will be taken over by others.

Yours very truly,
W.M. Flinders Petrie

5.40.

A Generous Life:
The Passing of Eckley Coxe

"The latest report from Mr. Fisher, written at the Ruins of Memphis and received the day before his death, lay under his pillow when he died."

— The Museum Journal, *September 1916*

On September 21, 1916, just days after the most recent exciting news from Fisher in Memphis, news of another sort reached Philadelphia. The great patron of the Museum, Eckley Brinton Coxe, "Eck," had died at Windy Hill, his home in Drifton, Pennsylvania. Coxe, at the young age of 44, had succumbed to Addison's disease. His obituary in the Philadelphia Inquirer shows him as gaunt and sickly, not at all the energetic, enthusiastic man who visited Egypt so many times. Even as his health had declined in his last year, Coxe had corresponded regularly with both Gordon and Fisher in the field, his passion for ancient Egypt unbroken.

ECKLEY B. COXE, JR., DIES; ILL FOR YEAR

Millionaire Student of Archaeology Was Principal Patron of University Museum

Financed Expeditions to All Parts of World, and Collected Many Treasures of Ancient Nations

ECKLEY BRINTON COXE, JR.

Archaeology student and backer of many Egyptian expeditions, who died yesterday.

After an illness of more than a year, Eckley Brinton Coxe. Jr., millionaire, student of archaeology, generous patron of the University Museum and member of a family widely known in Philadelphia society, died yesterday at his summer home at Drifton, Pa. Mr. Coxe was 44 years old. He is survived by his mother. His home in this city was at 1004 Locust street. Although no word has been received here regarding funeral arrangements, it is expected that he will be buried in this city.

Mr. Coxe's death was a shock to his many friends here, despite the fact that he had been in ill health for a long time Only recently he went on an automobile trip to Maine, in company with his aged mother and other relatives, and although it was known that he was not in the best of condition it was not suspected by his friends here that death was near News of his demise was contained in a dispatch received from Hazleton, Pa.

Named after one of the pioneer anthracite coal operators of this country, Mr. Coxe in his early life played a prominent part in the firm of Coxe Brothers & Co., Inc., which mined coal in Luzerne, Carbon and Schuylkill counties before the properties were leased to the Lehigh Valley Railroad. His uncle, Eckley B. Coxe, Sr., was the founder of the coal interests held by the family. He died in 1895.

The greater part of his life, however, Mr. Coxe devoted to the study of archaeology For many years he was the chief financial support of the University Museum and during the last ten years acted as president of the institution. He is said to have taken upon his shoulders the entire running expenses of the museum.

Long the head of the Egyptian Society, Mr. Coxe sent five expeditions to Egypt, the last one, the Eckley B. Coxe, Jr., expedition, only recently discovering the temple and palace of Meren-Ptah, who is believed to have been the ruler of Egypt during the time of Moses. Many other valuable discoveries have been made by archaeologists in various parts of the world through the generosity of Mr. Coxe, and it is said of the $2,000,000 worth of treasures in the University Museum that a large portion of them were donated by the patron who died yesterday.

5.41. *The Philadelphia Inquirer,* September 21, 1916.

5.41.

ECKLEY B. COXE, JR., DIES; FINANCED PENN'S EGYPTIAN RESEARCH

Son of Anthracite Pioneer of Pa., Ill Year, Gave Liberally to University.

Eckley B. Coxe, Jr., president of the University of Pennsylvania Museum, widely known in social and club circles of this city, and member of one of the pioneer families in the Pennsylvania anthracite regions, died today at the Coxe home in Drifton, Luzerne county, Pa. Mr. Coxe had been ill for about a year. He was unmarried, and is survived by his mother, Mrs. Charles Brinton Coxe.

The home of Mrs. Coxe in this city is 1604 Locust street. It was also the home of her son. Mr. Coxe was a graduate of the University of Pennsylvania, class of 1893, and for some years was interested in the Egyptian researches of the University, contributing liberally to many branches of this research work. The Eckley B. Coxe, Jr., expedition, financed by Mr. Coxe, is now in Egypt making excavations under the direction of Dr. Clarence S. Fisher.

In the early part of the present month a report was received from Dr. Fisher, in which he set forth that recent excavations made in Egypt show the palace of Merenpthah to have been twice as large as the original excavations indicated. Dr. Fisher had only uncovered the general outline of the work when the hot weather came on and made it impossible to finish.   5.42.

From First Codicil to
Will of Eckley B. Coxe Jr 80

I give and bequeath to the University of Pennsylvania the sum of Four Hundred Thousand Dollars ($400,000) in addition to the sums given by my said Will, the said $400,000 to be held and the income only to be applied exclusively for the Museum of the said University and so far as may be needed exclusively for the Egyptian Section and after meeting the needs of that section to aid in explorations and in defraying the expenses of transportation of the collections and also for defraying the expenses of the publications of the said Museum..

x3x x x x x x x x   Second Codicil

I give and bequeath a further sum of One Hundred Thousand Dollars ($100,000) to the University of Pennsylvania to be held exclusively for the Museum thereof and the income only to be used and applied as far as possible for the Egyptian Section as in the case of the legacy in the First Codicil of Four Hundred Thousand Dollars ($400,000).

5.43.

5.44.

Coxe, a principled and religious man throughout his life, had been active in the Episcopal Church both in Drifton and in Philadelphia. His funeral was held at St. James Episcopal Church in Drifton, then his body was brought for final services to St. James Episcopal Church at 22nd and Walnut Streets in Philadelphia. The service was reportedly attended by many in Philadelphia society. This grand Rittenhouse Square church was the one he attended while in the Coxe family's city residence at 1604 Locust Street.

Eckley Coxe was buried next to his father, Charles Brinton Coxe, in Woodlands Cemetery, 40th and Woodland Avenue in West Philadelphia. Dr. Gordon of the Museum was one of his pallbearers. Also in attendance were friends from the board of the Children's Hospital of Philadelphia to which he had contributed generously. He remains there alongside his father, Charles, and mother, Elizabeth ("Lizzie" who died in 1919), just a few blocks from the Museum to which he had devoted so much of his life.

5.42. *The Evening Telegraph*, New York, September 21, 1916.

5.43. A part of Eckley Brinton Coxe's will for the maintenance of Egyptological research, excavation, and publication at the University of Pennsylvania Museum.

5.44. Grave of Eckley Brinton Coxe at Woodlands Cemetery, 40th and Woodland Ave, Philadelphia.

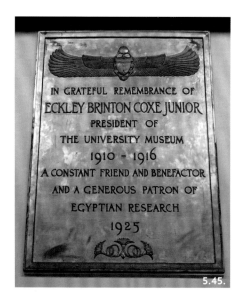

5.45.

5.45. Plaque commemorating the completion of the Museum's Egyptian Wing in honor of Eckley Brinton Coxe Jr.

5.46. Architect Wilson Eyre's sketch of 1923 showing the Museum with the Coxe Wing (left center) extending eastwards off of the Rotunda. The Coxe Wing was built from 1923–25 and opened in 1926. [UPM image # 133689]

Eckley Coxe had hoped to see many years of fruitful excavations in Egypt; however, his will made provisions for the continuation of the Coxe Expedition. From his bequests of close to a million dollars (the value of the dollar in 1916 was about twenty times what it is today), Coxe gave half a million to the Museum for Egyptian research: $400,000 to be used exclusively for the Egyptian Section and a further $100,000 for the Museum, but to be applied also for Egyptological work unless other pressing needs arose. Other beneficiaries were the Children's Hospital of Philadelphia where Coxe gave a further $100,000 above his already substantial donations, including an endowment of $10,000 to provide Christmas presents for children. He gave an additional $100,000 to the University of Pennsylvania for an increase in faculty salaries. Many other organizations in Philadelphia and in other parts of Pennsylvania also received gifts from his will.

Although his life was cut short, Coxe's generosity helped ensure the future of the Egyptian Expedition. For ten years after his death, major excavations under Clarence Fisher's direction continued at Memphis, Dendera, Dra Abu el-Naga in Thebes, and Beth Shan in Palestine. Objects from these sites constitute the largest and most important groups of material housed in the Museum's Egyptian collection. Upon the arrival of the impressive architectural works and other material from the Memphis excavations, the Museum completed the Coxe Wing to house the great Egyptological collection that Coxe had sponsored.

1926: The Sphinx Moves to the Coxe Wing

Fortuitously, Clarence Fisher's major discovery at Memphis was the palace of Merenptah, dating to exactly the same time period as the Sphinx. Now the Museum had a unique collection of architecture and sculpture from Memphis dating to the Ramesside Period (ca. 1200 BCE). Although Director Gordon's original hope of adding new colossal sphinxes to the Museum did not happen, in many respects the results were even better. The Museum had architecture that complemented the Sphinx perfectly. The Sphinx was to be reunited in Philadelphia

5.46.

with additional elements from the royal buildings associated with the great Ptah Temple at Memphis.

From 1923 to 1925 the Museum constructed the Coxe Egyptian Wing, named after the patron whose passion for Egypt had been the driving force in the Museum's excavations there. The wing was part of Wilson Eyre's original design for the Museum and was attached to the eastern side of the Chinese Rotunda. It was intended to eventually connect to a larger central rotunda which was never built. However, when it opened in 1926 the Coxe Wing, at 34,000 square feet, more than doubled the Museum's public gallery space. It was beautifully organized to present both large and small objects from ancient Egypt. Spacious central halls were intended to display large objects including the Sphinx and sections of Merenptah's Palace. Smaller side galleries were suited to the profusion of archaeological material that had come back recently from the excavations of Clarence Fisher.

The original design of the Coxe Egyptian Wing included two large halls, one atop the other. The upper one with a 60-foot ceiling was designed to accommodate the height of the columns and gateway from the South Portal of the Merenptah Palace, as well as space for the Sphinx. Unfortunately, the design of the Upper Hall had not taken into account the weight of the palace architecture and it was unclear if the floor was strong enough for all of this concentrated weight in its mid-section. Director Gordon was forever cautious about overtaxing the strength of the building.

In 1926 objects were installed in the now-completed Coxe Wing. These included the columns, doorways, and the mounumental South Portal gateway excavated near the Merenptah Palace, some parts of which had been restored to give a sense of their original appearance and colors. Given the questions about the combined weight of the palace architecture and the colossal Sphinx, Gordon decided to place them together in the Lower Hall. This necessitated displaying the South Portal gateway and columns in sections rather than at their full height.

After ten years of greeting visitors inside the Museum's main entrance, the Sphinx was now ready for its third and final move of the 20th century. The Sphinx was taken outside again and hauled around to the back of the Museum where an opening

5.47. The Coxe Wing's Upper Hall ("Upper Egypt"), originally designed to house the Sphinx and Merenptah Palace architectural elements. [UPM image # 31008]

5.48. In 1926, the Sphinx was again the center of attention at the opening of the new Coxe Wing; it was exhibited in the Lower Hall along with architectural elements from the palace of Merenptah at Memphis. The man in the fore-ground facing the Sphinx is Museum director George Byron Gordon. Gordon passed away the next year, 1927, having been at the helm of the Museum for seventeen years. [UPM image # 174874]

5.49a.

5.49a-c. Views of the Sphinx in the Coxe Wing sitting among columns and architecture from Merenptah's Palace found at Memphis, 1926. [UPM image #s 31027, 31026, 31025]

on the eastern side of the Coxe Wing's lower level allowed for the installation of the large architectural pieces. Here they set the Sphinx against the backdrop of the partially restored elements of Merenptah's Palace.

Nothing could be more fitting for the colossal Sphinx than to be united in the Museum with other remains of the great city of Memphis. Although the Sphinx came from the Ptah Temple and not from the Merenptah Palace, in a sense all of these elements belonged to the great royal buildings erected by Ramses II and his son Merenptah in honor of the god Ptah. Let us not forget too that thousands of years ago Merenptah had tagged the Sphinx as his own, something we will examine below.

The decision to install the Sphinx and elements from Merenptah's Palace in the Coxe Wing's Lower Hall was in every respect a compromise. It left the Upper Egyptian Hall looking oddly empty because Wilson Eyre had designed its soaring ceiling to house the columns and gateway of Merenptah's South Portal. Nevertheless, downstairs in the Lower Egyptian Hall, the overall ensemble of architecture fronted by the Sphinx forms a striking and evocative display. The Sphinx sits there resplendent, after thousands of years, still guarding the ruins of ancient Memphis. With small changes over the last century, this combination of objects from Memphis has remained the centerpiece of the Museum's Egyptian galleries.

Now, a hundred years later, the Museum is considering the possibility of moving the Merenptah Palace pieces to their intended location in the Upper Egyptian Hall. If this happens—and it would be a remarkable step in the reinstallation of the Egyptian collection—the Sphinx will remain downstairs. The Sphinx's entry point at the end of the Coxe Wing is now bricked over and sealed. New buildings were added in this area in the 1970s, and it would be very, very hard to get the Sphinx out again!

5.49b.

5.49c.

Strange Coincidences: Beth Shan and Chanhu-Daro

The story of the colossal granite Sphinx from Memphis is interwoven in myriad ways—both overt and subtle—with the history of the Penn Museum's work in Egypt before and after World War I. We have already seen how the Sphinx arrived during a transitional period for the Coxe Egyptian Expedition. The Sphinx became part of Director Gordon's vision for a grand Egyptian wing designed to exhibit the greatness of ancient Egypt through monumental sculpture. The story of the Sphinx also connects some of the people involved at the time, illustrating what a closely knit field archaeology was at the time (and still is to a certain extent today).

Remember Ernest Mackay? He is the man who, while working with Flinders Petrie for the British School of Archaeology, actually discovered the Penn Museum's granite Sphinx, as well as the even larger Alabaster Sphinx. It is doubtful that by the 1920s anyone (other than Mackay himself) would have remembered the real story of the Sphinx's discovery during the 1912 season of the British School of Archaeology. Strangely enough, in 1921 the very same man who had dug the Sphinx out of the mud of Memphis nine years earlier was hired by the Museum to take part in work then underway under Clarence Fisher's direction. How did this happen?

As the work at Memphis was winding down, Clarence Fisher had started excavating in 1921 at a site that promised new discoveries relating to Egyptian interaction with the Levant. This was the great tell site of Beth Shan in the Jordan Valley in what was then the British Protectorate of Palestine (now modern-day

5.50.

5.50. The 300-foot Tell of Beth Shan in the Jordan Valley. Beth Shan had been an Egyptian military center during the New Kingdom period. [Image courtesy of Dupy Tal and Moni Haramati, Rockefeller Museum]

Israel). In those days borders were much more easily traversed than they are today. Fisher simply packed up much of his equipment, other belongings, and his Egyptian workers and drove on up to Beth Shan from Egypt.

At Beth Shan, Fisher excavated atop the huge 300-foot-high central city mound and revealed buildings that dated to the same time period as the colossal Sphinx—the era of Ramses II and Merenptah. Beth Shan had been an Egyptian military and administrative center during the time of Egypt's New Kingdom, and there were Egyptian temples and other structures there. Remains of these are now part of the Penn Museum's Near Eastern collection,

It is here that the man who excavated the colossal Sphinx enters the story again. In 1919, just after World War I, Ernest Mackay had become Custodian of Antiquities for the Palestine Government. However, in 1921 funding problems with the position led Mackay to contact Director Gordon and offer his services at Beth Shan. Gordon responded positively and Mackay was hired as Fisher's assistant, working with him at Beth Shan during 1921–22.

Problems quickly surfaced. Letters in the Penn Museum Archives show that Mackay and Fisher did not get along. Fisher was very critical of Mackay and thought he was trying to undercut his authority. Fisher even accused him of being a Bolshevik. An assistant who Mackay had recommended, Miss Woodley, appears also to have come between the two men. Mackay ended up resigning in 1922 at

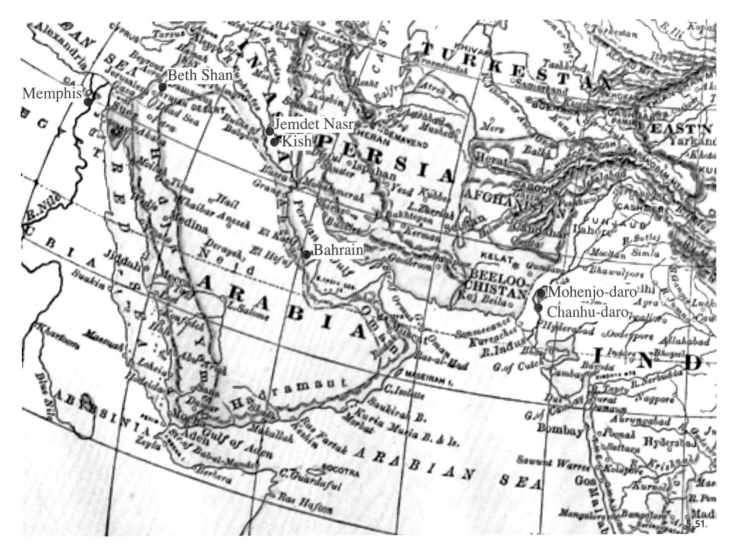

the suggestion of Miss Woodley. These events were among a number of personal disputes that Fisher became embroiled in later in his career at Penn. Such events damaged the relationship between Gordon and Fisher. Fisher eventually resigned in 1925, bringing to an end the great era of the Coxe Egyptian Expedition under his leadership.

After Beth Shan Ernest Mackay went on to work in Mesopotamia (Iraq), excavating the important sites of Kish and Jemdet Nasr for the Field Museum of Oxford University in 1922–1925. He worked briefly on the island of Bahrain in the Persian Gulf for the British School of Archaeology in Egypt (where Flinders Petrie was searching for connections between earliest Egypt and Mesopotamia). Then in 1926 he joined Sir John Marshall working on the Archaeological Survey of India. Marshall gave Mackay the task of excavating the important site of Mohenjo-daro in what is now Pakistan. And in 1932, he was hired by W. Norman Brown (Professor of Sanskrit at the University of Pennsylvania) as Field Director for the excavations at the large Harappan city of Chanhu-daro, south of Mohenjo-daro.

Mackay went on to publish important works on the archaeology of Mohenjo-daro and Chanhu-daro, as well as one of the first general books on the archaeology of the Indus Valley. Not surprisingly, Ernest Mackay is remembered mostly for his contributions to the study of the civilization of the Indus, but he has been lost to history as the actual "discoverer" of the Penn Museum's colossal sphinx.

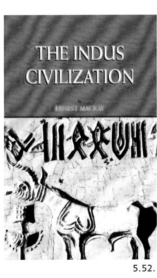

5.52.

5.51. Sites excavated by Ernest Mackay as his career took him east from Egypt to India.

5.52. Ernest Mackay wrote this popular book on the Indus Valley civilization in 1935.

CHAPTER SIX

Ancient Memphis:

The City of the Sphinx

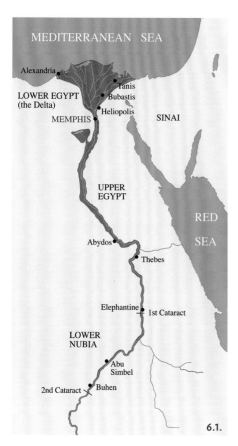

6.1. Map of Egypt.

The City of Memphis

How does the Penn Museum's Sphinx relate to the city in which it once stood? In this chapter we take a look at the archaeology and history of Memphis in order to understand the Sphinx's association with that important Egyptian city.

Over its 3,000-year history, ancient Egypt had many great cities. Among these are places like Heliopolis, city of the sun god Re; Thebes, the "southern capital" and location of the great temple of Amun at Karnak; and Alexandria, capital city of the Ptolemies on the Mediterranean coast. However, no city in ancient Egypt was as important, long-lived, and resilient as the city of Memphis. In order to understand the symbolic nature of the Penn Museum Sphinx it is important to understand the history and archaeology of the city where it came from. "Memphis" is the Greek version of an ancient Egyptian name, *Men-Nefer*; this is only one of many names used for Memphis over the years. Memphis endured for a remarkable time span—3,000 years—because in both real and symbolic ways it formed the very keystone of Egypt's identity.

Geographically Egypt is a country comprising two different regions: "Upper Egypt," the narrow ribbon of the Nile Valley as it snakes its way northwards through the Sahara towards the Mediterranean, and "Lower Egypt," the river delta formed as the main channel of the Nile breaks into a series of separate branches that empty into the Mediterranean. The regions are physically quite different; Upper Egypt is flanked along most of its length with majestic limestone cliffs that make a river journey up the Nile such a picturesque experience. Lower Egypt is a flat expanse of lush greenery, its northern edge giving way to marshes and lakes as you approach the sea. There were also cultural and linguistic differences between the people of Upper and Lower Egypt that reinforced the idea of two regions.

The Egyptians called their country *Tawy,* meaning the "Two Lands." From the beginning of history the pharaoh was the *Neb-Tawy,* "Lord of the Two Lands." An important role of the pharaoh was to keep Egypt unified in a state called *Sema-Tawy,* or "Union of the Two Lands." If the pharaoh maintained the *Sema-Tawy,* by extension he maintained Maat. Maat was an important idea in ancient Egyptian culture, a concept and a word that means "truth, justice, balance." Maat was embodied in the form of a goddess, herself named *Maat.* The idea of Maat, however, refers explicitly to the state of political harmony that exists when Egypt is strong and unified under authority of the pharaoh.

Memphis embodies this very idea of the *Sema-Tawy.* Its location is just slightly south of the point where the Nile Valley blossoms into the fan-like Delta, on the western side of the Nile. This location was no accident: this was the logical place to establish a political center from which to rule over both Lower Egypt to the north and Upper Egypt to the south. Memphis was founded in this location at the very time that Egypt made the transition from its Predynastic Period to the Early Dynastic Period (ca. 3000 BCE), an era when Egypt first defined itself as a unified nation state. Memphis and its location therefore are a direct expression of the concept of the *Sema-Tawy.* It became a royal capital designed explicitly for maintaining the unity of the Two Lands of Egypt.

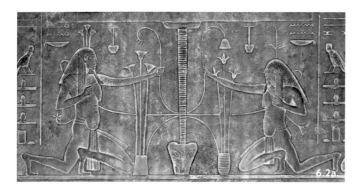

6.2a, b. Pharaoh maintains the union of the Two-Lands symbolically by defeating foreign enemies (center). The emblem of the *Sema-Tawy* (left) shows Upper and Lower Egypt (symbolized by the papyrus and lotus) bound together under the control of the king.

6.3. The king (right) offers Maat (divine order) to the gods. These scenes decorate parts of the palace of Merenptah from Memphis in the Penn Museum.

6.4. View of Saqqara with Step Pyramid of Djoser (3rd Dynasty, ca. 2700 BCE) in the upper center. Earliest Memphis may have lain quite close to Saqqara in the area now covered by the Nile cultivation. [Photograph by Eliot Elisofon, 1965, EEPA EECL 11164, Eliot Elisofon Photographic Archives, National Museum of African Art, Smithsonian Institution]

6.5a–c. The Step Pyramid of Djoser was Egypt's first royal pyramid. It is surrounded by an enclosure wall (above) and dummy buildings in stone (right) that may reproduce the living architecture of the city of *Ineb-Hedj*. [Images courtesy of Arian Zwegers, Berthold Werner and Adam Groffman]

6.6. Aerial view of the ruins of the center of Memphis. The pyramids of Saqqara are in the background, the modern village of Mit Rahina in the center. [Photograph by Eliot Elisofon, 1965, EEPA EECL 17373, Eliot Elisofon Photographic Archives, National Museum of African Art, Smithsonian Institution]

6.7. Ruins of the temples of Memphis among the palm groves. [Photograph by Eliot Elisofon, 1965, EEPA EENG 08388, Eliot Elisofon Photographic Archives, National Museum of African Art, Smithsonian Institution]

Archaeological and historical evidence tells us that Memphis was founded at the very beginning of the historical period, approximately 3000 BCE. From that point onwards, Egypt's history is organized into sequential groupings of kings: the dynasties. Egyptian traditions of later times consistently present the idea that dynasties of pharaohs started with a great unifier king named Menes. The texts tell us that Menes came from a town in Upper Egypt called Thinis. Despite this southern origin, he or his immediate successor established a new capital in the north, a royal residence city called *Ineb-Hedj,* or city of "The White Wall."

An Egyptian priest and chronicler of the Ptolemaic Period named Manetho recounted these traditions. About 250 BCE Manetho compiled a detailed history of Egypt's dynasties of kings based on records available to him. His work, the *Aegyptiaca,* has not survived directly. However, the *Aegyptiaca* is extensively quoted in an abbreviated version called the *Epitomes* of Manetho, copied down by a number of later writers from the Roman Period through the Middle Ages. Manetho tells us that the 1st Dynasty consisted of:

"Menes of Thinis together with his seven descendants: The king called Menes reigned for sixty years. He made a foreign expedition and won renown, but he was carried off by a hippopotamus. Athothis, his son, ruled for twenty-seven years. He built the palace at Memphis."

Here we have reference to the foundation of Memphis in its earliest form— the city called *Ineb-Hedj,* the "White-Wall," presumably so-named after the appearance of the whitewashed brick walls that surrounded the palace precinct of the pharaoh. Many archaeologists believe that a style of royal architecture that appears at this time called the *serekh,* or "palace-facade" is a form of mud-brick architecture that would also have appeared in the royal buildings of earliest Memphis. Characterized by narrow niches alternating in series with projecting buttresses, this style appears in its most grandiose expression in the Step Pyramid of Djoser at Saqqara, the necropolis site on the desert edge just west of Memphis. The vast enclosure of the Step Pyramid may be a monumental copy in stone of architecture that once existed in whitewashed mud brick in the city of Memphis.

Despite a lot of research, archaeologists have not yet identified the exact location and remains of earliest Memphis. The reasons for this are many, but essentially come down to the reality that the Nile River is not a static geological feature. It is an active, meandering river that is continually shifting location in its floodplain. Until the modern dams were built at Aswan in the 20th century,

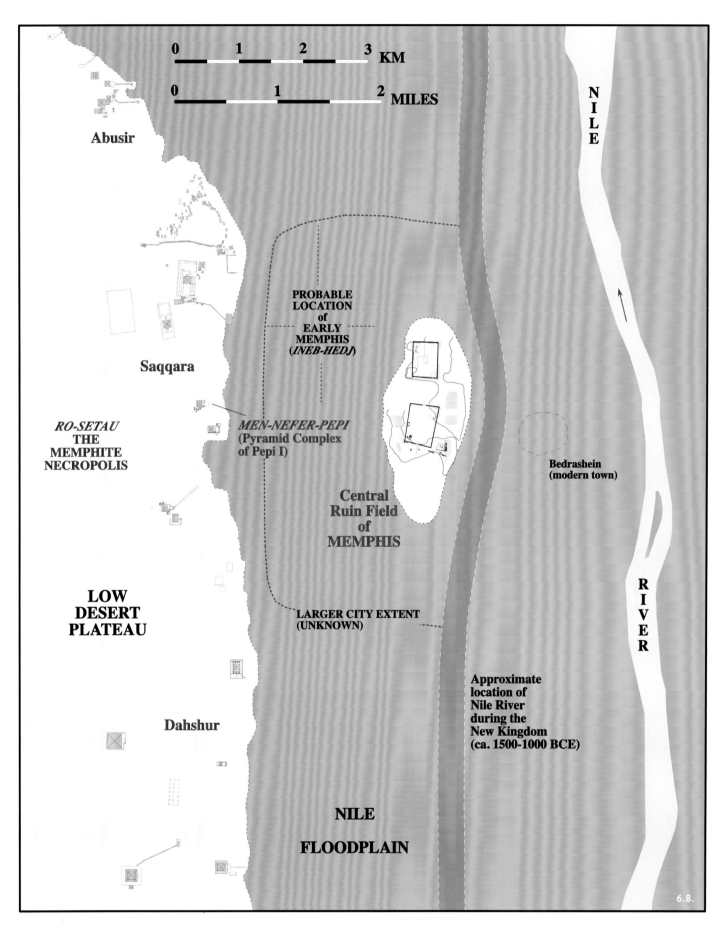

6.8. The region of Memphis. The Ptah Temple is the southernmost of the two rectangular enclosures at the center of Memphis.

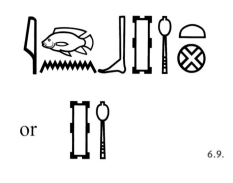

or

6.9.

6.10.

6.9. *Ineb-Hedj*, the original name of Memphis, means the city of the "White Wall." It could also be called "The Walls" for short.

6.10. *Men-Nefer*, the most common name for Memphis, derived from the name of the nearby pyramid complex of Pepi I of the 6th Dynasty.

the Nile would flood predictably every year. This annual Nile inundation arrived almost like clockwork between July and October. The inundation formed the basis for Egyptian agriculture and structured the calendar and rhythms of economic life. Ongoing deposition of silt replenished the fertility of the land but also gradually raised the elevation of the floodplain.

The rate sounds infinitesimal: something like less than a half inch (1 cm) every decade. But this adds up over the passage of time: 4 inches (10 cm) every century, 3.3 feet (1 meter) every thousand years. And so, something like 16 feet (5 meters) or more of silt has piled up since the days of *Ineb-Hedj*. Adding to this continual accumulation of silt, the river has migrated in its floodplain. Geological evidence suggests that in the region of Memphis the Nile has shifted about 3 miles (5 km) eastwards. Around 3000 BCE it ran quite close to the western desert escarpment and it was there that the early royal necropolis of Memphis was established in the 1st Dynasty: the site of Saqqara, which forms the core of what Egyptologists call the "Memphite necropolis." The great pyramid sites to the north and south of Saqqara, including Giza, Abu-Sir, and Dahshur, were all parts of the greater Memphite necropolis. The ancient Egyptians called this necropolis *Ro-setau*, a name we will examine later.

So, if Memphis once existed very close to Saqqara, what happened over Egypt's subsequent 3,000-year history as the river moved gradually eastwards? Because the Nile served as the primary artery of transport and communication for Egypt it was fundamental that the capital city be relatively close to the river. We now have identified archaeological remains of the city of Memphis from the time of the Middle and New Kingdoms. Memphis at that point was centered in the floodplain, about 2 miles (3.2 km) southeast of Saqqara. During that time something that served to anchor the location of central Memphis was the construction of large stone-built temples, particularly the main temple dedicated to Ptah, the patron god of Memphis. These long-lived religious institutions would have stabilized the core of the city in that location over its subsequent history. The center of Memphis maintained itself in this location for some 2,000 years. Although we know the Nile gradually migrated yet further eastwards, the city appears to have adapted with harbor areas that serviced the city from the river's edge. Today the ruins of Memphis are marooned in the middle of the floodplain, two miles from the modern course of the Nile.

The story of Memphis is a complex one. From its initial establishment around 3000 BCE, Memphis held sway as the preferred royal capital and governmental center of Egypt. The city had a heyday during the Pyramid Age of the Old Kingdom (4th–6th Dynasties, ca. 2600–2200 BCE). It served as a major administrative center during both the Middle Kingdom (ca. 2000–1750 BCE) and New Kingdom (18th–20th Dynasties, ca. 1550–1050 BCE). In the 18th Dynasty Memphis functioned as the primary royal administrative capital, although sharing many functions with Thebes in southern Egypt. Despite its importance, in many periods the pharaohs chose to establish royal residence cities elsewhere. During the Middle Kingdom a city named *Itj-Tawy* was the royal capital, thought to be about 30 miles (48 km) south of Memphis, but it has not yet been located by archaeologists. In the 19th Dynasty, Ramses II built a new royal capital at a site called *Per-Ramses*, "The House of Ramses," in the northeastern Nile Delta.

Despite these political fluctuations, the gravitas of Memphis endured. This city was still the geographical balancing point of the Two Lands; it survived long-term

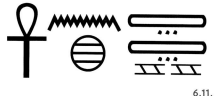

6.11.

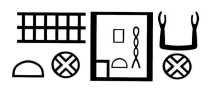

6.12.

environmental and political changes through a continual process of renewal over time. As pharaoh followed pharaoh, Memphis outlasted many other upstart cities as a center for political power.

One of the important changes over the history of Memphis is the city's name. From its initial foundation the city was known as *Ineb-Hedj,* but over thousands of years the Egyptians gave it additional names. A significant development in the city's name occurred when Pepi I (ca. 2290–2240 BCE), one of the pharaohs of the 6th Dynasty at the end of the Old Kingdom, constructed a pyramid complex on the desert edge at south Saqqara. The name of Pepi's pyramid complex was *Men-nefer-Pepi,* "Lasting-is-the-beauty-of-Pepi." The cult of Pepi in fact (true to the name) lasted for many centuries. Within a short period of time we find that the name of Pepi I's pyramid in its abbreviated form—*Men-nefer*—began to refer to the whole city of Memphis. Indeed, by the time of Egypt's Middle Kingdom, responding to the gradual eastward shift of the Nile, the center of Memphis had moved further south and east. The city center at that time lay directly eastwards of the location of Pepi I's pyramid.

Here we have the genesis of "Memphis." Forever thereafter the city remained *Ineb-Hedj,* but in day-to-day parlance it was first and foremost Men-nefer. There were other names applied to Memphis and the region around it. Also common in the Middle and New Kingdoms was the name *Ankh-Tawy,* meaning "Life-of the Two-Lands." The name is also one that employs a pun (of which the Egyptians were fond), as the word *ankh* also means sandal strap, and so the name also casts Memphis as the element binding together the Two Lands. *Ankh-Tawy* may refer specifically to the area of mortuary temples that lay between the city proper and the desert necropolis of Saqqara. However, it too had a wider connotation that encompassed the region of Memphis.

Despite other names, after the Old Kingdom, *Men-nefer* was the name that stuck. During the 1st millennium BCE when Greeks came and visited and settled in Egypt, they began to refer to the city using a Greek version of the Egyptian name *Men-nefer.* During the Ptolemaic Dynasty (323–30 BCE), Egypt was effectively a bilingual country using both the Egyptian and Greek languages and thus many cities and gods had Greek names derived from their Egyptian ones. To the Greeks *Men-Nefer* was Memphis. Consequently, from classical texts in Greek and Latin we have the name Memphis that derives from the name of one Old Kingdom pharaoh's pyramid.

6.11. *Ankh-Tawy,* "Life of the Two-Lands," was commonly used as a reference to the region of Memphis.

6.12, 6.13. The district of *Hut-Ka-Ptah* in hieroglyphs. The district of *Hut-Ka-Ptah* on a relief from the palace of Merenptah in Memphis, now in the Penn Museum.

There is another way in which the city of Memphis and its name is important to the history of Egypt. At the heart of ancient Memphis stood the temple dedicated to Ptah, the city's patron god. Throughout Egypt's long history, and due to the political prominence of Memphis itself, Ptah emerged early on as one of Egypt's great state-gods. Over time, many pharaohs added to and embellished the Ptah Temple, which became an anchor for the city as a whole.

The Ptah Temple was not a single shrine, but rather an evolving complex of connected religious buildings dedicated to Ptah in his various forms and other associated gods. The temple's name in ancient Egyptian was *Hut-Ka-Ptah*, meaning "The-temple-of-the-spirit-of-Ptah." Such was the size of the Ptah Temple that the Egyptians often used the name *Hut-Ka-Ptah* to refer to Memphis as a whole. Sometimes the name appears with a city symbol after it implying the temple of Ptah was a veritable metropolis in its own right; it was indeed a separate administrative district.

The Ptah Temple existed over thousands of years, although it shifted location with the migrating city until it became anchored during the New Kingdom by the great stone temples of that era. By the time of Egypt's Late Period (ca. 664–332 BCE) the Ptah Temple was so prominent that its name became synonymous with the country of Egypt as a whole. *Hut-ka-Ptah* was pronounced as "Hikupta" in the Demotic phase of the Egyptian language that was then used. This became Greek "Aigyptos," or as we say today in English, "Egypt."

When the Greeks came to Egypt, particularly from about 600 BCE onwards, Memphis was a city with thousands of years of history behind it. The city was still intact and its great temples were still open and functioning. During the Greek and Roman periods, the now foreign rulers of Egypt added to the city of Memphis. Indeed, the city flourished during the period of the Ptolemaic kings who descended from Alexander the Great's general Ptolemy, son of Lagos. Alexander himself was crowned pharaoh of Egypt when he came to Memphis in 332 BCE after having captured Egypt from the Persians. For that reason, some of the descriptions of the city, written by classical writers both before and after the time of Alexander the Great, provide a contemporary viewpoint on the design and layout of Memphis as it then existed. Descriptions of Memphis occur in Classical Greek texts including the writings of Herodotus (ca. 484–425 BCE). Although Memphis continued as a major city well through the period of the Roman Empire, things began to change. The enduring city of *Ineb-Hedj* was not to last forever.

During the Late Roman and Byzantine periods the administrative and military capital of Egypt was shifted across the Nile to a site called Babylon (not to be confused with the famous city of Babylon in Mesopotamia). This site began to siphon away the power and influence of Memphis. Then, in 389–390 CE the Late Roman emperor Theodosius I issued a series of decrees for the proscription of pagan religion through the Roman Empire. The proscription of paganism had lasting impact throughout the Mediterranean and especially in Egypt where the gods' temples had still continued to function even as Christianity had spread. During Theodosius I's reign Egypt's great temples were closed, many of them systematically purged of their pagan images. This represented a major blow to a city like Memphis, which lived and breathed around the great temple to Ptah. During the succeeding Byzantine Period Memphis underwent a long and relentless decline. Like a great warrior whose legs have been cut from beneath him in battle, Memphis slowly toppled.

Two and a half centuries after Theodosius, in 640 CE, the Arab general Amr Ibn el-As, one of the companions of the prophet Muhammed, invaded Egypt bringing an end to control by the Byzantine Empire from Constantinople. Significantly, when Amr Ibn el-As signed the treaty of surrender from the Byzantine governor of Egypt he did so at the site of Memphis, Egypt's ancient capital. The story of Memphis therefore bookends the very beginnings of ancient Egyptian history, as *Ineb-Hedj*, ca. 3000 BCE, and its end in the Middle Ages with the arrival of Christianity and then Islam in 640 CE. Amr Ibn el-As established a new capital city named Fustat on the eastern side of the Nile, quite close to Roman-Byzantine Babylon and just south of the center of Cairo. Fustat grew significantly for 500 years but Cairo proper, which was founded in 969 CE, later eclipsed it.

The building of these new capitals, first Fustat and then Cairo, during the Middle Ages served as the final death knell for what remained of ancient Memphis. The city and its great stone monuments stood derelict after the abandonment of the gods' cults. The city's population had shriveled as Memphis was deprived of its political and religious importance. Memphis became a convenient stone quarry for the construction of Fustat and then Cairo. The same fate befell the city of Heliopolis located farther to the northeast of Cairo. Huge amounts of ready-made stonework existed in the great standing temples and palaces of both Memphis and Heliopolis. In the 7th century CE both cities began to be substantially deconstructed and the masonry hauled away for reuse in the construction of Egypt's medieval capitals. Many of the buildings of medieval Cairo—its mosques, city walls, and other stone structures—are composed of the stones of Memphis. Still, some things remained in the devastated ruins of the Ptah Temple and those vestiges are what attracted archaeologists in the last two centuries to excavate and reconstruct ancient Memphis.

The Ruins of Memphis

For a long time the excavation of ancient Memphis has been kind of a holy grail for Egyptian archaeology. Ancient Memphis is not like Pompeii or Macchu Pichu, cities abandoned and frozen in time. Memphis was one of the great cities of the ancient world, even though it has been severely denuded by natural and human factors. How do we come to understand the characteristics of this lost city on the Nile? Let us look briefly at the history of archaeological work at Memphis that led up to the period of work when the Sphinx was discovered.

During the Middle Ages, as the ruins of Memphis became a building quarry for new capitals at Babylon, Fustat, and then Cairo, the site increasingly slipped into obscurity. There are descriptions of the ruins and their location included in the writings of various medieval authors. Among these are the Jewish traveler Benjamin of Tudela in the 12th century; the Moroccan explorer Ibn Battuta in the 14th century; and the Egyptian historian el-Maqrizi in the 15th century. These writers were content with describing the location and landscape surrounding the remains of Memphis. Although interesting and sometimes informative they provide little direct information relevant to understanding ancient Memphis, a quest that requires archaeological excavation.

6.14.

6.15.

6.14. Map of Memphis and its region from *Description de l'Égypte,* vol. 5 (1809).

6.15. Napoleonic scholars recording the hand of a fallen colossus at Memphis, from *Description de l'Égypte,* vol. 5 (1809).

6.16.

6.17.

6.16. Painting published by Lepsius of the colossal Ramses II which Caviglia and Sloane discovered at Memphis in 1820. The statue was later raised up and now is partially restored in the Memphis Museum.

6.17. Early 20th century view of the colossal Ramses II, Abu el-Hol, discovered in 1820 (antique postcard).

Modern interest in the archaeology of Memphis dates to the era of Napoleon Bonaparte's French Expedition to Egypt (1798–99). As part of the scientific commission that produced the celebrated *Description de l'Égypte (1809–1828)*, French scholars made the first attempt at mapping the ruin field of Memphis. Throughout the early 1800s Memphis attracted attention primarily as a location to conduct unsystematic digging for antiquities to sell. However, it was the haphazard process of digging in Memphis that began to reveal remnants of the city's storied past and which eventually gave way to systematic excavation.

Discoveries during the 1800s attracted people's interest, particularly the large-scale statues that still lay among the ruined temples of Memphis. In 1820, an Italian, Giovanni Caviglia, working with Charles Sloane, the British Consul in Cairo, made the most famous discovery at Memphis of the early 1800s. Their discovery was the fallen colossus of Ramses II, which is popularly called Abu el-Hol (the "father of awe," a term also applied to the Great Sphinx at Giza). When the famous decipherer of hieroglyphs Jean Francois Champollion went to Memphis during a trip in 1828–30, he was so inspired by this great statue that he planned to return and conduct his own work around it. He never did so, as he died just two years later in 1832.

The German Egyptologist Karl Richard Lepsius made the first systematic attempts at excavation of Memphis in 1843. Lepsius's plan of the ruins and area of Memphis remained the standard plan of the site until the excavations of Flinders Petrie in 1908. In the 1850s, an Armenian engineer Joseph Hekekyan followed Lepsius. Hekekyan, who at the time was conducting a survey for the Geological Society of London, undertook the first significant excavations in the central ruins of Memphis. He made several major discoveries including a second colossus of Ramses II, one that was later removed to adorn the square in front of the main train station in downtown Cairo, "Maidan Ramses."

The late 19th century saw an increasing pace of archaeological activity, particularly focused on the ruins of the Ptah Temple at the center of Memphis. Auguste Mariette, the founder of the Egyptian Antiquities Service, and his successor, Gaston Maspero (a man who played a prominent role in the story of the Penn Museum Sphinx), excavated areas of central Memphis. At that time the site was increasingly under threat from agricultural development and the removal of *sebakh* (fertilizer dug out of ancient sites). Memphis was in dire need of systematic planning and salvage excavation. In 1908, Flinders Petrie began six years of work there on a larger scale than anyone had attempted previously. His work rescued information from parts of Memphis that have long since vanished beneath modern villages and fields.

The Penn Museum's colossal Sphinx came from Petrie's discoveries in the Ptah Temple at Memphis in 1912, his fifth year of work at the site. Since then, the Penn Museum itself has played a major role in the excavations of Memphis. As we have already seen, one of the most significant discoveries of the Coxe Egyptian Expedition, just a year after the arrival of the Sphinx in Philadelphia, were the well-preserved remains of a huge palace complex at Memphis belonging to pharaoh Merenptah, son and successor of Ramses II. Clarence Fisher excavated this palace in 1915–20 and major parts of it came to Philadelphia a decade after the Sphinx. The University of Pennsylvania also conducted further excavations at Memphis in the 1950s. The Museum's long association with the archaeology of Memphis continues to this day, since Memphis forms such an important part of the Museum's Egyptian collection and galleries.

The investigation of Memphis continues to draw archaeologists applying new field techniques, such as remote sensing, and geoarchaeological techniques. Since the days of Petrie and Fisher, other institutions have tackled the site of Memphis, most importantly the Egyptian Antiquities Organization and the long research program of the Egypt Exploration Society's Survey of Memphis project, which has assembled a comprehensive study of the landscape and structure of Memphis over its long history. Yet because of its complexity, its longevity, and its limited preservation, Memphis remains a work in progress.

We now turn to the gods of ancient Memphis because they and their temples are intimately connected with the Sphinx, which once stood guard over Ptah's great temple.

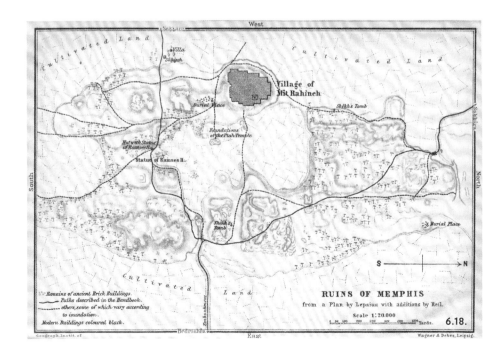

6.18. Plan of the ruins of Memphis after Baedekers *Egypt* (1914). This map was based on the first systematic map of the site made by Lepsius in 1843.

The Gods of Ancient Memphis

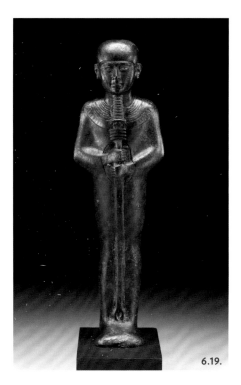

6.19. Bronze figure of Ptah. [UPM object # E14294]

6.20. Detail of a limestone relief of Ptah. [UPM object # E13579]

Patron deities who were worshiped in temples both large and small protected most ancient Egyptian town and cities. The deities in these temples tended to be arranged in family groupings consisting of a father, mother, and child god. The city of Memphis was no different. For much of its history it was a capital city. Even during times when the main royal residence lay elsewhere, Memphis remained an important administrative and religious center. A major factor in the continuing prominence of Memphis is the particular group of gods who were worshiped there. The religious significance of these gods, and the wealth and influence of their temples as they developed over centuries and millennia, came to define the essence of Memphis as a major religious and urban center.

Ptah was an ancient deity known from texts as far back as the Early Dynastic Period, the time of the foundation of Memphis (ca. 3000 BCE). With a multi-faceted and complex persona, Ptah was the great creator god. However, he also had popular aspects; for example, he was a patron god of craftsmen (connecting with his role as a creator). Ptah was the chief god of Memphis and, as noted above, the name of his temple at Memphis, *Hut-ka-Ptah,* "The Temple of the spirit of Ptah," was often synonymous with the city of Memphis itself. His role as craftsman led the Greeks and Romans to associate Ptah with their gods Hephaestus and Vulcan.

Ptah's iconography is unique. He appears as a mummiform human male. He wears a distinctive skull cap, a squared-off false beard, and holds a staff that often comprises three hieroglyphic symbols, the *ankh* (life), the *djed* pillar (stability), and the *was* scepter (dominion).

Over their long history, the ancient Egyptians developed a number of different creation myths to explain how their world began. One of the most important such myths is known as the Memphite Theology. In this complex, multi-layered account of the beginning of the world, Ptah of Memphis plays the central role as the primeval creator god. The Memphite Theology is known to us from a 25th Dynasty (ca. 700 BCE) text inscribed on a slab of black basalt known today as the Shabaka Stone. According to the text on the stone, King Shabaka found an old and damaged papyrus and wished to record the information he found there for posterity. He had the damaged text inscribed on a more permanent monument, which is the surviving stone itself.

The Shabaka Stone is illuminating as it allows the Egyptians themselves to talk about who Ptah was in their own words. The text on the stone tells us the origin of the religious knowledge inscribed on it (Lichtheim 1973 [1]:51–56):

> *This writing was copied out anew by his majesty in the House of his father Ptah-South-of-his-Wall, for his majesty found it to be a work of the ancestors which was worm-eaten, so that it could not be understood from beginning to end. His majesty copied it anew so that it became better than it had been before, in order that his name might endure and his monument last in the House of his father Ptah-South-of-his-Wall throughout eternity, as a work done by the Son of Re [Shabaka] for his father Ptah-Tatenen, so that he might live forever.*

The text explains Ptah's role in creation. Ptah, they say, created the world by means of thought and speech:

> As to the tongue, it repeats what the heart has devised. Thus all the gods were born and his Ennead was completed. For every word of the god came about through what the heart devised and the tongue commanded.

The text then enumerates what Ptah has created and further emphasizes one of his important relationships, his indivisible connection with another deity called Tatenen, the god of the "primeval mound" of creation:

> Thus it is said of Ptah: "He who made all and created the gods." And he is Tatenen, who gave birth to the gods, and from whom every thing came forth, foods, provisions, divine offerings, all good things. Thus it is recognized and understood that he is the mightiest of the gods. Thus Ptah was satisfied after he had made all things and all divine words. He gave birth to the gods, He made the towns, He established the nomes, He placed the gods in their shrines, He settled their offerings, He established their shrines, He made their bodies according to their wishes. Thus the gods entered into their bodies, Of every wood, every stone, every clay, Everything that grows upon him in which they came to be. Thus were gathered to him all the gods and their kas, content, united with the Lord of the Two Lands.

6.21.

6.21. The Shabaka Stone is now housed in the British Museum (EA 498). The stone was later used as a millstone and the hieroglyphs suffered damage. [Image © Trustees of the British Museum]

6.22. Relief on one of the columns from the palace of Merenptah at Memphis depicting the god Ptah in his shrine. [UPM object # E13577B]

6.22.

6.23. This over life-size statue from Memphis shows Ramses II seated with Ptah-Tatenen. It relates to Ramses' emphasis on the composite form of Ptah (Cairo Museum, CCG 554). [Image after Ludwig Borchardt, *Statuen und Statuetten von Königen und Privatleuten im Museum von Kairo, Nr. 1-1294, Teil 2: Text und Tafeln zu Nr. 381-653*, Berlin, 1925, pl. 93]

6.24. Image of Ptah-Tatenen from the tomb of prince Amunherkhepeshef in the Valley of the Queens.

Because Ptah was a great creator god the Egyptians frequently linked him with other deities who were thereby seen as manifestations of Ptah and his creative powers. As we see in the Memphite Theology, Ptah held a very close relationship to another primeval god named Tatenen. We first meet Tatenen in the Middle Kingdom. His name refers to the primordial mound that appeared out of the watery chaos called Nun at the moment of creation. His name literally means "The-risen-earth." The mythology of the primeval mound is rooted in the Egyptian environment. Life in Egypt was governed by the annual cycle of the Nile inundation. Every year the Nile would break over its banks and flood the area called Kemet, restoring the rich black alluvial soil of the Nile Valley. When it receded, having replenished the soil, the yearly cycle of growth would begin again. The idea of Tatenen mirrors the annual (re)appearance of the fertile soil. In cosmic terms, Tatenen was the embodiment of the first occurrence of fertile land from a watery nothingness at the beginning of time. He forms a key element in the physical basis for life's beginning.

The myth of the primeval mound recounted on the Shabaka Stone and other sources also discusses how life came into being when solid ground had risen out of the empty watery void. The first living thing to appear on Tatenen was a lotus flower called Nefertem. From Nefertem, the sun god himself appeared in a form called Atum. As he rises into the now fully formed sky with earth below, the sun god goes on to illuminate the cosmos with his radiant energy and make life possible. Because of this connection to the earth, Tatenen is also associated with the earth god Geb. Even though he is a nature deity, Tatenen is usually shown in anthropomorphic form, typically as a bearded man wearing a headdress with two tall plumes and ram's horns. Tatenen has many aspects to his cosmic creative powers and could also serve as a protector of the deceased king in the netherworld.

Tatenen existed for a long period of time separately from Ptah of Memphis. However, during the New Kingdom there was increasing interest in emphasizing the cosmic creative power of Ptah. As a result, during that time the Egyptians merged Ptah with Tatenen to create the composite form Ptah-Tatenen who is discussed on the Shabaka Stone. This god is still Ptah but now imbued with an enhanced cosmic creative power through his identification with the primeval mound of creation.

There is something quite interesting in the evidence for the merging of Ptah and Tatenen. Although the association between the two may go back in time, the period where we see it really being developed as an important part of the theology of Ptah is during the reign of Ramses II. Ramses II was the first pharaoh to discuss Ptah-Tatenen extensively in his inscriptions, and to create new temples, statues, and monuments at Memphis dedicated to the composite deity Ptah-Tatenen. We have some interesting evidence that the Penn Museum's Sphinx came from a part of the Ptah Temple where Ramses II seems to have built a whole new temple dedicated to Ptah-Tatenen.

The association between Ptah and Tatenen is, however, only one aspect of the god of Memphis. He has many other connections and identities, so before we further examine Ptah-Tatenen we will look at some of these other aspects of Ptah and the other members of the Memphite Triad (see below).

Aside from their formal names, most Egyptian gods were also known by distinctive epithets or nicknames that described a deity's special characteristics. These nicknames often reflect popular devotion to the gods. Some of Ptah's epithets reflect his close association with the city of Memphis, and where and how he was worshiped there. He is known frequently as the god who is "South of his Wall," referring to the position of his temple enclosure in Memphis. He is also known as the "Lord of *Ankh-Tawy*," which may correspond to a geographical location on the west bank of the Nile—the location of the royal mortuary temples including that of Pepi I who had given the name Men-nefer to Memphis. Some of Ptah's other nicknames include the "Lord of *Maat*" (the principle of order), "Great of Strength," and "Beautiful of Face."

One of the most important forms of Ptah at Memphis was "Ptah who hears prayers." This relates to the practice of petitioning and praying to Ptah. He was

6.25.

6.25. A small multi-colored faience figurine of Ptah wearing a special feathered garment and seated on a block throne. [UPM object # 29-84-482]

6.26a, b. Two examples of "hearing ear" stelae dedicated by pilgrims were found at the site of Memphis by the Coxe Expedition in 1916. The one on the left below [UPM object # E12506] has two large ears, while the one on the right [UPM object # E12507] features three pairs of ears.

6.26a.

6.26b.

especially venerated as a sentient deity who thought of and spoke the original names for the elements of the created universe. So, his attribute of listening was seen as a key way of connecting to his divine consciousness. Worshipers dedicated small stelae decorated with multiple images of ears. Perhaps by carving multiple ears on the stelae, the worshipers hoped that that god would be more likely to hear and answer their prayers. Some of these stela bear images of only a single pair of ears, others contain many pairs, or are covered with over 40 images of single ears—all the better for the god to hear the prayers of the dedicant.

Another aspect of Ptah connected with popular religion occurs in the form of the minor Memphite deity Pataikos, a manifestation of Ptah particularly associated with magical practices. Representations of Pataikos bear some similarities to the popular household god Bes. Both Pataikos and Bes normally appear in dwarf-like form. Pataikos appears nude with a bald head, and a large scarab beetle frequently sits atop his head. In some cases, images of Pataikos also share iconography with a type of artifact called the Horus cippus. Cippi of Horus are small stelae with images of the god Horus defeating threatening animals. They were used in magical rituals of protection. Pataikos similarly dominates threatening animals and often stands atop crocodiles while grasping snakes, reptiles, or other dangerous animals in his hands.

Another important god of the region of Memphis whose identity over time became increasingly merged with Ptah is the funerary god Sokar. Sokar was the primary god of the Memphite necropolis, the region called *Ro-Setau* which spread from Giza in the north to Dahshur in the south. One of Sokar's epithets was "He of Ro-Setau." Sokar's animal form was that of a falcon.

In funerary religion Sokar was associated with rebirth from a sandy mound called Imhet (perhaps symbolizing the sandy mounds of the desert necropolis). Sokar commonly adopts the form of a falcon head emerging from the sandy mound. The falcon-headed mound could appear sitting atop a sacred boat, the Henu barque. Sokar appears in the Pyramid Texts of the Old Kingdom where the deceased king is said to journey in the Henu barque of Sokar.

The Sokar Festival, celebrated at Memphis, took place in the season of *akhet* (time of the Nile inundation). Images of Sokar were carried during this festival, while the king took part in rituals connected to agriculture and irrigation. The 22nd Dynasty king Sheshonq II was buried (ca. 880 BCE) at the site of Tanis in the Nile Delta in an unusual falcon-headed silver coffin representing this funerary god.

Sokar is a good example of the way Egyptian religion could merge different deities to create composite forms. Perhaps because of his Memphite origins and his association with crafts, one of Sokar's primary connections was with Ptah. At a fundamental level, both were seen as having a role in the creative power that governed the genesis of life on earth and rebirth of life in the netherworld. We have already seen how Ptah was separately linked with the primeval mound Tatenen. Similarly, Sokar's powers connect with the afterlife centered on a mound, Imhet.

Consequently, Sokar merged with the god Ptah to form the composite deity Ptah-Sokar. By the Middle Kingdom, with the rise in importance of the funerary god Osiris, Ptah-Sokar then further joined with Osiris to become a triple deity: Ptah-Sokar-Osiris. Ptah in his unified form Ptah-Sokar-Osiris remained extremely popular for the rest of Egyptian history. This was a god whose powers subsumed the totality of human experience from birth to death to rebirth in the netherworld.

6.27

6.29.

6.30.

6.27. An amulet of Pataikos from Memphis. He stands on a pair of crocodiles and holds reptiles in his hands. Flanking him are goddesses and on the reverse side (right) a divine figure appears atop a lotus blossom. [UPM object # 29-83-275]

6.28. The small cippus stela shows the young god Horus trampling a pair of crocodiles and grasping dangerous creatures including snakes and scorpions. A head of Bes appears above the figure of Horus. [UPM object # E15270]

6.29. Wooden images of the falcon god Sokar were common funerary objects. [UPM object # E2156]

6.30. The Henu barque of Sokar depicted on the 22nd Dynasty cartonnage mummy case of Djedmaatesankh, now in the Royal Ontario Museum (910.10). [Image courtesy of Chris Irie]

6.31. Painted wooden statue of Ptah-Sokar-Osiris. The god typically wears a tall, feathered headdress, which also features a sun disk and ram's horns. The headdress and the statue in this image come from two different statues of Ptah-Sokar-Osiris. [Statue: UPM object # E1934; Headdress: UPM object # 29-71-824]

6.32. Stele from Memphis showing the king (right) offering incense before the triad of Memphis: Ptah (on shrine), Sekhmet (with lion head) and Nefertem (left) holding a pole capped with lotus. [UPM object # E13629]

6.32.

6.31.

6.33.

6.34a,b.

Images of the combined Ptah-Sokar-Osiris show a mummiform male wearing a feathered headdress. A very popular funerary object from the time of the New Kingdom onwards was the Ptah-Sokar-Osiris statuette. These were placed in tombs to assist the deceased magically in the journey to the afterlife. Frequently they contained papyrus scrolls with spells of the *Book of the Dead* written on them.

In the same way that Ptah, over time, developed many forms and connections with other deities, so, too, he developed a divine family which we call the Memphite Triad. This group of three gods was not always a unified family. However, by the time of the New Kingdom we find Ptah, Sekhmet, and Nefertem fully developed as the main gods of Memphis.

Sekhmet is a lioness deity and can take either full lion form or, more frequently, she appears as a woman with the head of a lioness. At Memphis, Sekhmet was the wife and consort of Ptah. However, she is a deity with a complex identity and a major role in Egyptian religion that extends well beyond Memphis itself. The ancient Egyptians associated felines—both cats and lions—with many different deities. Sekhmet, whose name means "The-powerful-female-one," was a fearsome deity with warlike tendencies. Sekhmet was thought to accompany the king into battle and to provide a protective force for him. Although Sekhmet could rage at her enemies, she was also a nurturing deity. One of her roles was that of divine guardian who could ward off illnesses, in particular a disease called the "plague of the year." She is perhaps best known through her statues that protected the gateways to certain temples during the New Kingdom.

Much of the ancient Egyptian world was understood in terms of complementary opposites, perhaps in response to the surrounding environment—the fertile Nile Valley and the dry desolate desert. Similarly, some ancient Egyptian goddesses had this dual nature. Perhaps the best example would be the goddesses Sekhmet and Bastet. Sekhmet's peaceful counterpart was Bastet. Shown as a cat or as a woman with a feline head, Bastet's place was in the home. She was probably primarily a protective domestic goddess who, like a mother cat with her kittens, took good care of the children in the house. Bastet was tremendously popular in daily religion and many amulets of her were produced, especially from the New Kingdom onwards.

6.33. Only the head and torso of this Sekhmet statue is preserved, but it would have originally depicted the goddess standing. The top of a papyriform staff appears between her breasts. Her sun disk with a rearing uraeus illustrates her connection to her father, the sun god Re. In Egyptian mythology, Sekhmet represents the "Eye" of the sun and can act on behalf of the sun god. [UPM object # E2049]

6.34a, b. Faience amulet of Sekhmet from Memphis [left: UPM object # E14357], and a bronze figurine of Bastet, also from Memphis [right: UPM object # 29-70-695].

6.35. Hundreds of over life-size statues of Sekhmet have been found fronting Theban temples where Sekhmet is associated with another leonine goddess, Mut, the consort of Amun, who was the patron deity of the Theban area. Most of these statues date to the reign of Amenhotep III. This seated example [UPM object # E2048] is one of four large diorite Sekhmet statues in the Penn Museum.

6.3

While both of these goddesses were feline in nature, they were opposite in activity and action. The ancient Egyptian myth of the Eye of the Sun alludes to this when describing the goddess Hathor-Tefnut: "She rages like Sekhmet and is friendly like Bastet." Bubastis, a site in the eastern Delta, was the center of Bastet's cult, but she also appears at Memphis because of her close association with Sekhmet.

The child in the Memphite Triad is the god Nefertem. Nefertem was primarily a solar deity whose role was central to several Egyptian creation myths. His name means "Atum is good" or "he who has newly appeared is perfect." He appears as a human male wearing a headdress composed of a lotus blossom flanked by two tall plumes. He also carries a sickle-shaped object in his left hand.

Nefertem is the son of Sekhmet and, beginning in the New Kingdom, he fills a key role as the child-member of the Memphite Triad, along with Sekhmet and Ptah. Because of the close connection between the aggressive lioness goddess Sekhmet and her more peaceful feline counterpart Bastet, Nefertem is sometimes described as the child of Bastet.

As the son of the fierce goddess Sekhmet, Nefertem sometimes takes on a warlike role and, in that form, he can be associated with other warlike gods such as Montu, Sopdu, and Hormenty, as well as with several other leonine deities in whose cults he was thought to participate.

6.36a, b.

6.37.

6.38.

6.36a, b. This necklace features a cast solid gold amulet of Sekhmet, thirty cowrie-shaped beads, one gold pomegranate-shaped bead, and two large and two small barrel-shaped beads (one of the large barrel beads is made of chalcedony). Excavators found this necklace in a cache at the palace of Merenptah in Memphis that dates to the reign of the 26th Dynasty king, Amasis. [UPM object # 29-70-19]

6.37. Bronze standing statue of the god Nefertem shown with his lotus crown. This statue was probably made in a Memphite workshop and features inlays of glass and gold work. [UPM object # E14286]

6.38. A scene on the Great Harris Papyrus (EA9999,43) depicts the Triad of Memphis. Nefertem is on the far left. His crown looks slightly different than it does on the statue above, but all of the elements are the same: the tall plumes, the lotus flower, and the *menats* (or necklace counterpoises). [Image © Trustees of the British Museum]

Because of his associations with the fragrant blue lotus flower (perhaps more correctly identified as the *Nymphaea caerulea*, or blue water lily), Nefertem is also thought of as a god of perfume. Some of his divine epithets include "Protector of the Two Lands" and "Lord of Provisions."

Nefertem plays an important role in Egyptian creation myths. The Egyptians believed that the lotus blossom was the first living entity to appear on the primeval mound, Tatenen, at the beginning of time. When the petals of the blue lotus opened, the sun god himself appeared for the first time. This creation image is beautifully embodied in a wooden statue of King Tutankhamun showing the head of the youthful king (who is likened in this case to the young sun god being born) appearing atop a lotus blossom (see Fig. 6.39).

The idea that the primeval mound, Tatenen, gave rise to the first living entity, the lotus blossom Nefertem, is central to the father-son relationship between Ptah and Nefertem. These cosmic associations were part of the way the gods of Memphis became linked over time with the primeval creative forces in the universe.

The Apis Bull was another fundamental Memphite deity whose origins lie in the earliest history of Memphis during the Early Dynastic Period. The Apis was one of the many ways that Ptah could manifest himself. The Apis was an actual living bull understood to be an incarnation or son of the god. There was only one living Apis at a time and when the Apis bull died, a search would take place throughout Egypt to find its replacement. According to the Greek writer Herodotus who may have visited Memphis in the 5th century BCE, Apis bulls were black, had special markings, and very specific physical characteristics. He notes, *"The Apis is the calf of a cow which is never afterwards able to have another. The Egyptian belief is that a flash of light descends upon the cow from heaven, and this causes her to conceive Apis. The Apis calf has distinctive marks: it is black, with a white square on its forehead, the image of an eagle on its back, the hair on its tail double, and a scarab under its tongue"* (Herodotus, *Histories* 3.28). When the Apis bull died, it was embalmed with great ceremony and buried in the Serapeum at Saqqara, a massive catacomb for the burial of these sacred bulls guarded by sphinxes. After death, the Apis bull became an Osiris-Apis, indicating that he had joined with the god of the dead.

During the Ptolemaic Period, a new presentation of this god is fostered by Ptolemy I in the hopes of uniting the religious beliefs of his bicultural kingdom. At this time, Egypt has a large Greek population, particularly around the cities of Memphis and Alexandria. Osiris-Apis is now worshipped as the deity Serapis who appears in human form as a classical-looking bearded man with flowing hair. Serapis appealed to the Egyptian population who recognized his cult as that of the traditional Osiris-Apis. He was also worshipped by the Greek population in Egypt who seemed to be more comfortable worshipping a god in human form, rather than in a "strange" fully animal or hybrid form.

One of the most important priestly offices in ancient Egypt was that of the High Priest of Ptah at Memphis. These men bore the title "Greatest of Craftsmen of Ptah." Prince Khaemwaset, the eldest son of Ramses II, held this office. Prince Khaemwaset is known particularly for his great interest in the Memphite area, its deities, and the monuments there from past ages of Egypt. In modern times, he is often referred to as one of the world's first archaeologists due to his efforts to restore ancient monuments, such as the 5th Dynasty pyramid of King Unas,

6.39. Painted wooden statue of the head of Tutankhamun emerging from a lotus blossom. Howard Carter found this head in the tomb of Tutankhamun. It now resides in the Egyptian Museum, Cairo (JE 60723). [Image from Carter, *The Tomb of Tut-Ankh-Amen*, vol. III, 1933, p. I]

6.40. The vibrant bloom of the *Nymphaea caerulea* water lily. [Uploaded by PalmBeaches974 on July 13, 2012 with a CC BY-SA 3.0 license; source is http://en.wikipedia.org/wiki/Nymphaea_caerulea#mediaviewer/File:Nymphaea_Caerula.jpg]

6.41. Bronze figurine of the Apis Bull, a living bull worshiped at Memphis, first as an avatar of Ptah (or his son), and then understood to be a living incarnation of Ptah himself. [UPM object # E14291].

6.42. Decorative handle from a terracotta oil lamp depicting the god Serapis. In appearance, he is bearded like Zeus, and is a deliberate fusion of Egyptian and Hellenistic deities. He wears a basket-like crown on his head in the form of a grain measure. He is a funerary deity, but fertility was also an aspect of his cult. [UPM object # E2521]

6.43. Gold ring bezel with the family group of Isis, Serapis, and the child-god, Horus. Here Serapis has taken the place of Osiris in the divine triad. [UPM object # 29-128-1039]

6.44. Faience stele of Prince Khaemwaset shown worshiping before the god Ptah. [UPM object # E13578]

6.42.　　　　　　　6.43　　　　　　　6.44

which bears an inscription in his name. Khaemwaset prepared a tomb for himself near the Serapeum, the burial place of the Apis bulls at Saqqara.

Khaemwaset's career as High Priest at Memphis would have brought him, on an almost daily basis, to the great temple of Ptah, *Hut-Ka-Ptah*. We can be sure that Khaemwaset would have regularly passed by the Sphinx there in its original setting. Let us now examine the temple of Ptah and the original location of the Penn Museum Sphinx.

Hut-Ka-Ptah and the Giants of Memphis

Ancient Memphis had many temples and an array of royal palaces that developed in and around its center. We know the names of some of these buildings from ancient texts. However, most of the Memphite temples recorded in ancient texts have never been physically identified due to the site's severely ruined condition. In reality only a handful of the religious buildings of ancient Memphis are attested through actual remains. The major group clustered in and around the temple enclosure of Ptah, *Hut-Ka-Ptah*.

Hut-Ka-Ptah was a complex that included a central temple dedicated to Ptah, as well as satellite buildings associated with the cults of other related deities and probably also deified kings. During most periods, a large enclosure wall surrounded the temple precinct. The location and size of the wall changed through time. The main temple dedicated to Ptah was oriented on an east-west axis. Its exact form and size is unclear, although the remains of the colossal statuary, such as the Abu el-Hol statue of Ramses II, indicate the mammoth size of the temple.

To gain a sense of the original size and appearance of the Ptah temple complex it is useful to look at the better-preserved ruins of the huge temple complex of the god Amun at Karnak in Thebes. Because Karnak did not undergo the extensive process of denudation that Memphis did, significant areas of Karnak are still standing. There we see the central temple of Amun-Re, added to over millennia

6.45a, b. Scale comparison of the temple complex of Karnak at Thebes with Hut-Ka-Ptah at Memphis.

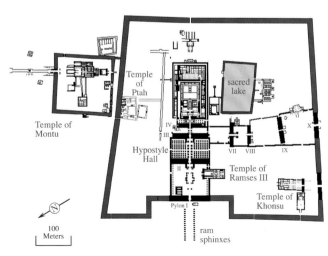

Precinct of Amun-Re at Karnak

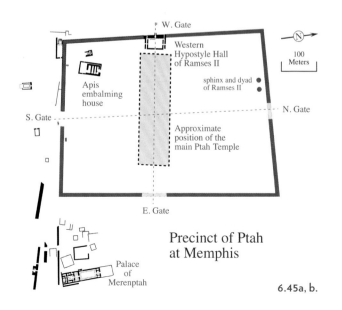

Precinct of Ptah at Memphis

6.45a, b.

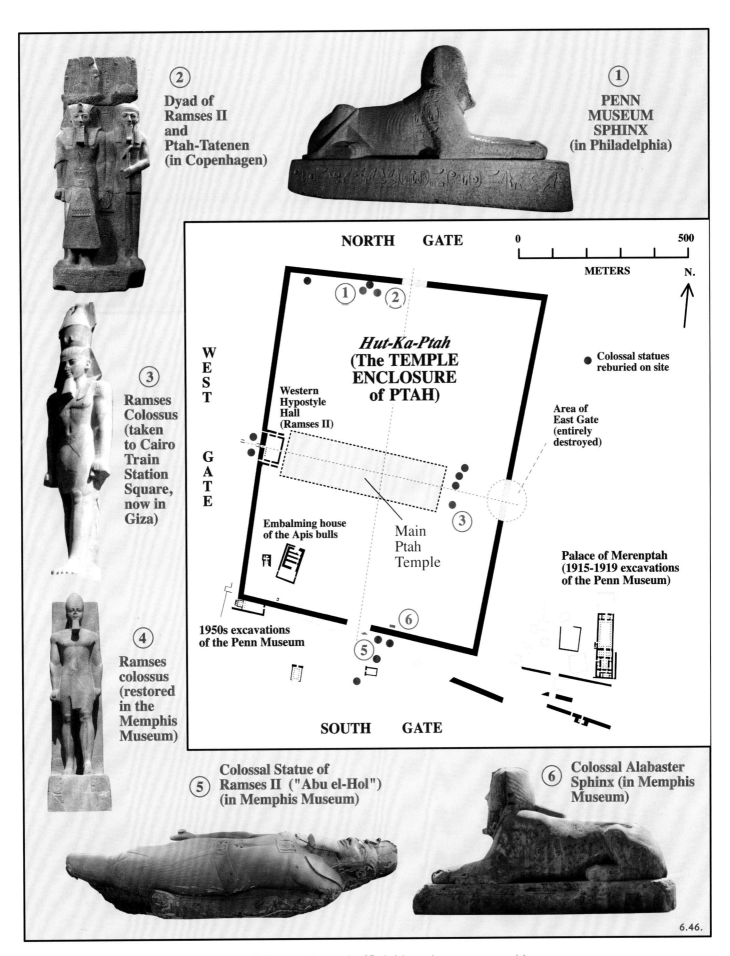

② Dyad of Ramses II and Ptah-Tatenen (in Copenhagen)

① PENN MUSEUM SPHINX (in Philadelphia)

③ Ramses Colossus (taken to Cairo Train Station Square, now in Giza)

④ Ramses colossus (restored in the Memphis Museum)

NORTH GATE

0   500

METERS

N.

Hut-Ka-Ptah (The TEMPLE ENCLOSURE of PTAH)

WEST GATE

Western Hypostyle Hall (Ramses II)

● Colossal statues reburied on site

Area of East Gate (entirely destroyed)

Embalming house of the Apis bulls

Main Ptah Temple

③

Palace of Merenptah (1915-1919 excavations of the Penn Museum)

1950s excavations of the Penn Museum

⑥

⑤

SOUTH GATE

⑤ Colossal Statue of Ramses II ("Abu el-Hol") (in Memphis Museum)

⑥ Colossal Alabaster Sphinx (in Memphis Museum)

6.46.

6.46. Some of the major colossal statues and their find spots in the temple of Ptah (object photos are not to scale).

5.50.

6.47. Vulcan on a Roman coin of 91 BCE. Vulcan, identified with Egyptian Ptah, appears with the tongs of a metalsmith behind him. [UPM object # 29-126-659]

by kings from the Middle Kingdom through the Ptolemies. The temple grew in scale by accretion. King after king added courtyards, halls, and pylons, gradually embellishing the temple outwards from the original temple core. Periodically, they created new entrances and axes that linked the main temple with satellite temples. At Karnak these were additional temples dedicated to other members of the Theban Triad—Amun's consort Mut and son Khonsu, as well as a number of other Theban and national gods.

Hut-Ka-Ptah would have been comparable to Karnak in scale and general appearance. The main Ptah Temple would have dominated the central part of the enclosure. It would have had a series of pylons and courtyards leading to the enclosed temple with the god's sanctuary on the western side. The main temple would have been linked with satellite buildings by processional avenues within the main enclosure, as well as other temples beyond the main Ptah enclosure. Some of these other structures focused on Ptah in his various manifestations, as well as other Memphite deities. Inside of the Ptah enclosure was the temple of the Apis and it is here the living Apis would have resided. Also within the precinct was the embalming house used when the Apis died. Still standing at Memphis are the great stone embalming tables used for preparing the sacred bulls of Memphis.

Littering the ruins of the Ptah Temple are the remains of colossal statues. Most are just shattered fragments lying now in the mud, disassociated from their original architecture. A smaller number are complete, indicating the scale of the temple. Some of these stone giants were left in place by archaeologists. A handful of others were removed to museums as occurred in the case of the Penn Museum Sphinx. These giants of Memphis provide a sense of the grandeur that once was the temple of Ptah.

The Father of History Visits the Temple of Vulcan

As we have seen, at the heart of ancient Memphis lay the great temple complex dedicated to the god Ptah, one of the cosmic creator deities of the Egyptian pantheon. This temple, which innumerable pharaohs added to and embellished over thousands of years, formed a kind of anchor for the core of Memphis. It is the Ptah Temple that has attracted the most attention by archaeologists. Yet, it remains a site that frustrates. The architecture of the Ptah Temple was so badly damaged during the Middle Ages that we must combine the fragmentary record of the site's archaeology with the written sources from ancient times to gain a picture of what it may have been like.

One source of information that many researchers have turned to for insight are the accounts of Memphis and its Ptah Temple in the writings of Greek and Roman authors. Three men are most important: Herodotus (who lived ca. 484–425 BCE), and the later Greek authors Diodorus Siculus and Strabo (who wrote in the 1st century BCE). Because these men lived toward the end of ancient Egyptian history, their accounts reflect Memphis at the end of its period of growth and development. The most important of these accounts of Memphis is that of

Herodotus. What he tells us about the Ptah Temple turns out to be important in the discovery of the Penn Museum Sphinx.

Sometime around 450 BCE, Herodotus apparently visited the land of Egypt (although some historians doubt this claim). He wrote a detailed description of Egypt in his most famous work, *The Histories*. Herodotus is often called the "father of history" due to his extensive writings about the inhabited world—what the Greeks called the *oikumene*—as it was then known. In his description of Egypt, Herodotus says he visited Memphis itself where priests at the temple of Ptah provided him with information on parts of that vast building, much of which would still have been standing intact. Herodotus did not specifically call it the temple of Ptah but rather identified the temple with Hephaestus. Since part of Ptah's identity was as patron god of crafts, the Greeks equated him with their own god of crafts and metalworking, Hephaestus. Later, the Romans connected Ptah with their god of metalworking, Vulcan, whom they also associated with Greek Hephaestus. For that reason, the Ptah Temple is called the "Temple of Vulcan" in Roman Period copies of Herodotus' *Histories* that have come down to us.

6.48. Statue thought to represent Herodotus. [Agora Museum, Athens, S270. Image courtesy of Giovanni Dall'Orto]

Whether or not he actually visited the "Temple of Vulcan" at Memphis, Herodotus was impressed by the immense statues that decorated the gateways into the temple of Ptah. He was especially interested in two colossal figures of Ramses II that still stood in front of the western gateway of the temple, some 800 years after the time of Ramses II. He identified these with a later Ramses (whom he calls Rhampsinitus). These seem to have been venerated by the Egyptians as the embodiment of the seasons "Summer" and "Winter." Archaeologists have never identified these exact statues but fallen colossal statues of Ramses II have been found in several locations, especially connected with the western and southern gateways of the temple. One of these is the gigantic figure popularly called Abu el-Hol. It can be seen today in the Open Air Museum at Memphis. Another is a giant figure from just inside the heavily destroyed East Gate that was taken to downtown Cairo in 1954 and set up next to the Cairo train station, which was then named "Ramses Station." A third fallen giant figure of Ramses II was restored during the 1980s and stands today at the Memphis Museum. Which of these might have been the statues of "Summer" and "Winter"? That remains uncertain but many giant statues of Ramses and other pharaohs certainly guarded the Ptah Temple. Maybe the Egyptians had names for many of these colossi, and perhaps this echoes today in the local name for the place where many of these figures were found: Kom el-Rabi', "The mound of Spring."

The description that Herodotus wrote of the "Temple of Vulcan" has both fascinated and frustrated historians and archaeologists. He describes the kings who were the most important builders as well as some aspects of the temple's architecture, particularly focusing on the gateways, which evidently were the most impressive elements of the temple. The description, although it contains some specific information, is vague enough to allow only the barest image of the Ptah Temple. Nevertheless, many archaeologists who have worked on the Ptah Temple, including Flinders Petrie, have tried to incorporate Herodotus' description of the temple. Here is what Herodotus had to say about the Ptah Temple and the colossi that decorated its gateways:

> *The priests said that Asychis became king of Egypt, and that he built the eastern portico of the temple of Vulcan, which is by far the most beautiful and the largest...*

The priests also informed me that Rhampsinitus (Ramses III) succeeded Proteus in the Kingdom: he left as a monument the portico of the Temple of Vulcan, fronting to the west; and he erected two statues before the portico, both 25-cubits high. Of these, the one standing to the north the Egyptians call 'Summer,' and that to the south 'Winter.' The one that they call Summer they worship and do honor to, but that one called Winter they treat in a quite contrary way. In the next place, they relate that he built in it the temple of Vulcan, which is vast and well worthy of mention. Of the other kings they did not mention any memorable deeds, nor that they were in any respect renowned, except one, the last of them Moeris; but he accomplished some memorable works, as the portal of Vulcan's temple, facing the north wind.

— Parts of the description of the temple of Ptah at Memphis by Herodotus

Herodotus confirms for us that the East Gate (which one entered coming from the direction of the Nile River) was the main entrance. This gateway he says was "by far the most beautiful and the largest." Excavations in the area of the East Gate have produced badly smashed fragments of a number of colossi; most were left in the ground. Areas of pavement and pedestals for pillars or statues suggest this was indeed an impressive entrance. The best-preserved colossus from this area is the one taken to Cairo in 1954. It is one of the largest colossal statues in existence. Its size confirms Herodotus' statement about the grandeur of the East Gate.

In addition to his description of the gigantic figures guarding the East and West Gates, Herodotus also mentions the temple's North Gate. This gate is the most important one for us because this is the area where Mackay and Petrie excavated the Penn Museum Sphinx in 1912. When Flinders Petrie began excavations at Memphis, it was natural for him to try to relate actual finds with Herodotus' ancient description. In his first season's work (1908) he had excavated the Western Hypostyle Hall of Ramses II and the West Gate.

In 1912 he turned his attention to the North Gate. Petrie was actually using Herodotus as a guide for what he might find there. Herodotus tells us, in a short and somewhat cryptic statement, that no other kings before "Rhampsinitus and Proteus" had done anything memorable, except for a king named Moeris who added the northern portal to the temple. Moeris is the Greek name for a legendary pharaoh of Egypt's Middle Kingdom (11th–13th Dynasties, ca. 2050–1750 BCE). The name Moeris is usually linked to Amenemhat III, the longest reigning king of the 12th Dynasty and a prolific builder. When Petrie uncovered a block inscribed with the name of Amenemhat III at the north side of the temple he took this as confirmation of Herodotus' account. We have seen in Chapter 2 how the 1912 newspaper reports about discoveries near the North Gate highlighted the substantiation of Herodotus through archaeology.

Although Herodotus names a number of pharaohs, and perhaps confuses which ones were the actual builders, archaeology tells us something interesting. Many kings contributed to the temple of *Hut-Ka-Ptah*, or the "Temple of Vulcan." However, none of them compares with Ramses II. Many of the colossi that have been excavated at Memphis belong to Ramses II. His fallen colossi occur near all four of the great gates. He also added the Western Hypostyle Hall and added colossi of himself there as well. Ramses II evidently had a huge impact on the Ptah Temple. What was he doing there? Where does the Penn Museum Sphinx fits into the picture?

"Glorious is Ramses II in the Domain of Ptah"

Ramses II is often called "Ramses the Great." There were eleven pharaohs with the name Ramses who ruled during Egypt's 19th and 20th Dynasties, ca. 1250–1050 BCE (therefore we generally use the term "Ramesside Period" for the entire era). However, the second Ramses stands out head and shoulders among these kings. He is known not just for his impressively long reign of 67 years, his prolific family that included 120 children, and his valor on the battlefield. He is remembered especially for the astounding volume and scale of his monumental construction. These were monuments that really changed the face of Egypt. Temples were built in places where they had never before stood, such as the famous rock-cut temple at Abu Simbel in Nubia. Many older temples were given ostentatious new additions in the form of grand stone pylons, columned halls, and colossal statues of pharaoh and the gods. In this program of temple building Ramses II completed projects started by his father, Seti I, such as the immense Hypostyle Hall at Karnak. However, he carried the work to new levels of scale (although with a bit of a sacrifice in the quality of workmanship and artistry; many hasten to point out that Ramses II was interested more in quantity over quality). Such is his reputation that the British poet Percy B. Shelley chose Ramses II to illustrate the theme of a vainglorious pharaoh in his celebrated 1818 poem, "Ozymandias":

6.49. The statue of Ramses II called the "Younger Memnon" is thought to have inspired Shelley's poem "Ozymandias." [Image © Trustees of the British Museum, EA 19]

> I met a traveller from an antique land
> Who said: Two vast and trunkless legs of stone
> Stand in the desert. Near them, on the sand,
> Half sunk, a shattered visage lies, whose frown,
> And wrinkled lip, and sneer of cold command,
> Tell that its sculptor well those passions read,
> Which yet survive, stamped on these lifeless things,
> The hand that mocked them and the heart that fed:
> And on the pedestal these words appear:
> "My name is Ozymandias, king of kings:
> Look on my works, ye Mighty, and despair!"
> Nothing beside remains. Round the decay
> Of that colossal wreck, boundless and bare
> The lone and level sands stretch far away.

Although Shelley's poem suggests the impermanence and futility of political power, in the case of Ramses II the creation of great monuments in stone did result in a memory that has endured over three thousand years. Some of the most famous of those monuments have a lot to tell us about the Penn Museum Sphinx and how it relates to Ramses II's devotion to Ptah of Memphis.

The temple of Ptah at Memphis benefited tremendously from the "mighty works" of Ramses II. As we have seen, this temple was then known generally as *Hut-Ka-Ptah* ("temple of the spirit of Ptah"). Among the hieroglyphic records that survive from Ramses II's reign are texts informing us that Ramses II added extensive new architectural elements to the Ptah Temple. The archaeological remains and

6.52.

6.50. The rock-cut temple of Ramses II at Abu Simbel is probably Ramses II's most famous monument. Importantly, it also contains inscriptions detailing Ramses II's devotion to Ptah and his work at Memphis.

6.51. Ptah (left), Amun-Re (with feathered crown), Ramses II (center right), and Re-Horakhty (right) are enthroned together in the sanctuary at Abu Simbel. [Image courtesy of Mike Gadd]

6.52. The "Blessing of Ptah" in the temple at Abu Simbel. [Image courtesy of the Oriental Institute of The University of Chicago, P. 2479]

great statues remaining on the site today confirm the texts. However, more than just venerating the god, Ramses was interested in linking himself eternally with Ptah. Inscriptions from Ramses II's reign also tell us that he decreed that the Ptah Temple be given an additional new name: "Glorious is Ramses II in the Domain of Ptah."

In order to understand Ramses II's activities at Memphis, strangely enough we have to take a brief detour to another place: the famous temple of Abu Simbel in Nubia, 600 miles south of Memphis. The great rock-cut temple was dedicated to Ramses II in the company of three of Egypt's major gods: Amun-Re, Re-Horakhty, and Ptah of Memphis. These deities appear seated together with Ramses II in the sanctuary at Abu Simbel. The temple contains many scenes and inscriptions, but one of the most important there is a long text called the "Blessing of Ptah." In this Ramses spells out in detail his devotion to Ptah and the rewards and recognition that Ptah bestows on the pharaoh. The "Blessing of Ptah" tells us that Ptah was the symbolic father of Ramses II: *"I am your father who begat thee as one of the gods, all your limbs are of the gods. I assumed my form as the Ram, lord of Mendes and begat you in your noble mother since I knew that you would be my champion..."*

Most of the content of the "Blessing of Ptah" explains how Ptah showers Ramses II with happiness, the wisdom of a king, and power to rule Egypt. Along with these comes agricultural wealth through bountiful harvests and wealth through industry. So, how does Ramses reciprocate Ptah's generosity? With great buildings, of course. The king responds saying he has expanded the temple of Ptah at Memphis. Here in the midst of the "Blessing of Ptah" we find a description of some of the king's works at Memphis:

I enlarged your temple in Hutkaptah, constructed in eternal work of excellent workmanship in stone and finished it with gold and real precious stones. I embellished your temple enclosure on the North, with two noble twin halls opposite you, their doors like the horizon of heaven causing the people to adore you. I made for you a noble temple within Inbu [Memphis]. Divine is your image in the secret shrine, reposing on its great seat. I equipped it with priests and prophets, serfs, fields, and cattle. I made it festive with sacred offerings and myriads of things.

The "Blessing of Ptah" explains the thinking behind Ramses II's huge constructions at the temple of Ptah. As he transformed the place into a bigger and better version, his goal was evidently aimed at linking himself with Ptah forever. However, there is also something else that is important in this inscription. The form of Ptah that occurs here is not the generic Ptah of Memphis, but rather Ptah in his hybrid version, Ptah-Tatenen—Ptah merged with the creator god of the primeval mound. Ramses is here addressing both Ptah proper, but more specifically the composite creative deity Ptah-Tatenen. His text tells us that one of his achievements was construction of a grand new temple for Ptah-Tatenen "on the North." Here at Abu Simbel we may in fact have found an ancient description by Ramses II himself of the very area of Memphis once guarded by the Penn Museum's Sphinx.

The Sphinx and the Temple of Ptah-Tatenen at Memphis

Our brief look at the ruins of the Ptah Temple and the texts from the time of Ramses II provides us now with some crucial information for a greater understanding of the Sphinx and where it came from. Let us sum up what we know: as the remains of his many colossal statues show, Ramses II had invested a huge effort in reworking the temple of Ptah. He had gone so far as to add a new name to the temple: "Glorious is Ramses II in the Domain of Ptah." The idea of the Ptah temple appears now to have focused very much on the divine kingship of Ramses II celebrated in association with the creator god of Memphis. In the process of emphasizing his connection with Ptah, Ramses II chose to highlight one of the fundamental elements of that god: his potent, natural creative energies. To do this, Ramses II's theologians expanded on the idea of the interconnectedness between Ptah and the god Tatenen, embodiment of the primal earth at the beginning of time. It is here that the "Blessing of Ptah" inscription at Abu Simbel is so important to understanding the Sphinx and where it came from. As we have seen, Ptah in this text is not the generic version of Ptah, but rather Ptah in the specific hybrid form, Ptah-Tatenen.

When Ramses speaks of constructing a new temple in honor of Ptah-Tatenen he says that it was a

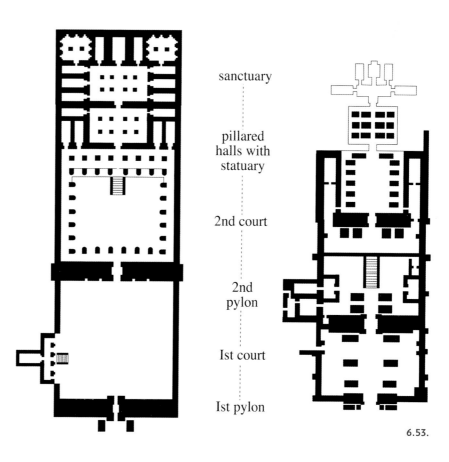

6.53. Temples of Ramses II at Abydos (left) and Wadi el-Sebua (right).

sanctuary

pillared halls with statuary

2nd court

2nd pylon

Ist court

Ist pylon

6.53.

6.54. What once existed: the Ptah Temple at Memphis is almost entirely destroyed. The Sphinx and its partner in Copenhagen likely derive from a satellite temple which Ramses II built on the north side of the temple enclosure at Memphis dedicated to the Ptah-Tatenen.

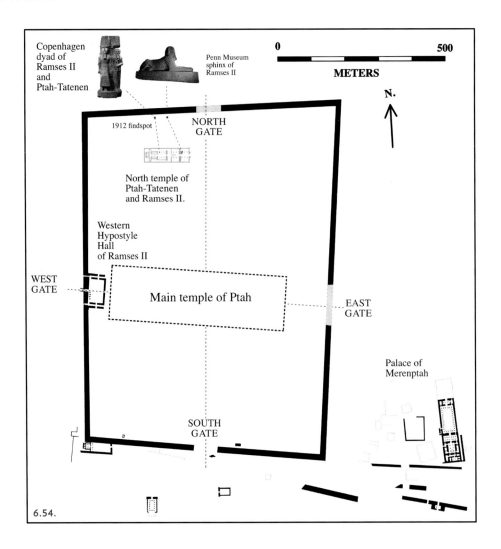

6.54.

specific building "in Hutkaptah." In other words it lay within the greater precinct of the already existing Ptah Temple. Something seems to have existed in its place before but under Ramses it was entirely rebuilt: a new temple. Its stonework was "finished with gold and real precious stones." This suggests the extensive use of colored inlay and gilded elements. More than that, he says there was a new temple enclosure "on the north" with a shrine for the god, and "two noble twin halls" opposite (the sanctuary). The doors were "like the horizon of heaven." The whole thing he describes as a "noble temple within Memphis."

Ancient texts like the "Blessing of Ptah" can be very hard to interpret, but in this case we can use the description, along with the archaeology of the Ptah enclosure, to form a picture of where the Ptah-Tatenen temple might have been and what it looked like. Ramses II's wording in the Abu Simbel inscription is not extensive but it does describe a format of temple that has survived at a number of other sites in Egypt.

Two good examples of this typical temple layout in the reign of Ramses II are found at Abydos in southern Egypt, and a small temple of Wadi el-Sebua in Nubia. As seen in these preserved examples, Ramses II's temples tended to follow a standard template composed typically of two open courtyards in succession. These usually have great pylons that are guarded by seated figures of the king and flanked by guardian sphinxes. As you move into the temple you then pass through one or two outer pillared courts containing colossal statuary, and finally the inner temple, usually with a tripartite sanctuary at the back. The description of the temple of Ramses II and Ptah-Tatenen in the "Blessing of Ptah" equates with this basic layout as seen in the Abydos and Wadi el-Sebua temples.

What the Abu Simbel text appears to tell us is that Ramses II had both greatly expanded the existing Ptah Temple, but also honored Ptah-Tatenen with a splendid new temple precinct that he constructed on the north side, but presumably still within the greater Ptah temple. The description could be understood to imply some other temple enclosure in the north part of Memphis as a whole. However, Ramses' statement suggests strongly this is a special new temple for Ptah-Tatenen in the north part of the existing enclosure of *Hut-Ka-Ptah*.

The area just inside the North Gate is, in fact, where Ernest Mackay and Petrie excavated the Penn Museum's colossal Sphinx and also the granite dyad statue of Ramses II and Ptah-Tatenen now in Copenhagen. It seems very likely these particular colossi, and other fragmentary ones that Ernest Mackay reburied in 1912, once belonged to this very temple discussed in the "Blessing of Ptah." This temple "in the north" appears likely to represent a special new building dedicated to Ptah-Tatenen together with Ramses II.

We may use the arrangement of these other temples to gain a sense of where both the Penn Sphinx and the dyad statue in Copenhagen once stood. The Penn Sphinx likely was one of a group that stood flanking the entrance into the temple of Ramses II and Ptah-Tatenen. Other colossal figures would have stood there as well. This certainly included large seated figures guarding the temple's pylons, as we see at sites like Luxor Temple or Abu Simbel. Sphinxes may also have flanked the approach through the outer courtyards such as those still nicely preserved in the Wadi el-Sebua temple. As you entered the temple proper you would have encountered a series of statues like the Copenhagen dyad, showing Ramses II with Ptah-Tatenen. In all likelihood, statues of other related gods would also have formed an overall composition of sculpture. The sanctuary would have been in the back. Here, in a shrine at the temple's rear would be a smaller statue of Ptah-Tatenen in precious materials. Images of Ramses II would probably rest in other sanctuaries on the side.

Based on a consideration of the fragmentary archaeology and the ancient texts we have developed a theory about the original location of the Penn Sphinx. It, and the colossal pair statue of Ramses II and Ptah-Tatenen, both come from a north temple built specifically to honor Ptah-Tatenen.

It would be wonderful if we could search the ground at Memphis for further evidence of the temple of Ptah-Tatenen. However, at this point we confront the realities of the archaeology of Memphis. The area has now completely vanished. In the years since Flinders Petrie's excavations, the modern town of Mit Rahina has engulfed the entire northern end of the Ptah Temple (which was already mostly destroyed).

We are left to connect the dots between ancient inscriptions and the evidence that Petrie rescued a hundred years ago. We can only envision in our mind's eye what it might have been like. Certainly it was a grand temple, one part of Ramses II's huge works in the *Hut-Ka-Ptah* at Memphis. All that remains of it are the Copenhagen dyad and the Penn Museum Sphinx. But, not to despair! More can yet be gleaned from looking at the Sphinx itself, so we now consider the fascinating world of Egyptian sphinxes.

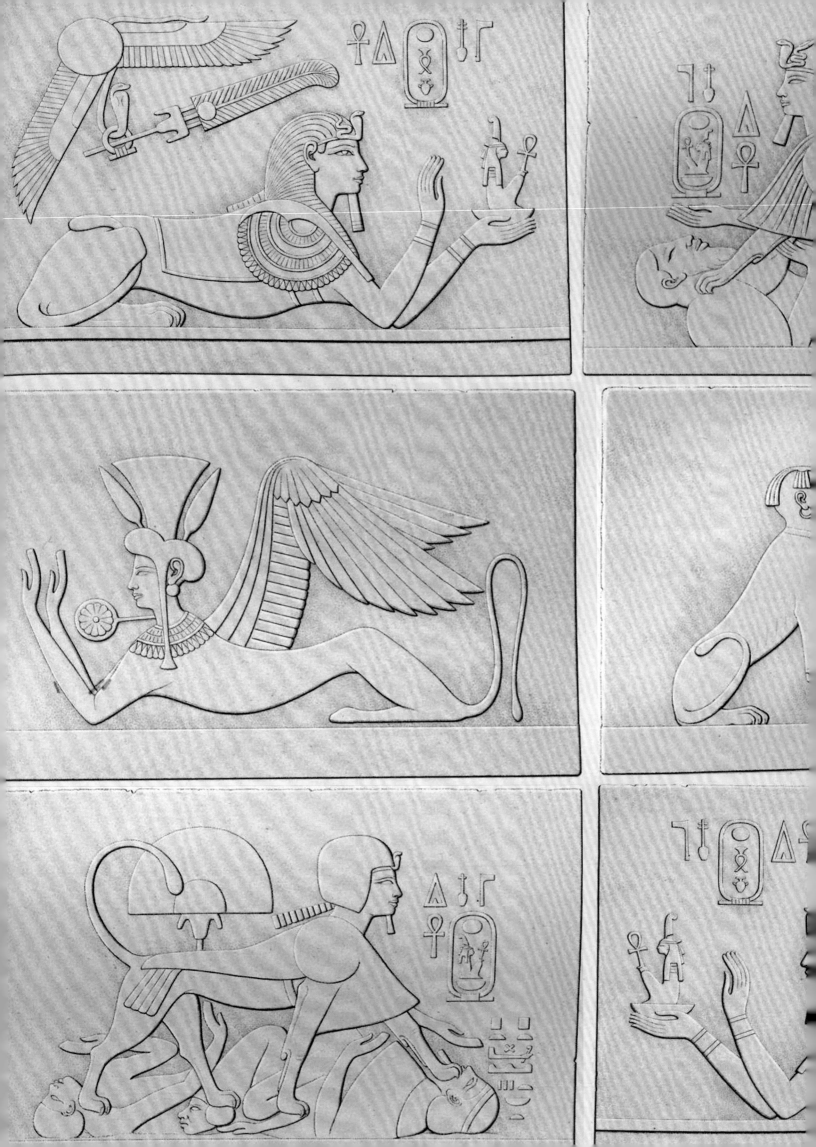

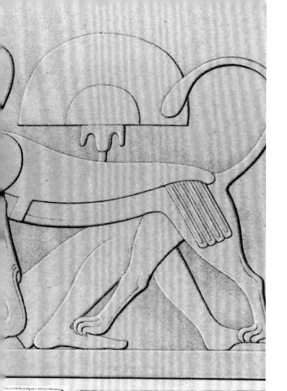

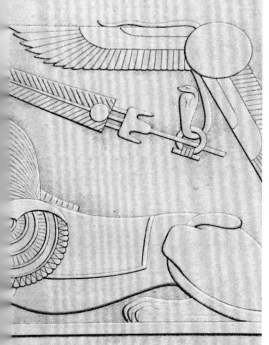

CHAPTER SEVEN

The World of Egyptian Sphinxes

What Is a Sphinx?

After years of waiting, it was before me at last. The great face was so sad, so earnest, so longing, so patient. There was a dignity not of earth in its mien, and in its countenance a benignity such as never any thing human wore. It was stone, but it seemed sentient. If ever image of stone thought, it was thinking. It was looking toward the verge of the landscape, yet looking at nothing—nothing but distance and vacancy. It was looking over and beyond every thing of the present, and far into the past. It was gazing out over the ocean of Time—over lines of century-waves which, further and further receding, closed nearer and nearer together, and blended at last into one unbroken tide, away toward the horizon of remote antiquity. It was thinking of the wars of departed ages; of the empires it had seen created and destroyed; of the nations whose birth it had witnessed, whose progress it had watched, whose annihilation it had noted; of the joy and sorrow, the life and death, the grandeur and decay, of five thousand slow revolving years...

The Sphynx is grand in its loneliness; it is imposing in its magnitude; it is impressive in the mystery that hangs over its story. And there is that in the overshadowing majesty of this eternal figure of stone, with its accusing memory of the deeds of all ages, which reveals to one something of what he shall feel when he shall stand at last in the awful presence of God.

— Mark Twain, *The Innocents Abroad* (1869)

Reading Mark Twain's recollections of his first encounter with the Great Sphinx at Giza over 100 years ago, we can understand the impressions he had. When confronted with the sphinx, it becomes more than a colossal carving of a long-dead king. Its size, its age, and its permanence lend it an air of mystery. It is not hard to imagine it as an otherworldly being. The same can be said for the Penn Museum's colossal Sphinx from Memphis. There is majesty about it—if anything, enhanced by its eroded features. The Sphinx speaks to us without uttering a single word, gazing out somehow seeming sentient:

Close-mouthed you sat five thousand years and never let out a whisper.

Processions came by, marchers, asking questions you answered with grey eyes never blinking, shut lips never talking.

Not one croak of anything you know has come from your cat crouch of ages.

I am one of those who know all you know and I keep my questions: I know the answers you hold.

— Carl Sandberg, *A Sphinx* (1916)

How does the Penn Museum's Sphinx relate to the wider world of Egyptian sphinxes? First, what is a sphinx?

The sphinx, an iconic image of ancient Egypt, was a hybrid creature. The archetypal Egyptian sphinx usually had the body of a lion and the head of a man, although female sphinxes are known. This combination of human and leonine elements endowed the sphinx with the intelligence of a human being united with

7.1.

7.2.

the awesome physical prowess of a lion. Although composite human-leonine creatures appear in many civilizations around the world, the sphinx is arguably an Egyptian creation and it differs in many ways from sphinxlike creatures in other cultures.

Typically, the sphinx wears a *nemes* headdress (or another variation of a royal crown) with a rearing cobra—the uraeus—at its brow. Often the sphinx will also wear a false beard. These iconographic elements are clues to the viewer that the individual represented is the king. Large statues of sphinxes fronted temple complexes as protective guardian figures. Smaller statues, amulets of sphinxes, or sphinx imagery on objects served similar protective functions.

Sphinxes appear early in the Egyptian artistic canon and remain an important royal and divine symbol for the rest of the Pharaonic Period. One of the earliest sphinxes from Egypt is also the largest. The Great Sphinx at Giza is 66 feet (20 m) tall and 235 feet (74 m) long. At the time of its creation, sculptors carved it largely out of the living limestone bedrock. The Great Sphinx has the head of a man wearing a *nemes* headdress with a rearing cobra at its brow. The body of the sphinx takes the form of a recumbent lion with massive outstretched paws. Its tail, like that of most sphinxes, curls around its back right haunch. During the New Kingdom a false beard was added (fragments of the beard are now in the British Museum).

But, who does this sphinx represent? Over the years there has been some debate whether the sphinx has the head of King Khufu, the builder of the Great Pyramid (located slightly to the northwest of the sphinx's enclosure), or represents the son of Khufu, King Khafre, the builder of the second pyramid at Giza. It seems likely that the Great Sphinx bears the features of Khafre and that it formed part of that

7.1. The Great Sphinx at Giza has the body of a lion and the head of King Khafre of the 4th Dynasty.

7.2. The Penn Museum's colossal sphinx is an example of a classic Egyptian androsphinx featuring the head of a man, in this case the pharaoh Ramses II, and the body of a lion.

7.3. Three different human-lion creatures. On the left is a 5th century BCE winged Achaemenid sphinx from a palace at Persepolis. Its horned crown indicates its divinity. [ME129381 © Trustees of the British Museum] In the center, a manticore, a dangerous hybrid creature from Persian mythology with the head of a man, the body of a lion, and a dragon or scorpion tail. This illustration is from the Rochester Bestiary (ca. 1230–1240 CE), an illuminated manuscript which described all types of common and exotic creatures. [Image courtesy of The British Archives Royal MS12 Fxii] The image on the right shows Narasimha, an avatar of the Hindu god Viṣṇu. He is also an example of a human-lion hybrid, but in this case with a lion head and human body. This sculpture is from the Hoysaleswara Temple in Halebidu, Karnataka, and dated to the 12th century CE. ; Viṣṇu as Narasimha kills Hiraṇyakaśipu. [Stone sculpture from the Hoysaleswara Temple in Halebidu, Karnataka; uploaded by Ramanathan.k.i on May 18, 2010 with a CC BY 3.0 license; source is http://]en.wikipedia.org/wiki/Narasimha#mediaviewer/File:Vishnu_narasimha.JPG]

7.3.

7.4.

7.5.

7.6.

7.4. The ancient Egyptians worshiped the sun god in many different forms. This Late Period wooden stela contains a hymn to two versions of the sun god: Re-Horakhty, the rising sun, and Atum, the setting sun. [UPM object # 93-7-1]

7.5. A marble Greek-style sphinx shown with the body of a lion, the head and bust of a woman, and eagle's wings. Probably a support for a table, it was found around 1780 at the villa of Anoninus Pius in Genzano di Roma, Italy. [1805,0703.40 Image © Trustees of the British Museum]

7.6. Cylinder seal in the Metropolitan Museum of Art [1991.368.4 Rogers Fund] depicting sphinxes and other Egyptianizing iconography. [Image courtesy of The Metropolitan Museum of Art, www.metmuseum.org]

king's mortuary complex, which also consisted of a pyramid, several associated temples, a subsidiary pyramid, boat pits, and a causeway. The sphinx is fronted by an Old Kingdom temple wherein worship of Khufu or of the sun god Re could have been carried out. The Great Sphinx therefore represents the living king, Khafre (as Horus), making offerings to his father, Khufu (as the sun god Re). As Khafre was the son of Khufu, in Egyptian mythology Horus was an offspring of Re. There are also adjacent later temples built in the New Kingdom to honor the sphinx.

From as early as the Old Kingdom, the god Horus is also called Horakhty, meaning "Horus of the two horizons." As a falcon deity—a sky god—he is closely associated with the sun god Re and can merge with Re to become the combination deity Re-Horakhty. We will see that the Great Sphinx is linked with this solar deity.

Later, Egyptian sphinx images were exported to Syria-Palestine, where they became an inspiration for local artists who re-imagined the sphinx and created them in female form. Cylinder seals of the Middle Bronze Age bear sphinx iconography. It is possible that the concept of the sphinx as a female figure was then later transferred into Greek mythology.

It is essential to keep in mind that the Egyptian sphinx was quite distinct from the sphinx found in Greek mythology. The Egyptian sphinx was a protective, positive entity, while the sphinx that appears in Greek mythology was a fearsome and dangerous creature. The word for sphinx in ancient Egyptian was *šsp-ꜥnḥ* (*shesep-ankh* in English), meaning, "living image." This word may well be the origin of the Greek word sphinx, or it is possible that the Greek word Σφίγξ "sphinx" may derive from σφίγγω which means "to strangle," an etymology which would hint at the dangerous nature of the Greek sphinx.

The Greek sphinx is best known to us thanks to the story of Oedipus. Oedipus' harrowing encounter with the sphinx could not be further from the meaning and purpose represented by the Egyptian sphinx—a protective figure, a symbol of kingly power, and later, with regards to the Great Sphinx at Giza, a deity in its own right.

OEDIPUS AND THE SPHINX

The mythical hero Oedipus was the son of King Laius and Queen Jocasta of Thebes in Greece (not to be confused with the Egyptian city of Thebes, or modern Luxor). Before Oedipus was born, the Oracle of Apollo at Delphi revealed awful news to the royal couple. Their son would first kill his father and then marry his mother, Jocasta. In an attempt to prevent this terrible event from occurring, his birth parents gave Oedipus up as a child and ultimately King Polybus of Corinth raised him. When Oedipus learned that Polybus was not his real father, he consulted the Oracle of Apollo to learn the truth. Horrified and in an attempt to avoid his revealed fate, he fled to Thebes.

While he was en route to Thebes, Oedipus became involved in an argument with a man who unbeknown to him was his birth father, King Laius. Oedipus killed the man in self-defense, thereby fulfilling the first part of the prophecy. Oedipus continued on to Thebes where he encountered the sphinx—a monstrous creature with the body of a lion, wings of an eagle, tail of a serpent, and head and bust of a woman. The sphinx had been sent by the goddess Hera to terrorize the city of Thebes because of an earlier wrongdoing by King Laius. Anyone who wished to enter the city had to answer a riddle posed by the sphinx. The riddle was "What goes on four legs in the morning, on two legs at noon, and on three legs in the evening?" If the traveler could not answer the riddle, the sphinx devoured them. Oedipus was the first person to be able to answer the riddle correctly. The answer was "man," because a man crawls on all fours as a baby, walks on two legs throughout his adult life, and then in old age requires a cane, or a third "leg" to walk. In an astounded rage at having been beaten, the sphinx killed herself. As a reward for releasing them from their fearsome guardian, the people of Thebes appointed Oedipus their king. He was also given the recently widowed queen Jocasta—his mother—as wife, fulfilling the rest of the prophecy.

Despite his victory over the sphinx, things do not end well for Oedipus. As the couple is at first ignorant of the actual relationship between them, they have four children together. After investigating the murder of King Laius, Oedipus learns that it was he who killed his father. After Queen Jocasta realizes that she has married her own son who is also a murderer, she hangs herself. In horror at what he has done, Oedipus blinds himself with pins from her gown and spends the rest of his life wandering in exile before dying in Athens.

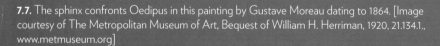

7.7. The sphinx confronts Oedipus in this painting by Gustave Moreau dating to 1864. [Image courtesy of The Metropolitan Museum of Art, Bequest of William H. Herriman, 1920, 21.134.1., www.metmuseum.org]

7.8. Drawing of an intaglio showing Oedipus and the sphinx. [2010,5006.1143 Image © Trustees of the British Museum]

7.9.

7.9. The *akhet* hieroglyph which is an abstraction of the form of the "horizon" (sun rising between two hills).

7.10. A view of the Great Sphinx at Giza from the late 1800s showing a view of it between two pyramids. The pyramids could take the place of the hills in the *akhet* glyph. The sphinx is then in the position of the sun disk. [UPM image # 1172]

7.10.

In Egypt, we have many references to sphinxes and what the Egyptians thought about them. The Great Sphinx at Giza is a particularly informative source. After the 4th Dynasty, the Giza necropolis was largely abandoned as a royal burial place. Kings of later periods constructed their tombs elsewhere. By the time of the New Kingdom, the pharaohs' tombs were being built at Thebes and were no longer in pyramid form. The Great Sphinx and the Giza pyramids were already a millennium old and at this time the Egyptians reimagined the sphinx at Giza as a god in its own right. The kings of the New Kingdom were very interested in the monuments to their royal predecessors at Giza, and the Great Sphinx became known as Hor-em-akhet (or Harmachis in Greek), meaning "Horus in the horizon."

During the New Kingdom, the ancient Egyptians may have come to think of the appearance of the Great Sphinx as a kind of gigantic hieroglyph dominating the landscape at Giza. The word for horizon was *akhet*, which contains a hieroglyphic sign which looks like a double hill with a sun disk in the center. At the Giza plateau, when one looks towards the west at the pyramids of Khufu and Khafre, the sphinx in between can easily be envisioned as the sun disk in the hieroglyph. The two pyramids flank it on either side like the hills in the horizon hieroglyph. This would be especially striking in periods when the sphinx was largely buried with only its head emerging from the sand. The sphinx, long-identified with the god Horus, is then quite literally Horus-in-the-horizon (Egyptian Hor-em-akhet), the very name for the deity which the Egyptians of the New Kingdom connected with the Great Sphinx at Giza.

Similar readings of the natural landscape as a three-dimensional hieroglyph can be seen with the name and location of the city of Amarna (ancient Akhet-Aten, the "Horizon of the Aten"). Amarna was selected by King Akhenaten for his new city in honor of his sole god, the Aten, because of a notch in the cliffs there wherein the sun (the Aten) would appear on the horizon. The Egyptians had many subtle religious concepts that governed the form and meaning of the Great Sphinx; one way to understand that is to look at the sphinx through their inscriptions and literature.

Ancient Encounters with Sphinxes

What do ancient Egyptian writings tell us about sphinxes? One period that is especially fruitful is the New Kingdom (18th–20th dynasties, ca. 1550–1050 BCE). We have already seen how Ramses II's son Khamewaset was interested in the ancient monuments of Memphis. There were others who had similar interests. In particular there are two princes of the 18th Dynasty (who later became kings: Amenhotep II and Thutmosis IV) who set up monuments in honor of the Great Sphinx at Giza.

As noted above, the Great Sphinx, carved in the 4th Dynasty (2625–2500 BCE), was initially planned to honor King Khafre, the builder of the second largest pyramid, and his father, King Khufu, the builder of the Great Pyramid. By the time of the New Kingdom, the Egyptians came to worship the Great Sphinx

7.11.

7.12.

as a manifestation of the god Hor-em-akhet ("Horus in the Horizon"), a version of the god Horus in the form of a solar deity. Both Amenhotep II and Thutmosis IV set up monuments in front of the Great Sphinx. The inscriptions on these monuments are interesting and informative.

7.11. Drawing of a New Kingdom stele of the scribe Montuher showing the pyramids and the sphinx. [Cairo Museum 72273]

7.12. Relief from Karnak of Amenhotep II showing the king in his chariot shooting arrows at bronze targets. His arrows have pierced the target. [Image courtesy of the Oriental Institute of The University of Chicago]

The Great Sphinx Stela of Amenhotep II from Giza

As a young prince, Amenhotep was well known for his athletic prowess. He resided in the city of Memphis and was given the responsibility of caring for and training his father's horses. Inscriptions record the young prince's athletic feats including his seemingly super-human abilities in archery, rowing, and in particular, horsemanship. While this may seem like a great deal of royal boasting or exaggeration, examination of the mummy of Amenhotep II indicates that he may have been close to 6 feet (1.8 m) tall (and he was buried in the Valley of the Kings with a great bow).

We learn from the text that as a young man, the prince often rode his horses near the Pyramids and sphinx at Giza (Lichtheim 1976 [2]:39–43): *"He would yoke them [i.e., the horses] with the harness at Memphis and would stop at the resting place of Hor-em-akhet [the sphinx]. He would spend time leading them around and observing the excellence of the resting place of Kings Khufu and Khafre, the justified. His heart desired to make their names live."*

The monuments at Giza were, by the time of the New Kingdom, already over a thousand years old and were undoubtedly interesting historical and religious attractions to the reigning (and future) kings of Egypt. When Amenhotep II came to the throne, he wished to celebrate and honor the area of the Giza plateau and ordered that a monument be erected there (Lichtheim 1976 [2]:39–43): *"Then his majesty remembered the place where he had enjoyed himself, in the vicinity of the pyramids and of Hor-em-akhet. One ordered to make a resting-place there and to place a stela of limestone in it, its face engraved with the great name of Aakheprure, beloved of Hor-em-akhet, given life forever."*

Amenhotep II built a temple dedicated to the god Hor-em-akhet at Giza which later became the center of a cult of royal ancestors, a cult which included the worship of Amenhotep II himself, as well as his son and successor, Thutmosis IV. The cult of Hor-em-akhet lasted into Roman times.

Thutmosis IV and the Dream Stela

A similar monument in honor of the sphinx was erected by Amenhotep II's son, Thutmosis IV. This text is inscribed on a large stele nestled between the paws of the Great Sphinx. In the text we learn that prince Thutmosis was, like his father, fond of horseback riding on the Giza plateau. One day, while out riding near the sphinx, the prince became tired and decided to take a rest in the creature's shadow. All of a sudden, while dreaming, the sphinx began to speak to him. As with Amenhotep II's stela, the sphinx is equated with a version of the sun god, Hor-em-akhet. The sphinx identifies himself as the young prince's divine father and promises the young man that he will wear the crown of Egypt one day (Breasted, *Ancient Records of Egypt II*, §§810–815):

> *One of those days it came to pass that the king's son, Thutmosis, came, coursing at the time of midday, and he rested in the shadow of this great god. A vision of sleep seized him at the hour (when) the sun was in the zenith, and he found the majesty of this revered god speaking with his own mouth, as a father speaks with his son, saying: "Behold thou me! See thou me! My son Thutmose. I am thy father, Horemakhet-Khepri-Re-Atum, who will give to thee my kingdom on earth at the head of the living. You shall wear the white crown and the red crown upon the throne of Geb, the hereditary prince. The land shall be yours in its length and breadth, that which the eye of the All-Lord shines upon. The food of the Two Lands shall be yours, the great tribute of all countries, the duration of a long period of years. My face is yours, my desire is toward you."*

It seems that the Great Sphinx had a problem and requests the young prince to help. The sphinx had become buried in the sand and would like to be freed from it. The sphinx appears to strike a bargain with Thutmosis. If Thutmosis clears away the sand that has engulfed his body, the Great Sphinx will in turn ensure that the prince comes to the throne as king:

> *You shall be to me a protector (for) my manner is as if I were ailing in all my limbs [--]. The sand of this desert upon which I am, has reached me; turn to me, to have that done which I have desired, knowing that thou art my son, my protector; come hither, behold I am with you, I am thy leader." When he had finished this speech, this king's-son [awoke] hearing this ------; he understood the words of this god, and he kept silent in his heart. He said: "Come, let us hasten to our house in the city, they shall protect the oblations for this god.*

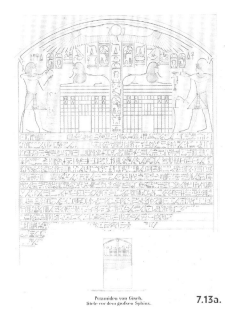

7.13a.

7.13b.

7.14.

7.14. Vintage photograph taken in the late 1800s showing the Great Sphinx at Giza blanketed by sand. The legend reads: "Henri Béchard (active 1870s & 80s); 'Le Sphinx Armachis, Caire' (The Sphinx Armachis, Cairo), about 1880." [Image courtesy of The National Media Museum]

7.15. One of the earliest representations of the sphinx at Giza by a European artist, George Sandys: "A relation of a journey begun an dom. 1610" (1615).

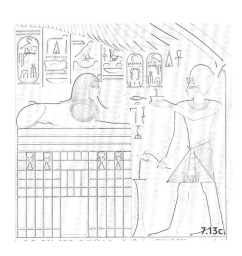

7.13c.

7.13a, b. Line drawing of the Dream Stele of Tuthmosis IV and a view of its position between the paws of the Great Sphinx at Giza. [Top image after Lepsius, *Denkmaeler aus Aegypten und Aethiopien* III, pl. 68]

7.13c. Detail from the Dream Stela of Tuthmosis IV (18th Dynasty, New Kingdom) showing the king making offerings to the god Horemakhet who is shown as a sphinx.

7.15.

7.16. An early engraving of the Great Sphinx of Giza by Olfert Dapper: "Description de l'Afrique" (1665). Here the Great Sphinx appears to be female and the overall image, although picturesque, is quite inaccurate!

7.17. Oil painting by Luc-Olivier Merson, "Le Repos pendant la fuite en Egypte" (1880). [Image courtesy of the Musée des Beaux-Arts de Nice. Photo by Muriel Anssens]

The end of the stele is unfortunately broken away, but it is fair to assume that Thutmosis arranged to have the sphinx freed from its sandy prison and we know that Thutmosis IV took the throne as promised.

When we read these texts in which the Egyptians envisioned the sphinx speaking to them it is clear we ourselves are part of a time-honored tradition lasting thousands of years. Many writers have attempted to give a voice to the Penn Museum's colossal Sphinx in Philadelphia. The 1913 "Interview with a Sphinx," as we have seen, makes the Sphinx into a bit more of a cheeky, wise-cracking character than we see in the Egyptian texts. But, by envisioning the thoughts of the great stone image, we are only following in the footsteps of the pharaohs of old!

As Thutmosis IV described on his Dream Stela over 3,000 years ago, the Great Sphinx was at that point encumbered by sand. Indeed, this would be an ongoing problem for even the largest sphinx on the desert's edge where Egypt's winds tend to deposit sand quite quickly. We know that at different points in its history, sand covered over the Great Sphinx at Giza. Engravings from the 17th and 18th centuries, as well as early photographs from the late 1800s indicate that this was the case quite late into modern times. Only relatively recently did archaeologists fully excavate the entirety of the Great Sphinx's body as Thutmosis IV claims to have done thousands of years in the past.

For most of its history the Great Sphinx was only a protruding head and shoulders. Interestingly, this same fate undoubtedly befell the Penn Museum's colossal Sphinx at Memphis. We see the same sort of weathering patterns on the Sphinx's head and face as we do on the Great Sphinx at Giza. It is clear that, like the Great Sphinx, the colossal Sphinx of Ramses II spent considerable time exposed to the elements (and was probably also vandalized) while its body was buried and protected below ground. Such is the way the wisdom of ages seems to have settled on the Sphinx's veiled countenance.

Before we leave the topic of the sphinx in literature, there is an interesting theme that we see in the ancient Egyptian texts that is echoed in people's encounters with sphinxes even in more modern times. In his Dream Stela, Thutmosis IV lay down and napped under the kindly shadows of the Great Sphinx. This idea of the sphinx as a benign, protective creature shows up in paintings inspired by the Biblical account of the flight into Egypt by Mary, Joseph, and the infant Jesus found in the gospel of St. Matthew (Matt. 2:13–14). A painting with this theme is housed at the Musée des Beaux-Arts de Nice. Painted by Luc Olivier Merson in 1880, the work features Mary and the baby Jesus resting nestled between the paws of a benign-looking sphinx who appears to gaze towards the heavens, while Joseph slumbers on the sands of the desert near a small campfire. The sphinx that appears in this painting seems to be more on the scale of the Alabaster Sphinx at Memphis rather than the Great Sphinx at Giza.

In the 21st century, the Penn Museum's colossal Sphinx from Memphis also has become (by coincidence or fate one cannot be sure) a comforting place to take a rest. One of the popular events at the Museum is "40 Winks with the Sphinx," where children of all ages sleep overnight in the Museum's Egyptian gallery beside the granite beast. Here again, we find that we are part of a tradition lasting thousands of years. From Thutmosis IV to the present, people have been drawn to find protection and solace beneath the comforting gaze of a giant stone lion.

The Power of the Lion

The ancient Egyptians, like many people both ancient and modern, were fascinated by the strength, power, and majesty of the lion. As early as the Predynastic period, leonine imagery was important in Egyptian art. Buried lions have been excavated in connection with royal tombs at the early sites of Hierakonpolis and Abydos. Lion deities were an integral part of the Egyptian pantheon from the earliest dynasties. Numerous deities including Sekhmet, Mut, Mehyt, Pakhet, Tefnut, and Mahes appear in leonine form. The sphinx is an adaptation of the lion. In order to understand Egyptian ideas and iconography of lions let's take a look at some of the other lion imagery from various periods in the Egyptian collection at the Penn Museum.

Delicately carved recumbent lions were found by Petrie during excavations at the site of Abydos. They may have been part of a gaming set. The royal tombs of the first pharaohs at Abydos contained many similar examples of lion-shaped gaming pieces, which occur as both lions and lionesses. These pieces may have been used as counters on a game board similar to our backgammon or "snakes-and-ladders." Excavators found the remains of seven lion cubs, probably kept as palace pets, in the funerary complex of King Aha (1st Dynasty, ca. 3000–2800 BCE) at Abydos.

Flinders Petrie excavated an ivory wand at the site of Rifeh. One end is decorated with the head of a jackal-like creature, while the rounded end features the face of a lion. In between are a series of knife-wielding protective deities, including a seated lion. Magical wands such as this one, created from a hippopotamus tusk, were an essential device used apotropaically during childbirth. Magicians would have drawn a protective circle around the bed of a birthing mother or her newborn child with the wand. The guardian figures decorating it would have warded off any evil forces that sought to harm the mother or baby.

In 1909–10, archaeologists David Randall-MacIver and Leonard Woolley found the necklace shown here, which is not strung in its original order, at the site of Buhen in Nubia. Gold clasps in the form of tiny lions decorate the ends of the necklace which is strung with gold seed beads and golden amulets which take the form of flies, falcons, and a pomegranate fruit. The lion clasps are very similar to a tiny electrum sphinx also in the collection (see the next chapter on sphinxes in the Penn Museum).

During the course of his reign Amenhotep III issued a series of large commemorative scarabs with texts on the back celebrating important events. One type is the so-called lion hunt scarab shown here. On the back of this scarab, eight lines of hieroglyphs record the king's hunting prowess and the number of lions killed during the first part of his reign.

The figures of the lion and king are intimately connected in the form of the Egyptian sphinx. Other associations between lions and royal figures are known, from royal lion hunts to scenes like the one we see on this relief. Here the king prepares to smite a group of enemies, while the lioness charges forward and bites the arm of one of the captives. Are we to understand that a royal pet lion accompanied the king into battle? Or is this scene to be understood symbolically, i.e., the king fights with the bravery and tenacity of a lioness? Or perhaps the king is

7.18b.

7.18a, b. Ivory lion gaming pieces from Abydos from the 1st Dynasty (ca. 3000–2800 BCE). [UPM object #s: left, E11520, right, E11522]

7.19. A Middle Kingdom magical wand made from a hippopotamus tusk and inscribed with magical figures; excavated at Rifeh. [UPM object # E2914]

7.20. Close-up of one of the lions seated atop *neb* baskets on the wand.

7.19.

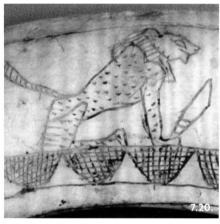

7.20.

7.21.

7.21. Lions appear often in Egyptian inscriptions and texts, as some hieroglyphic signs take the form of lions, or parts of lions. The lion has the phonetic sound of *rw* or *l*. The hieroglyph of the forepart of a lion has the sound *ḥȝt* and is found in words like *ḥȝty-c*, meaning "mayor." The final sign is that of the rear part of a lion and it reads *pḥ*.

7.22.

7.22. This delicate gold necklace with amulets and lion clasps at the ends, found at Buhen, dates to the Middle Kingdom. [UPM object # E10898b]

7.23. Bottom of a large commemorative scarab of Amenhotep III from Terraneh. [UPM object # E21]

7.23.

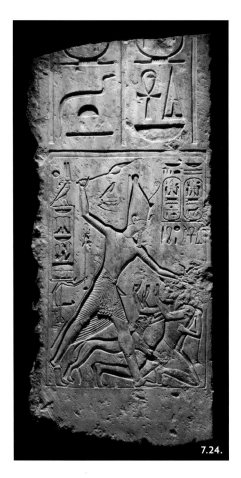

7.24.

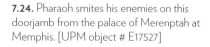

7.25.

7.24. Pharaoh smites his enemies on this doorjamb from the palace of Merenptah at Memphis. [UPM object # E17527]

7.25. Head of a lioness with inlaid eyes (now missing). [UPM object # E14225]

7.26. Fragment from the *Book of the Dead* of Neferrenpet from Thebes, 19th Dynasty. [UPM object # E2775A.4]

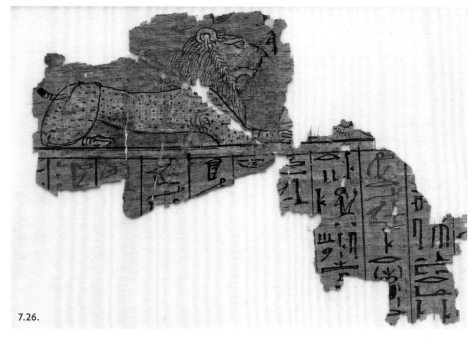

7.26.

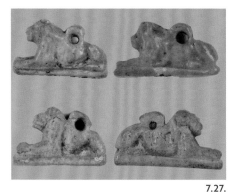

7.27.

7.28a.

7.28b.

7.29.

7.27. Faience amulets of recumbent lions such as these usually date to the Late Period and may have been used as part of a magical spell against snakes, which required the text to be said "over a lion of glazed composition threaded onto red linen." [UPM object # 29-81-256, -545, -764B and -474]

7.28a, b. Amulets of a double lion can be found in our collection as well. These may have been connected to Ruty, the twin lions featured in Chapter 17 of the *Book of the Dead*. It was believed the sun rose over Ruty's back each day. These amulets were popular because of their association with rebirth. [UPM object # E12759]

7.29. Funerary stele inscribed in Demotic dating to the Greco-Roman period from Dendera. [UPM object # E2983]

magically assisted in battle by one of the leonine deities such as Sekhmet? A limestone doorjamb comes from the palace complex of King Merenptah at Memphis which was excavated by the Penn Museum's Coxe Expedition in 1915.

Discovered at Memphis in 1915, the blue lioness above formed part of a larger object whose original form is unknown. Originally, artisans would have incorporated inlays of a different material to fashion the eyes. Because there are a number of leonine goddesses, it is difficult to say for certain which one this figure may depict. However, since it comes from Memphis, it may well be a representation of the goddess Sekhmet.

The funerary texts known as the *Book of the Dead* are often accompanied by vignettes or scenes that illustrate the text's magical spells. The papyrus fragment shown here comes from a *Book of the Dead* belonging to a man named Neferrenpet who lived at Deir el Medina. It joins with another part of the papyrus now housed in Brussels which contains Chapter 17, one of the most popular *Book of the Dead* spells. If the scene were complete, it would show the deceased in a pose of adoration before the lion. In this case, the lion may be a representation of Ruty, the twin lions who guard the horizon.

7.30a, b. Painted limestone statue of a stylized seated lion dated to the 26th Dynasty, with a close-up of the lion's benign "smile." [UPM object # E14306]

Among the treasures in the tomb of Tutankhamun were a series of animal-shaped beds. One of these beds took the form of a lioness and perhaps represents the little-known goddess Mekhyet. The shape of Tutankhamun's lion bed is exactly like the bed shown in the scene at the top of this funerary stela which Petrie discovered at Dendera, dating about 1500 years after the death of Tutankhamun. The mummy of the deceased on the bed is being attended to by the god of mummification, Anubis. On either side of the bed, the goddesses Isis and Nephthys kneel in a pose of mourning. As a desert dweller, the lion was thought to have regenerative powers and this connection with rebirth may explain the presence of lion imagery on funerary biers.

This limestone statue of a friendly looking, stylized seated lion has, painted on its chest, the catrtouche of Necho I, ruler of the delta city of Sais under the Assyrian kings Esarhaddon and Assurbanipal. Given the animal's benign appearance, it is possible that this statue represents a royal pet.

Tamed lions were not limited to the Early Dynastic period. There are later examples of scenes that may show tamed or pet lions. A depiction of what may be a tame lioness can be seen on the side of the small golden shrine from the Tomb of Tutankhamun, where the king is depicted shooting arrows while the lioness sits by his side. Ramses II appears with a tame lioness on the walls of the temple

7.31.

7.32.

7.31. Visitors to the Giza Zoo in Egypt sometimes get the chance to experience what it may have been like to handle tamed lion cubs. This young lion graciously posed for a photo in 2004. [Image courtesy of Stephen R. Phillips]

7.32. Ostracon from Abydos with an ink drawing of a lion. [UPM object # 69-29-341]

7.33. Limestone head of a lioness from Gurob with traces of pigment. [UPM object # E317]

7.34. One of the two red granite lions originally from Soleb in the British Museum [EA2]. Its companion [EA1] bears the original inscription of Amenhotep III and the text names the king's temple of Soleb in Nubia. [Image © Trustees of the British Museum]

7.33.

7.34

at Beit el-Wali in Lower Nubia. The Ptolemaic queen Berneice II is also reported to have had a tame lioness, or so the story goes. New Kingdom scenes of foreign tribute bearers include figures leading leashed lions. While African lions may have been familiar to the Egyptians, the animals depicted in the tribute scenes were an imported species from western Asia.

Egyptian artists frequently practiced their drawings on flakes of limestone or pottery. Known as ostraca, these trial pieces frequently have animal and human imagery. This ostracon from Abydos (Fig. 7.32) has a naturalistic-looking lion drawn on it in black ink. In some cases, pilgrims dedicated ostraca with images of deities to temples.

Flinders Petrie excavated this lovely limestone lioness head at the site of Gurob. It is an architectural element that probably was part of a balustrade (Fig. 7.33). It dates to the reign of Amenhotep III. Many depictions of the lioness-headed goddess Sekhmet date to the reign of this king, as do the impressive pair of lions from Soleb found at Gebel Barkal in Nubia (Fig. 7.34). Each measures more than 7 ft (2 m) in length. These lions were originally placed in the temple at Soleb in Nubia, but a Merotic king moved them south to the site of Gebel Barkal.

Our brief survey of lions in ancient Egyptian religion and art in the Penn Museum's collection shows what a powerful icon the lion was. The Egyptians truly managed to capture the essence of these big cats in many ways: sitting, standing, and attacking.

All Kinds of Sphinxes: Lions and Falcons and Rams, Oh My!

When we think about Egyptian sphinxes, we tend to call to mind a fantastical creature that has the head of a king (wearing a *nemes* headdress) and the body of a recumbent lion. Although this is the classic Egyptian form, sphinxes come in a dazzling array of variations. Since the sphinx is a hybrid creature, it must by definition contain elements from at least two distinct beings. The most common combination of a human head on a lion body gives us a form called an *androsphinx*. But this is not the only possible form. Sometimes sphinxes are made of a combination of two (or more) different types of animals. Two very common variations are *hieracosphinxes* which feature the head of a falcon and the body of a lion, and *criosphinxes* comprising the head of a ram and the body of a lion. There are also examples of crocodile sphinxes and sphinxes with a lion's body and a snake's head.

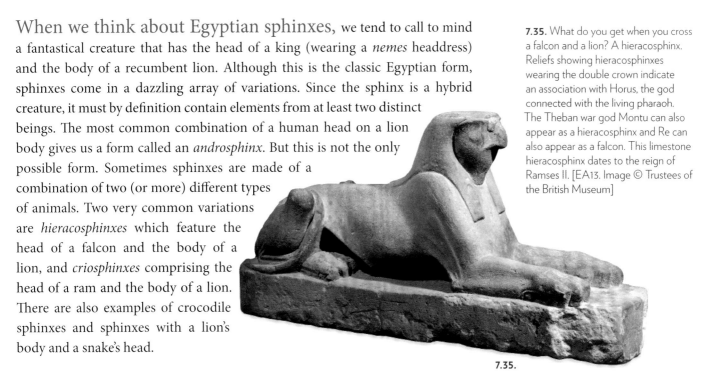

7.35. What do you get when you cross a falcon and a lion? A hieracosphinx. Reliefs showing hieracosphinxes wearing the double crown indicate an association with Horus, the god connected with the living pharaoh. The Theban war god Montu can also appear as a hieracosphinx and Re can also appear as a falcon. This limestone hieracosphinx dates to the reign of Ramses II. [EA13. Image © Trustees of the British Museum]

7.35.

7.36.

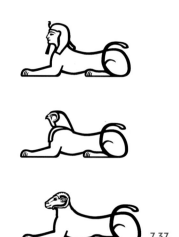

7.37.

7.38.

7.39.

7.36. Another popular sphinx form is the criosphinx. This composite creature has the body of a lion and the head of a ram. The god Amun could take the form of a ram and most criosphinxes represent this deity. [EA64534. Image © Trustees of the British Museum]

7.37. Three common forms of sphinxes.

7.38. A Late Period amulet depicts an unusual example of a seated snake-headed sphinx. [EA64610. Image © Trustees of the British Museum]

7.39. A creature that is part lion and part crocodile seems particularly awe-inspiring. There is a rare example of such a croco-sphinx at the site of the mortuary temple of Amenhotep III at Kom el-Heitan in Thebes. Unfortunately, the head is damaged. Perhaps this sphinx was meant to honor the crocodile god Sobek. [Image courtesy of Hannelore Siegmeier]

7.40. This photograph of Karnak Temple shows the avenue of criosphinxes that lined the processional way into the temple.

7.41. Identified as a sphinx of Queen Hetepheres II, this recumbent, maned sphinx is perhaps the earliest representation of a sphinx from Egypt. The statue bears traces of yellow pigment traditionally used to represent female skin tone in Egyptian art. [Egyptian Museum, Cairo JE35137]

7.40.

7.41.

Androsphinxes can be male or female. Certainly depictions of male kings as sphinxes are more common, but sphinxes of queens are also well known. In fact, the earliest representation of a sphinx in Egypt is one identified as Queen Hetepheres (Fig. 7.41). There are a number of anonymous Middle Kingdom female sphinxes presumably representing queens or princesses. In the New Kingdom, Queen Hatshepsut is depicted in a number of sphinxes (although she is a special case, since she was a woman carrying out the role of a male pharaoh). During the Amarna Period, Nefertiti can appear as a sphinx, and we also see a sphinx of the daughter of King Piye of the 25th Dynasty, Shepenwepet II, who held the important position of the God's Wife of Amun (Fig. 7.53).

Androsphinxes can be maned, semi-maned, or unmaned. With a maned sphinx, the sphinx has the head, including the ears and mane (or ruff) of a lion with only the face of a human being. We find maned sphinxes throughout Egyptian history. However, the most common form is the semi-maned sphinx. The Penn Museum's colossal Sphinx is a classical example of this form, as is the example from Hatsehsput shown in Figure 7.42. The semi-maned sphinx has the lion's ruff on its shoulders but in front the mane is reduced to a flat bib-like element descending to the sphinx's arms. It normally is capped by a *nemes* crown. Unmaned sphinxes have a fully human head topped with a headdress, crown, or tresses.

Sphinxes can be active or passive in their pose. Passive sphinxes are recumbent, with their forepaws stretched out straight in front of them. They can also sit on their back haunches and their forepaws are depicted in an almost vertical position that resembles a seated cat. In both cases, the tail is usually curled close to the body curved around the right flank. Sometimes passive sphinxes stand with their legs together; no movement is indicated by the position of their limbs, but the tail is erect and the pose suggests alertness.

Active sphinxes, in contrast to their seated or recumbent counterparts, are shown striding or trampling an enemy, and in at least one case, in the act of grasping an enemy with its front paws. These active sphinxes fully display the

7.44. Amulet of a seated female sphinx wearing a curious hairstyle. Termed the "Nubian style," this coiffure seems to be connected to birth and nursing mothers. [EA59851. Image © Trustees of the British Museum]

7.45. Bronze figure of a sphinx perhaps representing the protective deity Tutu who is often shown in sphinx form. [EA64556. Image © Trustees of the British Museum]

7.46. The excavator Theodore Davis found this wooden chair [30.8.45a-c, Theodore M. Davis Collection, Bequest of Theodore M. Davis, 1915] in the tomb of Tuthmosis IV in the Valley of the Kings. The king appears as a sphinx trampling enemies underfoot. [Image courtesy of The Metropolitan Museum of Art, www.metmuseum.org]

7.47. On this scarab, a human-headed sphinx is depicted striding above two bound enemies. [UPM object # E11049]

7.48. This brilliant blue faience androsphinx [1972.125, Purchase, Lila Acheson Wallace Gift, 1972] depicts Amenhotep III offering two *nw*-jars. It has been suggested that this figurine was part of an Egyptian temple model. [Image courtesy of The Metropolitan Museum of Art, www.metmuseum.org]

7.49. Dating to the 9th–7th centuries BCE, ivory plaques excavated at the site of Nimrud in modern Iraq often bear Egyptianizing designs. Here, two striding human-headed sphinxes face a central cartouche [62.269.4, Rogers Fund, 1962]. The sphinxes are female and wear the so-called Nubian style hairdo. [Image courtesy of the Metropolitan Museum of Art, www.metmuseum.org]

7.47.

7.44.

7.45.

7.46.

7.48.

7.49.

potential for power possessed by a creature that is half lion. We find scenes of trampling sphinxes decorating the sides of royal thrones and royal chariots, and these trampling scenes are popular motifs on scarabs. Depictions of ostrich feather fans often accompany trampling sphinxes (see Fig. 7.46). The fan represents the breath of life and indicates that the sphinx is alive.

Another form of active sphinx is one in which the front legs of the lion are replaced by human arms and hands. With this type of sphinx, the arms usually hold offerings, or are raised in a pose of devotion, while the rear haunches are at rest as in the normal recumbent sphinx.

Sometimes sphinxes are shown with the addition of wings and a tail that is raised (indicating action) instead of being curled around the right flank, as it normally does. In the case of winged hieracosphinxes, the figures resemble griffins, which have the body, tail, and legs of a lion and the head and wings of an eagle.

TUTU

A special example of the active sphinx is the god Tutu who entered the Egyptian pantheon during the Late Period; he continued to be worshiped through the Greco-Roman period. His iconography is undeniably sphinx-like. He is usually shown as a human-headed striding lion. Sometimes he has wings and often lion, crocodile, or falcon heads sprout from his back. His tail can take the form of a snake. His name means "image" or "collection" and he was thought to be the son of the powerful goddess Neith. Tutu had power over demons and as such was a protective deity. He was worshiped throughout Egypt, but his main cult center was in the Dakhla Oasis in Egypt's Western Desert where there is a temple dedicated to him. Votive plaques like the one shown here were erected to curry this god's favor and to prevent him from unleashing evil forces.

7.52.

7.52. Limestone relief of the god Tutu shown as a human-headed sphinx wearing a *nemes* headdress with horns and sun disk. Tutu sprouts a lion's head from his back, has a snake for a tail, and grasps knives and scorpions in his paws. [UPM object # 65-34-1]

7.53.

7.54.

7.55.

7.56.

7.57a.

7.57b.

7.53. Shepenwepet II was the daughter of King Piye and held the position of God's Wife of Amun. Here she is shown as a sphinx with human arms. She wears a full Hathor wig and holds a vessel topped with the ram's head of Amun. (Found during excavations near the Sacred Lake at Karnak [Berlin 7972.]) [Image courtesy of Miguel Hermoso Cuesta]

7.54. A recumbent winged hieracosphinx with human arms held in the position of devotion adorns this ivory plaque. Atop his head, the falcon bears a sun disk with uraeus. Because of this solar imagery, the god represented here is likely Re. [UPM object # 65-3-3]

7.55. A carnelian openwork carving [26.7.1342, Purchase, Edward S. Harkness Gift, 1926] depicting a winged female sphinx with human arms. She holds the cartouche of Amenhotep III, reading "Neb-maat-re." The female is usually identified as Queen Tiye. Her headdress is unusual and may have a foreign origin. [Image courtesy of The Metropolitan Museum of Art, www.metmuseum.org]

7.56. On this cloisonné pectoral from the Middle Kingdom, a pair of hieracosphinxes with wings trample their enemies. Found at Dahshur in the tomb of princess Mereret, the sphinxes here wear the horned and feathered crown often seen on Montu. In the center is the cartouche of Senwosret III, reading "Kha-kau-re." [Egyptian Museum, Cairo, CG52.002. Image after de Morgan, *Fouilles à Dahchour, Mars-Juin 1894* (1895, pl. xix)]

7.57a, b. A striding winged criosphinx decorates this ivory plaque [64.37.7, Rogers Fund, 1964] from Nimrud (top). It was probably an element from a piece of furniture. [Image Courtesy of The Metropolitan Museum of Art, www.metmuseum.org] Another ivory plaque excavated at Fort Shalmaneser at Nimrud (bottom). This example shows a striding winged androsphinx wearing a *nemes* headdress and a stylized double crown. [134322. Image © Trustees of the British Museum]

7.58.

7.59.

7.58. A temple model of the 19th Dynasty (reign of Seti I, father of Ramses II) in the Brooklyn Museum (49183) shows, by way of the remaining recesses, the location of sphinxes in front of a temple pylon. It was found at the site of Tell el-Yahudiya.

7.59. The reconstruction of the model (above) restores the identified elements in the recesses.

Guardian Sphinxes

Egyptian sphinxes came in a great variety of sizes and carried out various functions. For large stone sphinxes the most typical role was as a guardian figure flanking the entryways into the temples of Egypt's gods. The Penn Museum's colossal Sphinx would once have been part of a pair or a larger formation of sphinxes guarding a gateway in the Ptah Temple at ancient Memphis.

Because of this custom you could say that a single sphinx is a lonely sphinx. Actual lions are gregarious animals living in the family pride. Sphinxes' "gregarious nature" is connected to their architectural use and symbolism. Ancient Egyptian architecture is always very symmetrical: what happens on the left is usually mirrored on the right. Sphinxes tend to occur in pairs guarding each side of a temple entrance (which the Egyptians thought of as mirroring the horizon of the daily rebirth of the sun). A typical pattern would be to have larger groupings of sphinxes facing one another placed right outside a temple's entrance.

We see an example of such an arrangement of such guardian sphinxes in a rare object on display in the Egyptian galleries of the Brooklyn Museum (Figs. 7.58–7.59). From the site of Tell el-Yahudiya in the Nile Delta is a slab that once had a model temple mounted on its surface. The actual model elements are gone but there are recesses showing what was once there: a gateway flanked by pylon towers with a ramped stairway in front. On either side are square bases for obelisks each fronted by a statue, as well as two different pairs of sphinxes (their identity is made clear by the characteristic elongated shape with rounded posterior). One sphinx pair stood right in front of the temple pylons (one per pylon); another larger pair stood in front of the obelisks. Not every temple gateway would have looked exactly this way but the Brooklyn model gives an idea of the characteristic form in which sphinxes guarded temple gateways.

It's not surprising then that many of the known colossal sphinxes form couples. We'll see some of these colossal sphinxes below. They include the magnificent St.

7.60a–c. The small temple of Wadi el Sebua in Lower Nubia was built during the reign of Ramses II. It still retains a group of eight guardian sphinxes in front of the temple's pylon. [Images courtesy of Mike Gadd (a and c) and Andrew M. Johnson]

Petersburg sphinxes from the mortuary temple of Amenhotep III in Thebes, and a colossal sphinx in Paris (the Louvre colossal sphinx), whose mate exists as a fragmentary sphinx in the Cairo Museum. A smaller sphinx (the Louvre "Lesser Sphinx") also has its counterpart in a nearly identical sphinx that stands today in the garden of the Cairo Museum. The examples in Paris and Cairo may once have stood in the capital city of Per-Ramses (Ramses II's capital city in the Nile Delta) fronting a temple. Later on, these sphinxes were taken from that site to the nearby city of Tanis where they were set up again, fronting temples there. The Penn Museum Sphinx, however, like the even larger Great Alabaster Sphinx which Petrie also found in 1912, remains a solitary statue. For the time being at least—quite possibly for all eternity—these remain lone sphinxes, bereft of their partners. Still, the most famous sphinx of all, the Great Sphinx at Giza, has no partner either!

We do not have to rely on just the Brooklyn model to gain a sense of the typical arrangement of opposing sphinxes in front of temples. Because Ramses II was such a major temple builder there are many preserved remains of his temples. Among the best preserved were the temples of Lower Nubia, including the famous rock-cut temples at Abu Simbel near the Second Cataract of the Nile. Often forgotten is a smaller but still very impressive temple that Ramses II built at a site today called Wadi el-Sebua. The formation of guardian sphinxes in front of it provides a good model for the sphinx grouping that the Penn Museum Sphinx may once have belonged to.

Like the temples at Abu Simbel, Wadi el-Sebua was threatened in the 1960s with destruction by the rising waters of Lake Nasser. Today it has been disassembled and moved to higher ground not far from its original location where people can visit it. This temple has a grouping of eight guardian sphinxes in front showing Ramses wearing the *nemes* and double crowns. Behind stand four additional hawk-headed sphinxes (hieracosphinxes), each protecting small figures of Ramses. These figures emphasize the king's connection with the falcon god Horus, the main deity of the temple at Wadi el-Sebua. The set of sphinxes create a grand entrance to the pylon of the temple, a smaller version of the type of grand approach which would have characterized the large temples like Ptah's at Memphis.

By looking at this other evidence from the time of Ramses II we gain a sense of the way sphinxes were deployed as guardian statues in front of temples. We can be certain that the Penn Museum's colossal sphinx is one of the main guardian figures like those on the Brooklyn temple model. Presumably it once stood in or near the

North Gateway of the temple of Ptah at Memphis, not far from where Flinders Petrie's assistant Ernest MacKay excavated it in 1912. The Philadelphia sphinx probably had at least one partner, but quite possibly there would have been a large cluster of sphinxes. Other statues of Ramses II, like the large seated or standing figures, might also have stood in that location. Later pharaohs like Merenptah probably added their own statues.

Like the Louvre's colossal sphinx, or the sphinxes in St Petersburg, the Penn Museum sphinx probably had a partner that was never found. The sphinx's counterpart might have been destroyed long ago, along with much of the rest of the Ptah temple. Alternatively, it might still be there—somewhere at Memphia—perhaps to be found some day by a future archaeologist.

Divine Boats and Sphinx Avenues

The Egyptians expanded the idea of guardian sphinxes to other architectural and religious forms as well. Many temples had sacred processional avenues that connected them to other nearby temples. These avenues were used for periodic processions in which the statue of a god would be carried out of his temple usually to visit other gods' temples. These were major festive events for the people of ancient Egypt, a time for people to encounter the gods whose statues would normally be secluded inside the temple sanctuary, accessible only to the priests.

In the New Kingdom and other periods, the great gods were carried in a "divine barque," a model boat with a shrine on its deck containing a statue of the god. At select locations on their journey, the barque would stop. The gods could then be approached and asked questions. The deity would respond through an oracle. It is astounding how elaborate these divine barques could be: miniature versions of the temple itself with the god's statue in a gilded shrine on top. And, just as with the actual temple, the god's shrine was guarded in front by small sphinxes.

The best documented sacred barques in ancient Egypt are those that belonged to the Theban Triad, the three chief gods of Thebes in southern Egypt. These gods

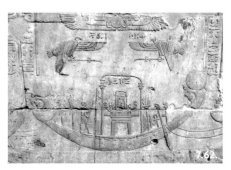

7.61. The barque of Amun (the ram heads on prow and stern symbolize this god) borne by priests during a procession shown in a scene on the Red Chapel of Hatshepsut at Karnak. Note the sphinxes (one recumbent and one striding) on the front of the sacred boat.

7.62. The divine barque of Khonsu on his temple at Karnak.

7.63, 7.64. The barque of the god Amun on the wall of the Hypostyle Hall of Ramses II at Karnak. Here you see several sphinxes, standing and recumbent, protecting the god's barque. Detail above: the standing sphinx guards the prow of the barque.

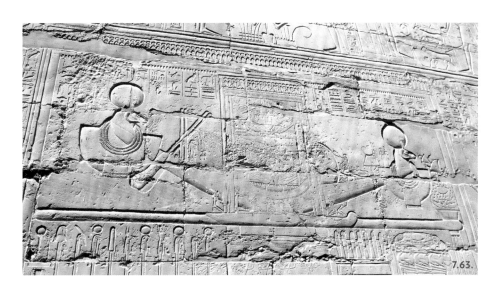

7.65. A replica of the barque of Horus sits today in the sanctuary of the Edfu temple where many visitors confuse it with the actual ancient boat miraculously preserved.

7.66. Tutankhamun's Restoration Stela (in the Cairo Museum) which mentions the statue and barque of Ptah at Memphis. [Image after Lacau, *Stèles du nouvel empire* [1926], pl. 70]

were Amun-Re, the "king of the gods" and chief god of Egypt by the time of the New Kingdom, Amun-Re's consort Mut, and their son, the moon-god Khonsu. In the temples of Karnak we see many images of the divine barques of the Theban triad, each with the head of the god decorating the prow and stern, and the shrine protected by sphinxes. It was common to have a figure of a standing sphinx on the prow.

Frequently, the gods in procession would traverse water as well as land. In that case the divine barques (which were not actual functioning boats) would have to sail on a full-scale functional barque. We have scenes on temple walls of these "boats on boats" and sometimes divine barques of several gods tethered together and moving in a convoy.

The role of sphinxes as guardians of the gods while on the sacred processional routes is another important aspect that helps us to understand the Penn Museum sphinx and its setting at Memphis. At Memphis, the god Ptah had a barque that allowed his cult statue to be carried on the sacred routes of that city. The name of this divine barque (all of the gods' barques had special names) was *Neb-Neheh*, "The Lord of Eternity." Unfortunately, no actual depictions have survived of the barque of Ptah at Memphis. Certainly the temples in Memphis would once have contained detailed carved reliefs showing the barque (like the well-preserved ones at Thebes and Edfu). However, the severe destruction of the Ptah temple has left us no images of *Neb-Neheh*.

During the reign of the famous boy-king, Tutankhamun, we get a picture of how impressive Ptah's barque was. The statue of Ptah and his divine barque had both been destroyed during the reign of the heretic pharaoh Akhenaten. At that time Akhenaten had closed the gods' temples and instituted the sole worship of the sun, the Aten. Tutankhamun, Akhenaten's successor, ordered the restoration of the traditional gods of Egypt. In Tutankhamun's "Restoration Decree," it states: *"He refashioned Ptah, South-of-his-wall, Lord-of-Ankhtawy, his noble statue being of electrum on eleven carrying poles, his sacred image being of electrum, lapis-lazuli, turquoise, and every kind of precious stone, whereas formerly the majesty of this noble god had been borne on seven carrying poles only."* Tutankhamun had made Ptah's statue and divine barque even better than before. In the same decree, he states that he had also upgraded the barque of Amun-Re from nine to eleven carrying poles, slightly bigger than that of Ptah. Amun-Re was, after all, the chief god of the empire.

In the Penn Museum's collection is a stela excavated at Memphis by the Coxe Expedition and dating to the

7.66.

Ramesside Period (Fig. 7.67). The stela belonged to a man named Kauemperptah, whose title was "Skipper of the barque of Ptah." This unusual job would have put him in charge of the operations of Ptah's divine barque. Strangely, his stela shows him worshiping the god Amun, and the barque of Amun, not of Ptah, appears at the top of the stela. We know that Ptah's barque would at times have been carried out of the various gateways of the Ptah temple, including through the North Gate where the sphinx of Ramses II stood.

Kauemperptah is one man who almost certainly would have seen the Penn Museum's colossal sphinx in its original setting and probably passed by it on a daily basis as he carried out his duties in the temple of *Hut-Ka-Ptah*. How many questions Kauemperptah could answer for us about the sphinx!

We have seen that temple gateways were guarded by sphinxes that helped keep the forces of chaos at bay. So, too, the divine barques on which the gods' statues came and went had sphinxes mounted on their decks protecting the deity. What of the processional routes on which the gods traveled? How to guard these sacred passages? With sphinxes, of course! The Egyptians extended the idea of the guardian sphinx fronting the temple entrance to create the sphinx avenue—an entire sacred roadway lined on either side with a phalanx of sphinxes. Needless to say, these were not the colossal statues like the Philadelphia sphinx, but small- and medium-sized sphinxes—more economical when you need dozens or hundreds of them.

There are a number of fine examples of sphinx avenues still in existence, particularly in the well-preserved temples of Thebes (modern Luxor) in southern Egypt. Very well known to visitors to Egypt are the criosphinxes (ram-sphinxes) of the temple of Amun at Karnak. These do not depict the king, but rather the god Amun himself with a ram's head (one of the animal forms Amun could take) and sphinx body. The criosphinxes guard the main gateway into the temple, so the god is symbolically protecting his own temple. Originally, these flanked an avenue that led to a landing area beside the Nile.

One of the great builders of sphinx avenues was pharaoh Nectanebo I of Egypt's 26th or Saite Dynasty (so-called because these pharaohs had their ancestral capital

7.67.

7.67. Limestone stela of Kauemperptah, the "Skipper of the barque of Ptah," in Memphis. Kauemperptah stands here (holding a bouquet), in this case not before Ptah but rather in front of Amun, with the barque of Amun at the top of the stela. Excavated by the Coxe Expedition. [UPM object # E13609]

7.68. Ram-headed sphinxes guard the route from the Nile to the gateway of the temple of Amun at Karnak, as shown in a postcard ca. 1910.

KARNAK, SPHYNX STREET

7.68.

7.69.

7.69. The ram-headed sphinxes lining the entry to Karnak today.

at the city of Sais in the Nile Delta). Nectanebo ruled during the Late Period, at a time when Egypt was relatively stable and there was renewed interest in temple building. One of his projects was the impressive phalanx of sphinxes that line the processional way between the Karnak and Luxor temples. This particular sphinx avenue originally contained about 800 sphinxes that ran along both sides. The Egyptian Supreme Council of Antiquities currently has an impressive, ongoing project to excavate and restore the sphinx avenue between the Karnak and Luxor temples. Not surprisingly, this work has been going on for many decades. Quite often it takes archaeologists longer to excavate, document, and study ancient ruins than it did for the ancient people to build them in the first place.

Ancient Memphis would have had many sacred processional routes, some of which, over time, would have been lined with sphinxes like those at Thebes. One of the sacred routes of Memphis connected the Ptah temple with the necropolis of Saqqara on the desert's edge. From the foundation of Memphis as the city of *Ineb-Hedj*, Saqqara had been the primary necropolis serving the city. Many kings and high officials built their tombs there. Also buried there from very early on was the sacred bull of Memphis: the Apis, whose religious importance at Memphis we examined in Chapter 6. Saqqara had many catacombs and burial grounds for sacred animals, but the Serapeum was by far the most important.

The Apis was an animal manifestation of Ptah. When the Apis bull died, it was mummified and buried in a great stone sarcophagus. Ramses II established a

7.70.

7.71.

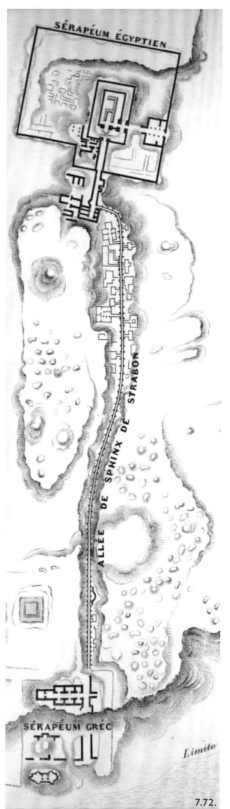

SÉRAPÉUM ÉGYPTIEN

ALLÉE DE SPHINX DE STRABON

SÉRAPÉUM GRÉC

Limite

7.72.

7.70. One of the sphinxes of Nectanebo I in front of Luxor temple.

7.71. A view of the avenue of sphinxes in front of Luxor Temple.

7.72. Mariette's map of the sphinx avenue at the Serapeum. [After A. Mariette, *Choix de monuments et de dessins découverts ou exécutés pendant le déblaiement du Sérapéum de Memphis*, Paris, 1856, pl. 1]

7.73a, b. Drawings of a Serapeum sphinx. [Images from Ebers, *Egypt: Descriptive, Historical, and Picturesque* (1878)]

7.73a.

SPHINX FROM THE SERAPEUM.

7.73b.

7.74.

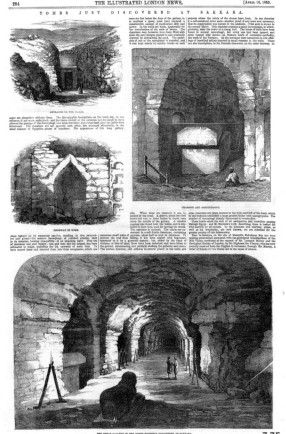

7.75.

special catacomb for the Apis bulls (which had formerly been buried in separate tombs)—the site we know as the Serapeum. The Serapeum grew over time as each successive bull was interred and new chambers were cut for succeeding Apis burials. During the Late Period, the kings Nectanebo I and II added a grand sphinx avenue much like the one at Luxor. The French Egyptologist Auguste Mariette, who established the Egyptian Antiquities Service, discovered the Serapeum in 1851—his first major discovery in Egypt and the one that made him famous—by excavating and following the sphinx avenue. It led from the desert's edge out to the entrance to the underground catacombs of the Serapeum. Some of the sphinxes that stood along the avenue are today in the Louvre where they stand, fittingly, in a row re-creating their original arrangements as guardians of the sacred Apis catacombs.

This brief survey of sacred barques and processional routes helps us to understand a little more about the Penn Museum's sphinx and the kind of religious structures it once belonged to at ancient Memphis. Its primary role was that of guardian figure associated with the temple dedicated to Ptah-Tatenen near the North Gate of the Ptah enclosure. This was a place where the image of Ptah came and went from his sanctuary on processions that took him to other parts of the religious landscape of Memphis. Sphinxes were the guardians of the gods at the doorways to their temples and along the routes of their periodic journeys, as they moved in and out of those sacred spaces.

7.74. Sphinxes from the sphinx avenue at the Serapeum on display in the Louvre, Paris. [Uploaded by Janmad on July 26, 2009 with a CC BY-SA 3.0 license; source is http://commons.wikimedia.org/wiki/File:Six_sphinxes_Serapeum_at_Saqqara_Louvre.JPG]

7.75. Images from *The Illustrated London News* (1853) publication showing the Serapeum and burials of the Apis bulls which Mariette discovered by following a trail of sphinxes into the desert.

Traveling Sphinxes

Unless a sphinx is rooted to the earth (as in the unique case of the Great Sphinx at Giza), it is by definition a "portable sphinx": one that can be transported from one location to another. Throughout history, there has been a lot of interest in moving these magnificent stone beasts from place to place. The ancient Egyptians themselves frequently "recycled" sphinxes by adding new inscriptions to already existing ones carved during earlier eras. Such sphinxes were then normally moved to a new location: this was the fate of most of the colossal sphinxes, as we will explore in Chapter 8. The Penn Museum sphinx is itself an example of a sphinx carved most likely during the Middle Kingdom, but taken over centuries later by Ramses II for his monumental works in the temple of Ptah at Memphis. Part of its early history involved its portability.

Special cases of portable sphinxes are the ones that have traveled outside of Egypt. The Penn Museum sphinx is a member of this select group. Already in ancient times, Egyptian sphinxes had begun to migrate beyond the borders of Egypt. One important period in the movement of sphinxes occurred during the four centuries of the Roman Empire when the Caesars ruled Egypt (30 BCE–395 CE). The Roman emperors contributed many great monuments in Egypt: in fact, some of the most impressive standing temples in Egypt were built during the Roman Period. However, there was also an interest in bringing Egyptian monuments back to embellish Rome itself.

An interesting example of a sphinx that traveled outside Egypt during the Roman Period is a female sphinx dating to the Middle Kingdom, the head of which is now in the Brooklyn Museum of Art, New York. This sphinx is not a monolithic one, like many of the colossal sphinxes, but rather was a composite sphinx in which different parts were joined. Only the head now remains but the tail behind the wig shows it originally joined to a sphinx body. Egyptologist Bernard Bothmer completed a study of this sphinx and concluded the woman in question is probably a queen of the time of Amenemhat II in the middle of the 12th Dynasty. This sphinx was taken to Rome during the period when the cult of Isis was popular in the Roman Empire. It may have adorned a temple dedicated to Isis whose cult had spread throughout the Mediterranean in later antiquity. There it stayed through the Middle Ages until 1772 when William Petty, Second Earl of Shelburne, purchased it from the collection of Cardinal Alessandro Albani. After changing hands in the 1940s and 50s the sphinx head went to Brooklyn in 1956 where it is one of the masterworks of Middle Kingdom Egyptian royal sculpture. This is a very well-traveled sphinx!

Many Egyptian sphinxes, large and small, have traveled outside of the Nile Valley from ancient into modern times. However, there are not that many colossal sphinxes outside of Egypt itself. The world of sphinxes of this size is a select club indeed. Only a few may be seen in the United States. These include the sphinx of Ramses II in the Penn Museum and the sphinx of Hatshepsut (restored from fragments) in the Metropolitan Museum. There are many other large ancient Egyptian statues and other monuments (for instance, the Central Park Obelisk), but enormous sphinxes are a rare breed.

7.76. A colossal sphinx on the move: press release photo of the Louvre "Lesser Sphinx" being moved in 1987 for installation in the "Tanis: The Gold of the Pharaohs" exhibition.

7.77. Head of a female sphinx, 12th Dynasty, Middle Kingdom. [Brooklyn Museum of Art, New York, 56.85]

More colossal sphinxes can be encountered in museums in Europe. Foremost of the gigantic sphinxes in Europe are two originally from the site of Tanis in the Nile Delta, now in the Louvre Museum, Paris. These are the Louvre colossal sphinx and the Louvre "Lesser Sphinx." In addition, there are a superb pair of large sphinxes originally from Thebes in southern Egypt and dating to the reign of Amenhotep III of the 18th Dynasty. These are now located in front of the Hermitage Museum in St. Petersburg, Russia. Other large sphinxes can be seen in Berlin (another sphinx of Hatshepsut), and a sphinx of Ramses III in Turin, Italy.

Among the oversize sphinxes that have left Egypt, the Penn Museum's sphinx would rank as the fourth largest one outside of Egypt after the Louvre and St. Petersburg sphinxes. The chart below shows the relative sizes of some of the largest known sphinxes.

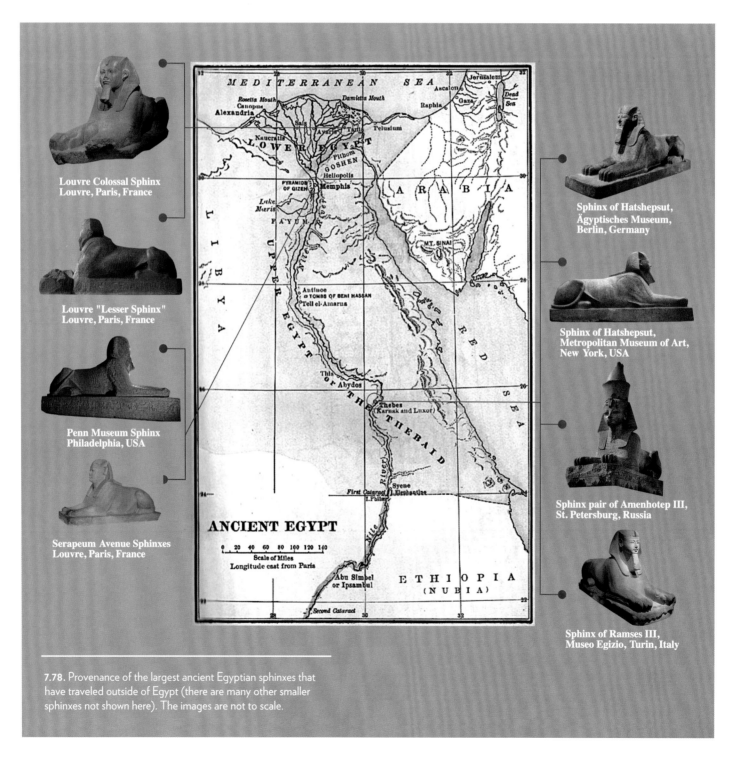

Louvre Colossal Sphinx
Louvre, Paris, France

Louvre "Lesser Sphinx"
Louvre, Paris, France

Penn Museum Sphinx
Philadelphia, USA

Serapeum Avenue Sphinxes
Louvre, Paris, France

Sphinx of Hatshepsut,
Ägyptisches Museum,
Berlin, Germany

Sphinx of Hatshepsut,
Metropolitan Museum of Art,
New York, USA

Sphinx pair of Amenhotep III,
St. Petersburg, Russia

Sphinx of Ramses III,
Museo Egizio, Turin, Italy

7.78. Provenance of the largest ancient Egyptian sphinxes that have traveled outside of Egypt (there are many other smaller sphinxes not shown here). The images are not to scale.

HOW DO THEY COMPARE?
RELATIVE SIZES OF THE LARGEST EGYPTIAN SPHINXES

The Great Sphinx at Giza
Khafre, Dynasty 4, ca. 2400 BCE
Material: Limestone bedrock
Length: 260 feet (57 meters)
Height: 65 feet (20 meters)
Width: 20 feet (6 meters)

**The Alabaster Sphinx
at Memphis**
Possibly Hatshepsut (Dynasty 18)
Material: Calcite (Egyptian Alabaster)
Length: 8 meters
Height: 4.2 meters
Weight: estimated at 70-80 tons

HOW DO THEY COMPARE?
RELATIVE SIZES OF THE LARGEST EGYPTIAN SPHINXES

Sphinx Pair, St. Petersburg, Russia
Amenhotep III (Dynasty 18), Thebes
Material: Granite
Length: 4.9 meters
Height: (with crown) 4.5 meters
Width: 1.5 meters

Colossal Sphinx, Louvre, Paris
Tanis
Material: Granite
Length: 4.8 meters
Height: 2 meters

The Colossal Sphinxes of Alexandria
Length: 4 meters
Height: 2.2 meters

Philadelphia Colossal Sphinx
Ramses (Dynasty 19), Memphis
Material: Granite
Length: 3.83 meters
Height: 2.13 meters
Weight: 12.6 tons

Colossal Sphinx of Hatshepsut
New York, Metropolitan Museum of Art
Length: 3.43 meters
Height: 1.64 meters
Weight: ca. 7 tons (reconstructed)

"Lesser" Sphinx from Tanis
Paris, Lourve
Length: 3.2 meters
Height: 1.7 meters

The Colossal Sphinx of Paris

The Penn Museum's sphinx is the largest ancient Egyptian sphinx in the Western Hemisphere. However, even before it came to Philadelphia in 1913 there were three larger sphinxes taken to Europe during the 19th century. These sphinxes have their own interesting stories to tell and there are many aspects to them that help us to understand the granite sphinx of Ramses II from Memphis.

The first of the colossal sphinxes to leave Egypt in the 19th century was the rose granite sphinx now in the Louvre, Paris. The Louvre sphinx was first discovered in 1802 by the English diplomat William Hamilton at the site of Tanis in the Egyptian Delta. The sphinx remained at Tanis until 1825 when Henry Salt, then British Consul General in Egypt, removed it along with another smaller sphinx and included it in a collection of Egyptian antiquities offered up for sale to an interested museum. None other than Jean-Francois Champollion, the decipherer of Egyptian hieroglyphs, examined this collection and recommended its purchase to King Charles X of France on behalf of the Louvre. The sphinx, which had remained in Alexandria until the purchase was confirmed, was then sent to Paris

7.79. Jean Francois Champollion (1790–1832), decipherer of Egyptian hieroglyphs and curator of Egyptian antiquities at the Louvre. Portrait taken in 1831. [Public domain image; source is http://en.wikipedia.org/wiki/Jean-Fran%C3%A7ois_Champollion#mediaviewer/File:Leon_Cogniet_-_Jean-Francois_Champollion.jpg]

7.80. The colossal sphinx of Tanis in the Louvre (A23). It measures 1.83 m in height, 4.8 m in length, and weighs approximately 24 tons. [Uploaded by CJ on January 11, 2007 with a CC BY-SA 3.0 license; source is http://commons.wikimedia.org/wiki/File:Louvre_sphinx.jpg]

7.81.

7.83.

7.81. The Louvre "Lesser Sphinx" (A21). [Image courtesy of Wally Gobetz]

7.82. Its matching sphinx in front of the Cairo Museum (CG 1197). [Image courtesy of Danee Sarman]

7.83. Egyptian Hall of the Crystal Palace, *The Illustrated London News*, July 22, 1854.

7.84. Work on a cast of the Louvre colossal sphinx during the move of the Crystal Palace from Hyde Park to Sydenham Hill (1853). [Photograph by Philip Henry Delamotte]

7.85. During the First World War, 1914–1918, approximately 125,000 men and women of the Royal Navy trained at the Crystal Palace. Image from *The Graphic*, February 4, 1915, of trainees in the Egyptian Hall.

7.82.

7.84.

7.85.

7.86. Members of the Royal Navy sitting on one of the two copies of the Louvre colossal sphinx at the Crystal Hall's entrance.

7.86. Members of the Royal Navy sitting on one of the two copies of the Louvre colossal sphinx at the Crystal Hall's entrance.

7.87. Sphinxes still guard the entrance of the now vanished Crystal Palace, Sydenham Hill, London. These are full-size copies of the great sphinx from Tanis in the Louvre, Paris. [Image courtesy of Barry Welch]

and arrived in November of 1828. Champollion personally examined it when he inventoried the Louvre collection in 1830.

Today the Louvre colossal sphinx sits in its own subterranean chamber, the "Crypt of the Sphinx," beneath the museum. In terms of its preservation, this sphinx is in some respects the opposite of the Philadelphia sphinx. The Louvre sphinx has a more heavily damaged body and base but a beautifully preserved head. In contrast, the body of the Philadelphia sphinx is in pristine condition, while its eroded head dramatically shows the effects of time.

The great sphinx of Tanis was not the only sphinx to go to Paris as part of the Salt Collection in 1828. Another colossal sphinx often called the Louvre "Lesser Sphinx" also came from Tanis. Like the larger sphinx, the Louvre Lesser Sphinx is a Middle Kingdom statue that was reused by later pharaohs. It weighs only 8 tons. Both the great and lesser Louvre sphinxes have matching partners which remained in Egypt and are now in the Cairo Museum. The partner to the Lesser Sphinx stands in the courtyard in front of the Cairo Museum. The partner of the great sphinx used to stand, impressively restored, on a dais outside the Museum, but it was not maintained and now is reduced to fragments in the storeroom of the Cairo Museum.

The Louvre colossal sphinx has an interesting history connected with the interest in ancient Egypt—sometimes called "Egyptomania"—that swept Europe during the 19th century. The Louvre sphinx was a "sphinx model" in 1850 during the construction of the famous Crystal Palace in London. Built for the Great Exhibition of 1851, the Crystal Palace contained an impressive Egyptian Hall with immense figures of seated pharaohs, modeled after the four seated statues of the temple of Ramses II at Abu Simbel. In front of the seated colossi was an avenue of sphinxes all produced from a cast of the one in the Louvre. The damaged elements of the original were restored in the copies and painted to give a semblance of the original appearance of the great sphinx from Tanis.

After the Great Exhibition of 1851, the Crystal Palace was deconstructed and moved from Hyde Park to Sydenham Hill in south London. It reopened in 1854 with an even grander arrangement and with cast concrete versions of the Louvre sphinx guarding the entrance. In 1936, the Crystal Palace burned to the ground leaving few remnants. Still standing today, however, are the sphinxes, testifying to the passion for things Egyptian that developed in the Victorian Period.

7.88.

The Colossal Sphinxes of St. Petersburg

In 1832, just four years after the Louvre had acquired its colossal sphinx, two magnificent granite sphinxes arrived in St. Petersburg, Russia, as a gift to Tsar Nicholas I. These sphinxes were installed on the embankment of the Neva River in front of the Winter Palace of the Russian tsars (now the Hermitage Museum). The St. Petersburg sphinxes date to the reign of Amenhotep III, pharaoh of the 18th Dynasty, and originally decorated that king's mortuary temple at Thebes (modern Luxor) in southern Egypt.

The St. Petersburg sphinxes were discovered in 1831 by an Italian excavator, Giovanni d'Athanasi, who was excavating in Upper Egypt on behalf of Henry Salt, the British Consul General and the same man who had moved the Louvre colossal sphinx from Tanis in 1825. D'Athanasi discovered the two sphinxes about 600 feet behind the famous "Colossi of Memnon," the seated figures of Amenhotep III still standing at the main pylon gateway of Amenhotep III's temple. The two sphinxes originally must have guarded one of the inner gateways of the badly destroyed temple. D'Athanasi was evidently proud of his achievement in moving these monstrous statues. He described their transport to the Nile as follows:

> *The two sphinxes which were discovered at the temple of Memnon have been sold to Russia. These colossal pieces are the most magnificent and weighty that have ever been removed to the European continent from Egypt. The head of the younger Memnon, of which Belzoni boasted its enormous size is nothing in comparison with these sphinxes. Mr. Belzoni in the account of his travels boasts of having removed a monolith weighing twenty or twenty-five thousand pounds; but what would he have said if he had seen these two sphinxes, each of which weighs two hundred and fifty thousand pounds, and had he known that the spot on which they stood was farther from the sea than was the head of the younger Memnon? He would have been overwhelmed with astonishment on learning that in less than a month*

these two sphinxes were removed from the place they were found in, behind the two colossi, to that where I shipped them by the sycamore trees. I took less than three hours to deposit each of them in the vessel.

— Giovanni d'Athanasi, *A Brief Account of the Researches and Discoveries in Upper Egypt Made under the Direction of Henry Salt Esq.*, London, 1836

The project of moving these huge sphinxes in 1832 is a story that deserves its own book. These sphinxes are larger than any others to have left Egypt. Moreover, there are two of them. And they were moved in the early 1800s in the days of sailing ships rather than steam ships, as had helped considerably in the journey of the Penn Museum's sphinx to Philadelphia in 1913. It should be noted, however, that d'Athanasi in his account greatly exaggerated their weight. His statement that they each weighed 250,000 pounds would make them 125 tons each and both much heavier than the Great Alabaster Sphinx at Memphis. Their weight is not entirely known, but is probably around 35 tons based on their dimensions.

The sphinxes in St. Petersburg are now the northernmost of those to leave Egypt and the only ones displayed outside (by comparison, the Penn Museum sphinx only stayed outdoors for three years). Considering the harsh winters of northern Russia, and the amount of time they have been there, it is remarkable that they remain in almost perfect condition.

7.89. Sphinxes of Amenhotep III on the Neva River embankment near the Winter Palace, St. Petersburg. This 1835 painting, by Maksim Vorobyov (1787-1855), "Sphinxes lining a quay in front of St Petersburg Academy of Arts," was made just three years after the sphinxes arrived in St. Petersburg. [Public domain image; source is http://commons.wikimedia.org/wiki/File:Sphinxes.jpg]

7.90. View of the St. Petersburg colossal sphinxes opposite the Hermitage Museum. [Image courtesy of Flickr.com/Russian Brothers]

7.91. St. Petersburg colossal sphinx with its double crown. [Image courtesy of Konstantin M. Koryakoff]

7.92. Limestone block originally from the mortuary temple of Amenhotep III at Thebes; it was reused in the temple of Merenptah where it was recovered by Flinders Petrie. [UPM object # E2096]

Before we journey onwards in the world of sphinxes there is an interesting object in the Egyptian collection of the Penn Museum that is related to the colossal sphinxes in St. Petersburg. This is a decorated block which Flinders Petrie excavated at Thebes in southern Egypt (Fig. 7.92). The block was part of the division material from Petrie's work for the Egypt Exploration Fund in 1897. Petrie discovered the block reused in the Theban mortuary temple of pharaoh Merenptah of the 19th Dynasty (he reused a lot of material, including labeling the Penn Museum sphinx with his own name).

However, this block originally came from the mortuary temple of Amenhotep III: it has the cartouches of Amenhotep III on it. It was from the site today called Kom el-Heitan, and it is precisely the same place where d'Athanasi excavated the St. Petersburg sphinxes. The block is the left half of a huge doorway lintel, originally 8 feet across. It shows two sphinxes, each on a podium, with decorative collars and wearing the double crown. The sphinxes face inwards holding the cartouches of the pharaoh between their paws. Behind them are images of the goddesses Wadjet (left) and Nekhbet (on missing side). The sphinx pair on this block in the Penn Museum are identical in appearance to the ones now in St. Petersburg, complete with the double crown. The Philadelphia block may even be a representation of those sphinxes from the temple of Amenhotep III in which they originally stood.

Sphinxes Turn Up in Strange Places

There are some places where you might not be surprised to encounter a sphinx. It is not unusual to find modern versions of Egyptian sphinxes used as monuments in cemeteries, or adorning buildings constructed from the 1830s–1930s in the United States. Other locations, such as a Las Vegas casino, might seem a little more incongruous. The sphinx is a symbol of the exotic and an icon of ancient Egypt. Sphinx imagery usually goes hand in hand with the term "Egyptomania," which describes the modern fascination with ancient Egypt. For centuries, the lure of ancient Egypt has inspired artists, designers, and decorators. This is not a new phenomenon; we know that interest in collecting objects with Egyptian motifs began as early as the Roman period when wealthy Romans decorated their villas with Egypt-inspired elements.

Interest in ancient Egypt soared during the Napoleonic era when scientists and artists accompanied Napoleon to Egypt and recorded their experiences. Shortly thereafter, in 1822, Champollion was able to use the Rosetta Stone (discovered in 1799 by Napoleon's troops) to decipher hieroglyphic writing, and scholars were able to begin to read hieroglyphs for the first time in over 1500 years.

Serious scientific work in Egypt began during the latter part of the Victorian era and is typified by the work of W.M. Flinders Petrie who was active in Egypt from 1880–1924. With all of these new archaeological discoveries made by Petrie and his contemporaries, ancient Egypt again entered the imagination of the West. The discovery of King Tutankhamun's tomb in 1922 ushered in a craze for all things ancient Egyptian—from furniture to clothing, jewelry to housewares, Egyptian motifs were all the rage. Later, Hollywood helped fuel the fire with a series of films set in ancient Egypt including "The Egyptian" (1954), "Land of the Pharaohs" (1955), and of course, the Egyptian epic of all times, the 1963 "Cleopatra" with Elizabeth Taylor and Richard Burton. Movies like "The Mummy" (1992) and "The Scorpion King" (2002) continue to introduce ancient Egypt to a new set of moviegoers.

Egyptianizing elements can also be seen in the architecture of cities around the world and downtown Philadelphia is no exception. Egyptian elements are found in the building of the original Wanamaker's department store (now Macy's department store), the Egyptian Hall in the Masonic Temple on Broad Street, on the façade of 508–510 Walnut Street, and even the pyramid-shaped top of the BNY Mellon Center at 1735 Market Street (which houses the aptly named Pyramid Club).

However, not all modern representations of sphinxes are quite so serious or artistic, nor is their use rooted in a historical appreciation of the meaning and symbolism of the ancient Egyptian sphinx. These sphinxes are often described as "kitsch." According to the German philosopher Walter Benjamin (1892–1940), kitsch, unlike art, "offers instantaneous emotional gratification without intellectual effort, without the requirement of distance, without sublimation." Clearly, Benjamin did not view kitsch in a positive light. Alternatively, one could argue that kitsch is a way for the average person to celebrate an individual of the past, a bygone era, or a place that is far away. Kitsch makes all of these things readily accessible and arguably a lot of fun! Let us celebrate some examples of sphinx kitsch.

While the Penn Museum's sphinx is the largest ancient Egyptian sphinx in the Western Hemisphere, it is by no means the largest sphinx in the United States. That honor goes to the large sphinx at the Luxor Hotel and Casino in Las Vegas. The main part of the Luxor hotel is a 30-story pyramid sheathed in dark glass. The tip of the pyramid features a fixed-position spotlight that shoots a 42.3 billion candle power beam straight upwards at night. The hotel is fronted by a 140-foot high obelisk and a 110-foot tall re-creation of the sphinx at Giza. The Great Sphinx is "only" about 63 feet high, so the Las Vegas sphinx dwarfs the real thing. But, then again, the real Great Sphinx is also 4,500 years old. Will the Las Vegas sphinx make it to such a venerable old age?

7.93. Erected in 1872, the American Sphinx in Mount Auburn Cemetery, Cambridge, Massachusetts, is a monument to those who died in the American Civil War. [Public domain image; source is http://en.wikipedia.org/wiki/Martin_Milmore#mediaviewer/File:Mount_Auburn_Cemetery_-_Martin_Milmore_sphinx.jpg]

7.94. One of a pair of sphinxes greets arriving visitors at the Masonic Temple in Philadelphia, which was dedicated in 1873.

7.95.

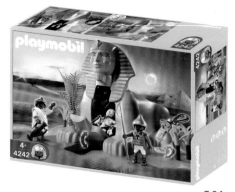

7.96.

7.97.

7.98.

7.99.

7.95. The sphinx at the Luxor Hotel and Casino in Las Vegas. [Image courtesy of Don Houser]

7.96. Ancient Egypt is always popular with children. With this Playmobil set, kids can explore the sphinx from the comforts of their playrooms.

7.97. A treasure trove of sphinx kitsch!

7.98. With sphinx and pyramid salt and pepper shakers, you can always feel like you are dining in ancient Egypt.

7.99. The sphinx has been featured in a number of comic books. It is certain that ancient sphinxes did not shoot laser beams from their eyes.

7.100. A vintage 1980 Ezra Brooks bourbon decanter hand decorated in 24 karat gold and with a Masonic emblem in the sun disk between the wings on the base.

7.101. Do you need a sphinx that always agrees with you? This sphinx bobblehead will always nod "yes" to any question you ask it.

7.100.

7.101.

Sphinxes Make Good Salesmen

When advertisers want to sell products, they seek iconic images to help persuade buyers that the commodity they are selling will deliver what the advertisement promises. For well over 100 years, advertisers of everything from cigarettes to soda, toilets to typewriter paper have relied upon the image of the sphinx to attract the consumer's attention. Vintage ads from the 1920s, 30s, and 40s often depict a sphinx (the most popular being the Great Sphinx at Giza). The sphinx is a convenient "strong and silent type:" you can make it say anything you want it to!

What messages do these ads wish to send? In some cases, the appearance of the sphinx may be used to offer a hint of the exotic, or as an icon for Egypt itself. The advertisements using sphinx imagery often highlight the longevity and durability of the sphinx. Sometimes the sphinx's silent and stoic nature fits with the particular products being offered.

7.102. Egypt is exotic and in the past smoking was seen as something exotic and stylish. In the early 1900s, the Egyptian Tobacco Industry was a major exporter of cigarettes worldwide. Many examples exist of vintage Egyptian-themed cigarette tins. Here a stylized Great Sphinx and two pyramids decorate the lid of this tin.

7.103. Citrus labels from the 1880s–1950s often featured images of exotic locales, ancient monuments, and famous figures from history. These labels were affixed to wooden crates that were sent off to markets. The attractive colorful labels helped growers, packers, and shippers market their produce across the United States. Here we see two "Sphinx" brand citrus labels and a "Cleopatra" label with two small sphinxes used as decorative motifs.

7.102.

7.103.

7.104.

7.106.

7.107.

How to make a Sphinx talk

AMONG your friends there is probably a quiet, reserved fellow who's practically a sphinx when it comes to praising anything.

Well, next time he drops in, serve him a highball made with Four Roses.

We sincerely believe that after the first sip, the "sphinx" will speak right up and say that he's never tasted a whiskey like Four Roses.

That's because Four Roses is an exclusive combination of specially distilled whiskies, selected to achieve a smooth, mellow *distinctively different* flavor.

Nor has the quality of Four Roses been changed. It is still the same great whiskey it was before the war.

FOUR ROSES

The same great whiskey today as before the war

• • •

A blend of straight whiskies— 90 proof. Frankfort Distillers Corporation, New York City.

7.105.

7.104. The sphinx is silent. A desirable feature in toilets is a silent flush. With this 1920 advertisement, Maddock toilets celebrated being the "first in America to make the silent action closet."

7.105. Have a friend who is quiet and reserved like the sphinx? This 1945 advertisement suggests to make him talk, serve him some Four Roses whiskey.

7.106 Advertisers often include promotional collectibles with their products. Starting in the 1840s, the Liebig Company produced beef extracts and stock cubes, and beautifully illustrated trading cards were included with the purchase of the product. This card (ca. 1900) features a fanciful illustration of a royal procession passing in front of a sphinx.

7.107. In 1923, even the inscrutable sphinx would smile when given some delicious, creamy, and sweet Honey Scotch candy.

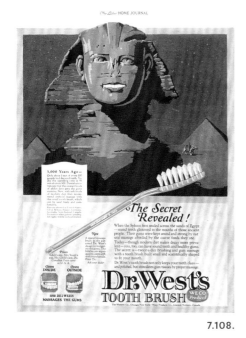

7.108.

THE STABILITY OF METLIFE IS MONUMENTAL.

We've proven we can stand the test of time. For over 100 years, MetLife has served customers promptly and conscientiously. So come to us for insurance and financial services. We plan to be around for centuries to come. For more information, call your MetLife representative.

GET MET. IT PAYS.
◆ MetLife®

7.109.

7.110.

7.112.

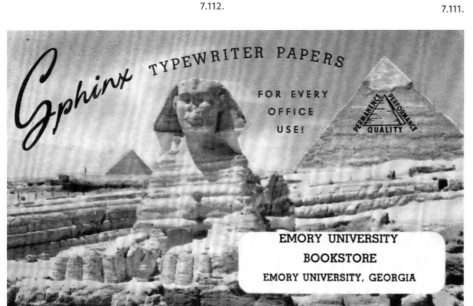

7.111.

7.113.

7.108. Sphinxes always seem to have secrets. This 1924 advertisement for Dr. West's toothbrushes reveals what that secret might be. The ancient Egyptian's diet was such that not many people had tooth decay. With one of these special toothbrushes, you can smile like the sphinx did 5,000 years ago!

7.109. From its desert perch on the Giza plateau, the Great Sphinx is a symbol of stability. In 1990, the equally iconic and beloved cartoon character Snoopy cast aside some of his canine tendencies and posed like a sphinx to help advertise the services of the long-lived MetLife company.

7.110. The refreshing taste of Pepsi Cola is able to make the silent sphinx sing in this 1947 advertisement.

7.111. Oddly enough, the sphinx has even been used to sell acne medication! The desert sun can be drying, and so can other types of acne medicines. In this 1980 ad, Topex promises not to make your face feel as dry as a sphinx's.

7.112. Another canine, this time a dog associated with Hush Puppies brand shoes, took to posing like a sphinx while advertising the durability of that brand of shoe in this 1994 advertisement in Spanish.

7.113. Three characteristics of the sphinx— permanence, performance and quality—are shared by the "Sphinx" brand typewriter paper. Too bad the Egyptians used papyrus, not paper, as writing material.

Getting to Know the Sphinx

8

One Big Cat

You might be tempted to say a sphinx is just a giant hunk of rock. Sure, the Egyptians sculpted it into a lion with a pharaoh's head, but what more is there to say? Aside from its interesting history, the Penn Museum Sphinx has lots to tell us about Egyptian culture, society, writing, religious beliefs, and technology.

We can pose many questions about the Sphinx: some easily answered, and some more difficult to answer conclusively. In this chapter we will examine the statue itself, looking at where and how it was carved, and how much it weighs. We will study the inscriptions on the Sphinx and discuss their significance. Was the Sphinx painted? Did it once have a crown? And who originally carved it? For, there is evidence on the statue that it did not originally belong to Ramses II, but to some earlier pharaoh.

Let us begin our look at the Sphinx by examining some of the features of its carving. Over thousands of years of creating sphinxes, the sculptors of ancient Egypt developed some interesting conventions in the way they represented the combination of lion body with human head. Few sculptors would have ever had the opportunity to see a living lion, although familiarity with the omnipresent small domestic cats may have helped in understanding a big cat's physique.

Sphinx sculptors tended to learn from and copy styles of portrayal handed down over generations from master to apprentice. We do not know much about the details of how sphinxes were copied and sculpted. However, many of them are artistic masterpieces. You have to suspect that there must have been some specialized sculptors who had a reputation for their sphinx artistry: the ones who as students really aced "Sphinx Carving 101."

One of the artistic elements of the Sphinx that you immediately notice are the powerful-looking paws. Although the Sphinx is resting, or recumbent, it looks like it might easily rise up and attack with its huge claws. This is something sphinx sculptors wanted to emphasize. Lions, like all felines, have five toes on each foot. Four of the toes are up front, but the fifth—the equivalent of our thumb—is farther back, on the inside of the paw. Viewing a recumbent lion's paw from the front, it appears to have only four toes because the fifth one is hidden. Sphinx sculptors idealized the actual form of the front paws to make the toes and claws more prominent. They shifted the inner "thumb" forward so that most sphinxes

---

ON PAGE 195

8.1. Diagram showing the measurements of the Penn Museum's Sphinx.

8.2. Ready to pounce! The powerful paws and sharp claws are prominently on display on the Sphinx.

8.3. The Sphinx's left paw.

8.4. Actual lion paws have four toes in front and one on the inside. [Image courtesy of Emmanuel Keller]

8.5. The Sphinx's tail curling over the right haunch and onto its rump.

8.6. Not all sphinxes are pretty. The sculptor of this "rustic"-looking limestone sphinx won no prizes in sphinx-carving! Still it is a sphinx and his tail curls up properly on the right side of its body. From Memphis, excavated by the Coxe Expedition in 1916. [UPM object # 29-75-422]

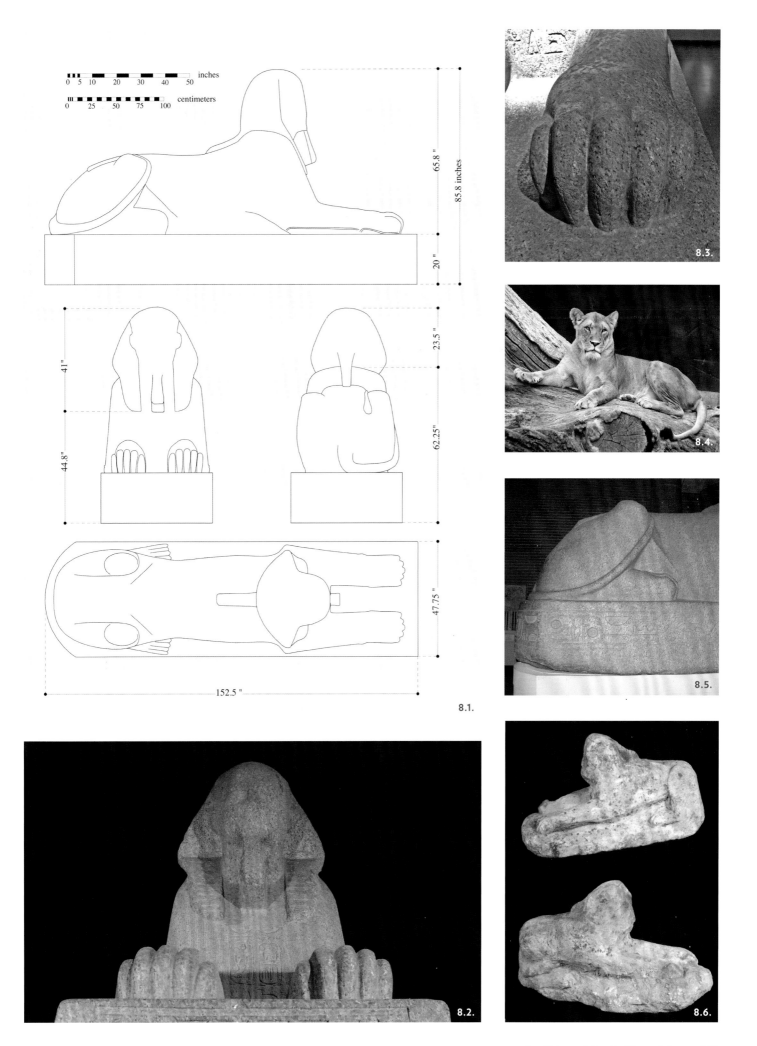

inches
0 5 10 20 30 40 50

centimeters
0 25 50 75 100

85.8 inches

65.8 "

20 "

41"

44.8"

23.5 "

62.25"

47.75 "

152.5 "

8.1.

8.2.

8.3.

8.4.

8.5.

8.6.

you see have five toes prominently on display on each front paw. This makes the sphinx's paws a little bigger, especially with the addition of the claws, which sculptors usually carved on the front of each toe.

If you walk around to look at the Sphinx's hindquarters, you will see that he has a long, impressive tail draped over his rump. Another artistic convention is the way the tail appears. Whether it is a colossal sphinx in granite or a miniature sphinx in terracotta, sphinx sculptors nearly always show the sphinx with its tail wrapped up around the right side of its body (there are only one or two aberrant left-wrapped sphinx tails, mostly of the Ptolemaic Period, among hundreds of right-wrapped ones). Why this is the case is hard to explain. Often sphinxes are placed to balance each other in front of temple pylons or along sphinx avenues. Therefore, you might logically expect that half of the world's sphinxes would have their tails on the left, and half on the right. However, that is not the case. Sphinx artists followed the artistic convention that the tail should curve up on the right side of the body.

The sculptors of this colossal Sphinx really captured the essence of a big cat in stone. How did they do that? Let us look at where the Sphinx was "born:" the granite quarries of Elephantine at the southern end of Egypt.

The Granite Quarries of Elephantine

As we saw earlier, the Penn Museum's colossal Sphinx once stood in front of a temple dedicated to Ptah-Tatenen at Memphis. However, the Sphinx's history goes back before its time at Memphis. For one thing, it is likely the Sphinx originally belonged to another pharaoh and Ramses II altered it (something Ramses the Great was well known for). Regardless of which pharaoh originally carved it, however, we can be certain that the sculpture originated in the great granite quarries of Aswan in Egypt's deep south, 500 miles (805 km) south of Memphis.

The stone used for the Sphinx is the characteristic red granite of Aswan that Ancient Egyptians especially prized for the architecture of their great temples and the statues that decorated them. The ancient town at Aswan the Egyptians called Abu, meaning "Elephant island." We know it as Elephantine. It is the northernmost of a group of islands that together form the First Cataract of the Nile, a rugged landscape characterized by outcroppings of hard granite and other igneous stones that interrupt the northward flow of the river. For that reason, early in Egypt's history Elephantine developed as a frontier town and gateway to the land of Nubia that lies immediately south of the First Cataract. Its other importance was for its stone. Over thousands of years, the Egyptian pharaohs developed numerous quarries around Elephantine, but the main granite quarries are an extensive area on the eastern side of the Nile, extending south and east of Elephantine. It is from these quarries that workers cut the Penn Museum Sphinx.

How do we know that the granite of the Penn Museum Sphinx must be from Aswan? Simply put, that is the only place in Egypt where there are outcroppings of granite. Geologically speaking, Egypt is a very young country. Most of what

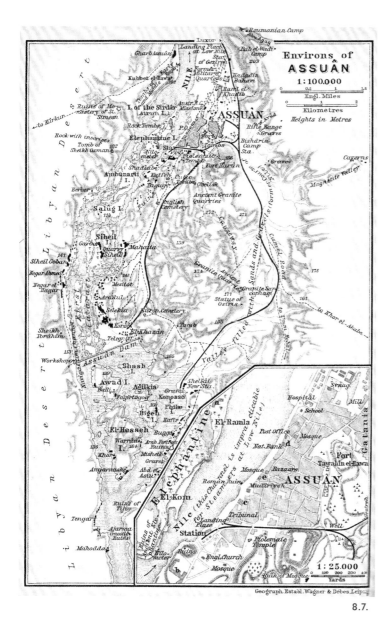

8.7.

8.8.

8.9.

8.10.

8.7. Aswan and the First Cataract, after Baedeker's *Egypt* (1914). The granite quarries from where the sphinx comes are located on the eastern side, about two miles from the Nile River.

8.8. The unfinished obelisk in the granite quarries at Aswan. [Image courtesy of John and Linda McMackin]

8.9. An unfinished sphinx, abandoned in the sandstone quarries of Gebel el-Silsila north of Aswan. Obelisks, sphinxes, and other large stone sculptures were often rough-cut in the quarry and then fine-dressed after transport. Sometimes, however, there were flaws in the stone or damage that led the masons to abandon their project. [Image courtesy of Chris Irie]

8.10. Artisans at work finishing stone statues, including a sphinx. These scenes are in the tomb of the vizier Rekhmire at Thebes dating to the 18th Dynasty. [Image courtesy of David P. Silverman]

is now Egypt was once under the Tethys Sea. Dense layers of limestone formed during this period, and when the sea receded and the Nile began flowing (ca. 15 million years ago), the river cut rapidly through the soft limestone and created the characteristic soaring limestone cliffs of the Nile Valley. The First Cataract where Aswan is located is the southern limit of the reach of the Tethys Sea. Here more ancient igneous (volcanic) granite protrudes up to the surface, as well as metamorphic stones like sandstone and quartzite.

There are different color varieties of granite in and around the First Cataract region but the red "Aswan granite," often called Syenite, is typical of the heavily used quarries on the east bank near Elephantine. The close proximity of these quarries to the Nile made it easy to load stone for monument building onto barges where they could then be floated northwards to various building sites in Egypt.

Egypt's stone quarries are wonderful places to find all kinds of abandoned monuments, as well as ancient inscriptions and graffiti left by the officials and workers responsible for the building projects of the pharaohs. The most famous of the abandoned monuments is a huge obelisk that sits partially carved in the Aswan granite quarries (Fig. 8.8). This massive obelisk, still rooted to the bedrock, developed a crack as workers quarried it, resulting in its abandonment (if completed it would have been Egypt's largest obelisk). North of Aswan in the sandstone quarries of Gebel el-Silsila we find an abandoned sphinx that was roughed out by ancient stone sculptors but left in the quarry (Fig. 8.9). Fissures through the rock suggest that, like the obelisk at Aswan, this unfinished sphinx had defects in the stone so the carvers abandoned it.

The unfinished sphinx at Gebel el-Silsila gives us a good indication of how the Penn Museum Sphinx may have looked when it left the quarry at Elephantine. Ancient builders were practical men. Why move more stone than you need to? We know that workers generally roughed out sculptures first in the quarry, lightening the block of unnecessary mass. The stoneworkers would have started with a rectangular block but then chiseled away the basic shape for the statue using a grid. The unfinished statue could then be transported to the building site and its final carving and decoration finished there.

In the case of the unfinished sphinx at Gebel Silsila, notice how the beard and crown are still in rough, blocky shape. The sphinx's front legs and paws have not yet been cut from the base. This same approach would have been important for the Penn Museum Sphinx since the block from which it was cut would originally have been at least 13 feet (4 m) long, 4 feet (1.2 m) wide, and over 7 feet (2.1m) high, weighing in at something like 60,000 pounds (30 tons).

How Much Does the Sphinx Weigh?

The sculptors of the Sphinx would have started with a huge block and carved it down to create the statue. How much stone did they remove, and what is the weight of the Sphinx? Here is an odd fact. A hundred years ago, the Penn Museum Sphinx traveled thousands of miles from Egypt to America. Many

QUARTZ
(white crystals)
silicon dioxide

ORTHOCLASE
(red crystals)
(KAISi3O8)

BIOTITE MICA
(black flecks)

8.11. The composition of the Sphinx's characteristic Aswan granite.

people were involved in moving it using hand power, cranes, trains, and a ship. At least one horse-drawn wagon was used: the wagon that hauled the Sphinx across the Schuylkill River to the Museum. Despite all that, until recently we did not actually have a precise figure for its weight. When Flinders Petrie first wrote to the Museum's director, George Byron Gordon, about the Sphinx he mentioned that the statue weighed about 11 tons. Later on, the company who moved the Sphinx to the Suez Canal, Congdon and Co., stated that it weighed "at least 12 tons." In both cases these tons are probably British tons (of 2,250 pounds), rather than American tons (of 2,000 pounds). Therefore, 11 and 12 British tons are equal to 12.5 or 13.5 American tons. We know that the various people involved in moving it were consistently dismayed when they saw the stone monster and realized how much it weighed; they all complained and charged extra fees due to the Sphinx's size.

When the Sphinx arrived in Philadelphia, the newspapers reported the Sphinx to be about 11 or 12 tons. However, in one letter Director Gordon stated the Sphinx to be 14 tons. Later when the Sphinx was moved indoors, the riggers stated it to be 14 tons. Why all of the disagreement on its weight? It is not surprising that no one ever actually weighed the statue directly.

In order to calculate the weight of the Sphinx accurately it is essential first to know something about the geology of its material. The Sphinx, as we have seen, comes from a single block of Aswan granite or Syenite. Granite is an igneous stone formed from volcanic magma and composed of a group of different minerals that formed crystals as the magma cooled. There are many varieties of granite and the relative proportions of its component minerals vary a lot depending on local geology.

The main components of granite are orthoclase, quartz, and biotite (a dark-colored form of mica). Around Egypt's First Cataract, there are different grades of granitic rock that vary in appearance and weight. The Penn Museum Sphinx is made of coarse-grained rose-colored granite in which the pink crystals (orthoclase) are quite large (giving it the appealing color the Egyptians favored). These are embedded in a surrounding matrix of smaller white crystals (quartz) with flecks of biotite. Granite of this particular type has a specific gravity (mass per volume) of 2.64 grams per cubic centimeter. Converted to English measures that equals 164.8 pounds per cubic foot of granite.

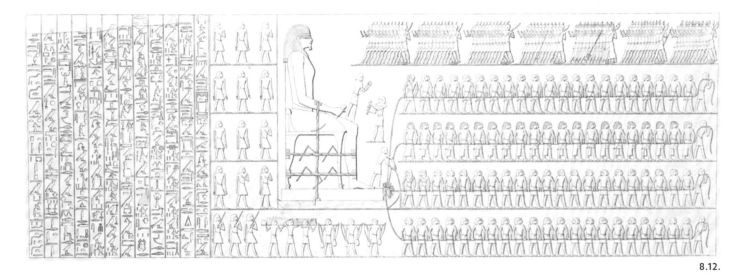

8.12.

8.12. The Egyptians were masters at moving colossal stone statues. Normally statues were lashed to sledges and pulled by as many men as required. In order to reduce the weight, sculptors normally roughed out statues at the quarry site. This scene shows a statue of Djehutyhotep II, governor of Bersheh, 12th Dynasty. The Egyptians would have moved the sphinx in the same way. [From Griffith and Newberry, *El Bershesh I* (1893), pl. xv]

In order to determine the Sphinx's total weight the next step is to calculate the total volume of granite in the statue. This is not an easy task since the Sphinx is a quite irregular shape. The Sphinx today is 12.66 feet long, 3.83 feet wide, and 7.12 feet high. The original rectangular block from which sculptors carved the Sphinx must have been *at least* 345.23 cubic feet (although probably larger since the quarrymen would have cut a larger, rough-cut block down to achieve those final, finished dimensions). At 164.8 pounds per cubic foot of granite, the minimum weight of the original block was 56,894 pounds (close to 28.5 tons).

To calculate the weight of the finished statue as it exists today, we can start with the easiest part, the Sphinx's base. This is primarily a rectangular slab but with a slightly rounded end at the back of the Sphinx. The main section measures 11.67 by 3.82 by 1.67 feet. Multiplying these together, we find that the main rectangular section of the base has a volume of 74.45 cubic feet. Add to this the curved end which projects out another 12 inches. The circular segment at the end has a volume of 2.85 cubic feet for a total of 77.3 cubic feet. At 164.8 pounds per cubic foot, the base alone weighs 12,740 pounds (6.37 tons). Of course, you might observe that the removal of the sunken relief hieroglyphs along the edges will reduce the actual weight of the base slightly but let's ignore that for the moment. You will already have observed that with a base weight of over 6 tons you only need 5 more tons for the Sphinx body itself to make it over the original estimate of 11 tons. So, what does the Sphinx's body weigh?

Because the Sphinx has a very complex geometry the simplest approach to estimate the volume of the figure is to subdivide the Sphinx's body into a series of simple shapes—stacks of slabs, prisms, cylinders, and spheres—fitted within the contours of the body. If you fit these shapes in slightly below the actual surface the resulting volume figures multiplied by the specific gravity for granite give you a minimum weight. Of course, the more finely grained the shapes are the more exact the volume estimate will be. A rough fitting of shapes to the Sphinx's body (leaving a lot of volume unaccounted for) produces a weight of 6 tons. But the volume unaccounted for easily adds another ton or two. These rough and ready calculations suggest the Sphinx is over 12 tons.

A similar approach to the Sphinx's volume can be taken by starting with the overall dimensions of the Sphinx and estimating the volume of material that was taken away to achieve the existing statue. In 2012, Penn Museum docent Dr. Benjamin Ashcom became interested in the weight of the Sphinx. He made

measurements on the base and upper parts of the statue in order to estimate how much volume the ancient sculptors removed. (This is the volume of the tailings, or waste material, discarded by the sculptors.) We can calculate the amount of stone removed and then subtract from the overall original block weight of 56,894 pounds. Students in Philadelphia's Lea School have spent many hours running their own calculations using this technique. Dr. Ashcom and the Lea School students' calculations put the Sphinx at a slightly higher weight of 15 tons.

So, 11, 12, 14, or 15 tons? No matter how you measure it the Sphinx is a colossal piece of granite, but careful measurement helps to define how colossal it is. Now more than a hundred years after the Sphinx arrived in Philadelphia we have a more accurate way to measure the weight of the Sphinx. Let us examine how modern technology can help.

Laser Scanning Solves the Mystery

As we have seen, the sphinx was never accurately weighed, and its irregular shape makes calculating its volume very difficult. Fortunately, there are modern techniques that allow us now to accurately calculate its weight without even touching it. In 2014 we used laser scanning to create a three-dimensional model of the sphinx. Using a Light Distance and Ranging (LIDAR) instrument we scanned the sphinx. This technique creates a three dimensional scan that can be rotated or viewed from any angle. With some further work a three dimensional scan of this type can then be transformed to a geometric model that permits one to precisely measure the volume of a complex object like the sphinx.

Laser scanning uses a rapidly rotating laser to measure distances to surfaces with tremendous accuracy. 3D laser scanners can measure millions of points in a short period of time. So many points are taken that shapes of objects are easily resolved by means of "point clouds." To survey the sphinx we used a Faro 3D Focus instrument. The sphinx was scanned from a number of different locations in order to allow the

8.14.

8.15.

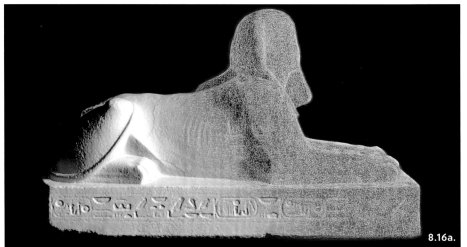

8.16a.

8.16b.

8.14. Josef Wegner scanning the sphinx in June 2014.

8.15. Old meets new: the sphinx and the LIDAR scanner used to make a 3D model.

8.16a, b. A 3D rendering showing the polygonal mesh fitted to the front of the sphinx. This image shows only 100,000 polygons. The actual volume calculation is based on a mesh of two million polygons.

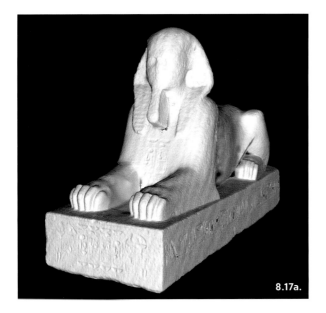

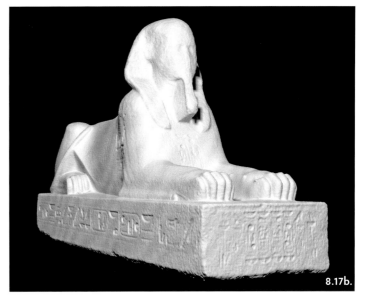

8.17a.   8.17b.

instrument to measure points over its entire body. Stationary white spheres were placed around the area in order to allow the different scans to be linked together. The point clouds from multiple scans were then merged together to create a single 3D model of the sphinx.

Penn Egyptology graduate student Paul Verhelst processed the sphinx scan data and created a final model of the sphinx. Although the point cloud that resulted from the scans can easily be viewed and rotated to any angle, using that data to calculate the sphinx's volume required some additional steps. The point cloud had to be converted into a geometric model that could be usable in Computer Aided Design (CAD) software.

Ross Davison, took the scan data that Paul had processed and cleaned the point cloud with a program Bentley's Pointools. Then, using a second computer program, Geomagic, he converted the point cloud into a polygonal mesh. The modeling of complex three dimensional shapes using polygons and NURBS (non-uniform rational basis spline) surfaces is the basis for 3D modeling and computer animation. In the case of the sphinx there were a few small areas where the laser scanning had not able to read points (like the base, and top of the head). These had to be extrapolated from the existing point cloud. Once that was done, however, the volume of the final mesh could then be calculated with great accuracy. The model created by wrapping a surface to the point cloud is composed of a mesh of two million polygons: a very accurate 3D model of the sphinx. From that Ross generated the measure of the sphinx's volume: 4.33 cubic meters.

Armed finally with a precise measure of the sphinx's volume we may now calculate the weight of the statue with a high degree of accuracy. As we have seen, the Aswan granite from which the sphinx is carved has a density of 164.8 pounds per cubic foot. The sphinx's metric volume is 4.33 cubit meters which equals 152.93 cubic feet. Multiplying this volume with the value of 164.8 pounds per cubic foot, the sphinx weighs in at 25,203 pounds (11,432 kg). At 2,000 pounds per ton this means the sphinx weighs exactly 12.6 tons.

Modern technology now allows us to see that the previous estimates were not too far off, but a bit on the low side. 12.6 tons is almost exactly half of the original size of the granite block from which the sphinx was carefully carved many thousands of years ago.

8.17a, b. 3D renderings of the sphinx created by a wire mesh fitted over the original point cloud. This 3D model is composed of two million polygons that very accurately wrap around the sphinx's complicated contours.

8.18.

8.18. The inscription on the base of the sphinx is symmetrical: it begins at the front of each side and ends on the curved back below the sphinx's rump.

8.19. At Abydos, Flinders Petrie found a pair of grave stele inscribed with the name of King Qa'a of the 1st Dynasty (ca. 3000–2800 BCE). The Penn Museum houses one of the pair. The king's name is found within the rectangular frame above the niched palace façade. A figure of the falcon god Horus sits atop the *serekh*. [UPM object # E6878]

What Does the Sphinx Say?

After the sculpting process was finished, an important step to giving the Sphinx identity was carving the inscriptions on it. The Egyptians abhorred the idea of statues and other images that were not given an individual identity with names and labels. What do the texts say?

The Penn Museum Sphinx's facial features are eroded away, yet it can still tell us something about the king whose visage it once bore. The Sphinx has an inscription running around its base that gives us the full five-fold name (or titulary) of King Ramses II. For much of Egyptian history, each ancient Egyptian ruler had more than just one name. By the time of the 5th Dynasty of the Old Kingdom, the ancient Egyptian king's full titulary consisted of five names. This tradition continued throughout the rest of pharaonic history. While many kings—like the eleven who bore the name Ramses—shared the same birth name, the full titulary for each king was distinct.

Why did the king have so many names and what was the purpose of these names? The full ancient Egyptian royal titulary reflected aspects of the king's reign and his role as ruler. One can think of these names almost as a king's "mission statement" because the statements found in the names conveyed the

8.19.

ruler's goals and his intended purpose as pharaoh. The king adopted the first four names upon taking the throne; the fifth name was the name he was given at birth. Significant relationships the king had with various deities could also be expressed in the title. For example, kings are called "beloved" of a particular deity, such as Maat, the goddess of truth, or Amun, a creator god who rose to the level of preeminent state god during the New Kingdom.

8.20. Cartouche of Merenptah from one of the columns from his palace excavated by the Penn Museum's Coxe Expedition and now in Memphis.

 The Horus Name

The first of the five names was the Horus name. This is the earliest of the king's names to appear in inscriptions and was traditionally enclosed within a rectangular frame known as a *serekh*, or "palace façade." The design at the bottom of the *serekh* echoed the form and design of the architecture found on palaces and other important royal buildings of the Early Dynastic Period. The *serekh* is topped by a figure of a falcon representing the god Horus. As king on earth, the pharaoh was a living representative of the god Horus, the son of Isis and Osiris.

The Horus name of many pharaohs incorporates the phrase, the "Mighty Bull," a reference to the ruler's strength, power, and potency.

 The Two Ladies Name

The Horus name was followed by the second name, known to us as the "Two Ladies" or *Nebty* name. These two ladies were the patron deities of Upper and Lower Egypt, the vulture goddess Nekhbet and the cobra goddess Wadjet. This name reflects the king's special relationship with these protective goddesses and his role as ruler of a united kingdom consisting of both the North and South of Egypt.

 The Golden Horus Name

The third name was the Golden Horus name. This name first appears in the 4th Dynasty. It may reflect the king's divinity, since gods were believed to have skin made of gold, as well as the triumph of the god Horus over his jealous uncle Seth celebrated in religious texts and stories such the "Contending of Horus and Seth."

The last two names, called the *prenomen* and the *nomen*—or the throne name and birth name—are found in cartouches, ⬭, the protective ovals that encircled a royal name. The Ancient Egyptian word for cartouche was 𓍷𓏤𓏭𓂋, coming from a verb meaning, "to encircle." Often the cartouche is decorated to look like a loop of rope that has been tied in a knot encircling the name. This magical circle would protect the name of the king, and by extension, the king himself.

The nswt-bity *Name (also known as the throne name or the prenomen)*

These hieroglyphs, which read *nswt-bity,* or "King of Upper and Lower Egypt" (literally "he to whom the sedge [plant]and the bee belong"), introduced the king's throne name and expressed the king's rule over the entire land of Egypt. Sometimes the epithet *nb t3.wy* "Lord of the Two Lands" introduces the throne name. The "two lands" referred to are northern and southern Egypt.

The Son of Re Name (also known as the birth name or the nomen)

The phrase "son of Re" (*s3 Rˁ*) usually came before the birth name. The name indicates that the pharaoh was thought to be a son of the sun god, Re. The epithet *nb hˁ.w* "Lord of Appearances" can also precede the birth name.

Most Ancient Egyptian names, both royal and non-royal, had meanings that Egyptologists can translate into words, short phrases, or full sentences. The throne name and birth name of Ramses II can be understood in the following way: the name User-maat-re Setep-en-re means "The Justice of (the sun god) Re is Powerful, Chosen of (the sun god) Re," and the name Ramses means "Born of (the sun god) Re." Mery-amun means "Beloved of (the god) Amun."

The last two names of Ramses's son and successor were Ba-en-re Mery-amun, Merenptah Hetep-her-Maat. His throne name means, "The ba of Re, beloved of Amun." His birth name means, "Beloved of Ptah, Joyous on Truth."

Now that we understand how the king's titulary works, let us take a closer look at the inscriptions on the Sphinx. What we see is that the texts contain the full five-fold titulary of Ramses II. On the front of the Sphinx's base, a symmetrically arranged inscription, meant to be read from the center outwards, contains the last two names (the throne name and birth name) of the king in cartouches.

The central two cartouches in this design give the king's birth name and read, "Lord of Appearances, Ramses Meryamun (*nb hˁ.w mry 'Imn Rˁ-ms-sw*)." On either side of those ovals, the other pair of cartouches gives the throne name of the king: "Lord of the Two Lands, User-maat-re Setep-en-re (*nb t3.wy wsr-m3ˁt-Rˁ stp-n-Rˁ*)."

On either side of the cartouches, in a rectangular *serekh* design, we find the text, "Mighty bull, beloved of Maat (*Ḥr k3 nḫt mry M3ˁt*)."

Depictions of the tutelary goddesses of Egypt appear on either side. These are the "Two Ladies" found in the titulary of the king. The cobra goddess Wadjet guards the left side of the composition and the text reads "Beloved of Wadjet, given life (*mry W3dt di ˁnḫ*)." Wadjet was the protective goddess of Lower Egypt who often wore the Red Crown. Nekhbet, the vulture goddess, guards the right and the text reads, "Beloved of Nekhbet, given life (*mry Nḫbt di ˁnḫ*)." Nekhbet guarded Upper Egypt in the south. She was the goddess of the White Crown and, in some myths, she was called the mother of the king. Together, these two goddesses

8.21. Photograph and drawing of the inscription on the front of the base of the Sphinx. [UPM object # E12326]

8.21.

8.22.

8.22. The goddesses Wadjet and Nekhbet appear together on this pectoral with the cartouche of Ramses II. [Louvre, E79; public domain image; source is http://commons. wikimedia.org/wiki/File:Pectoral_Rameses_II_ Louvre_E79.jpg]

watched over the Two Lands of a united Egypt. The *shen* (*šn*) hieroglyph meaning "eternity" appears before each goddess.

The hieroglyph for the word "sky" appears at the top of the entire inscription field. Another hieroglyph found in the word for "festival" appears under each cartouche.

Now let us look at the inscription on each side of the base. On the proper right side of the base, reading from right to left, we see:

ꜥnḫ Ḥr kꜣ nḫt mry Mꜣꜥt nb tꜣ.wy wsr-mꜣꜥt-rꜥ stp-n-Rꜥ nb ḫꜥ.w Rꜥ-ms-sw mry ꞽmn Ḥr nbw wsr rnp.wt ꜥꜣ nḫt nb tꜣ.wy wsr-mꜣꜥt-Rꜥ stp-n-Rꜥ nb ḫꜥ.w Rꜥ-ms-sw mry ꞽmn mꞽ Rꜥ

> May the Horus, the Mighty Bull, Beloved of Maat, Lord of the Two Lands User-maat-re Setep-en-re, Lord of Appearances, Ramses, Beloved of Amun, the Two Ladies: Defender of Egypt and Binder of the foreign lands, the Lord of the Two Lands, User-maat-re Setep-en-re, Lord of Appearances, Ramses, Beloved of Amun, live like Re.

On the proper left side of the base, the text reads from left to right and we find:

ꜥnḫ Ḥr kꜣ nht Mꜣꜥt nb tꜣ.wy wsr-mꜣꜥt-r-ꜥ stp-n-Rꜥ nb ḫꜥ.w Rꜥ-ms-sw mry ꞽmn Ḥr nbw wsr rnpw.t ꜥꜣ nḫtw nb tꜣ.wy wsr-mꜣꜥt-Rꜥ stp-n-Rꜥ nb ḫꜥ.w Rꜥ-ms-sw mry ꞽmn [mꞽ Rꜥ]

> May the Horus, the Mighty Bull, Beloved of Maat, Lord of the Two Lands User-maat-re Setep-en-re, Lord of Appearances, Ramses, Beloved of Amun, the Golden Horus: Strong of Years and Great of Victories, the Lord of the Two Lands, User-maat-re Setep-en-re, Lord of Appearances, Ramses, Beloved of Amun, live like Re.

Note that the two inscriptions share the signs ⌀ meaning "like Re."

The inscriptions around the base are not the only hieroglyphs on the Sphinx. Other texts appear in three different places. On the chest of the Sphinx, under the false beard, we find the cartouches of Ramses II (Fig. 8.23). On each shoulder of the Sphinx, his son and successor, Merenptah, added his own cartouches (Fig. 8.24).

8.23. The remaining inscriptions on the sphinx can be found on both shoulders. In this case, the cartouches do not belong to Ramses II, but rather to his son, the pharaoh Merenptah: "King of Upper and Lower Egypt, the son of Re: Ba-en-re Mery-amun, Merenptah Hetep-her-Maat *[nsw.] t [bꞽ]ty sꜣ Rꜥ bꜣ-n-Rꜥ mry ꞽmn mry n Ptḥ ḥtp ḥr Mꜣꜥt.*"

8.24. Ramses' nomen and prenomen also appear on the chest of the sphinx: "Lord of the Two Lands, User-maat-re Setep-en-re, Lord of Appearances, Ramses Meryamun, given life forever (*nb tꜣ.wy wsr-mꜣꜥt-Rꜥ stp-n-Rꜥ nb ḫꜥ.w mry ꞽmn Rꜥ-ms-sw dꞽ ꜥnḫ ḏt*)."

8.23.

8.24.

Merenptah and His Sphinx-Tagging Project

Merenptah was the thirteenth son of Ramses II. His father reigned so long (67 years) that twelve of the older princes died before their father. Merenptah was an active pharaoh who fought off an invasion of Libyans in Year 5 of his reign. He built extensively, often completing or adding to monuments of his father, Ramses II. He is also well known for his penchant for adding his own name to earlier monuments and statues. When it came to sphinxes, Merenptah's sculptors seem to have been given the task of systematically tagging each one with the king's name. Virtually every large sphinx then standing in Egypt's temples had the king's name added to its shoulders (buried sphinxes, of course, escaped this royal tattooing project). Many of the colossal sphinxes found at Tanis, including the ones in the Louvre and Cairo Museum, were tagged by Merenptah. Ramses II often added his titulary to the base and chest of the sphinx, Merenptah then followed with his name on one or both shoulders. In this way, the Philadelphia Sphinx looks very consistent with many of the large sphinxes reused in the 19th Dynasty by Ramses II and Merenptah. Often the names of the two pharaohs appear side by side: Ramses II's name in deeply sunk carving, Merenptah's in shallower carving. Part of the explanation for this may have been a filial devotion that Merenptah felt towards his illustrious father.

Another object in the Penn Museum, discussed below, also has inscriptions of Merenptah added to those of Ramses II: a granite column (Fig. 8.36) that tells us something about the reuse of existing monuments during the reigns of Ramses II and his son Merenptah. The addition of inscriptions raises one of the most important questions of all: Did the Sphinx originally belong to Ramses II or did he recarve a sphinx from some earlier pharaoh?

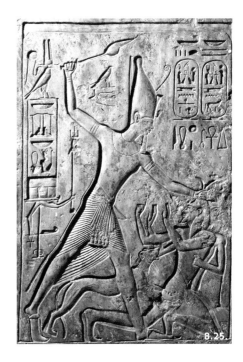

8.25. Pharaoh Merenptah smites his enemies in a scene on a decorated doorjamb from his palace at Memphis, excavated in 1916 by the Coxe Egyptian Expedition and on display beside the Sphinx in the Museum's Egyptian galleries. [UPM object # E17527]

8.26. Like ancient royal graffiti artists, Merenptah's sculptors added the king's name to the sphinx's shoulders.

8.27. A close-up of Merenptah's cartouches.

8.28.

8.28. This sphinx is the companion to the Louvre colossal sphinx. It used to stand reconstructed from fragments in the garden of the Cairo Museum, but is no longer there; the remaining fragments are kept in storage. Its shoulder bears the cartouches of Merenptah. [Cairo JdÉ 37478 + CG639, after H.G. Evers, *Staat aus dem Stein* II, pl. XI]

8.29. The Louvre colossal sphinx of Amenemhat II from Tanis, tagged by Merenptah.

8.30. A close-up of Merenptah's cartouches on the Louvre colossal sphinx.

8.31. The Louvre "Lesser Sphinx" from Tanis, tagged by Merenptah.

8.32. A close-up of Merenptah's cartouches on the Louvre "Lesser Sphinx."

8.33. Sphinxes of Amenemhat III from Tanis in the Cairo Museum, tagged by Merenptah. [Image courtesy of Hans Ollermann]

8.34. A close-up of Merenptah's cartouches on one of the Cairo sphinxes. [Image courtesy of Hans Ollermann]

8.30.

8.29.

8.32.

8.31.

8.34.

8.33.

Was the Sphinx Carved for an Earlier Pharaoh?

With the name of Ramses II on its base and chest and Merenptah's cartouches on the statue's shoulders, we can be sure that this Sphinx once adorned the significant additions that Ramses II and Merenptah made to the temple of Ptah at Memphis where it was found in 1912. In all likelihood, the Sphinx was one of a group of colossal guardian statues in front of the newly constructed temple of Ptah-Tatenen. But, does this mean that Ramses II actually commissioned the Sphinx? Did this Sphinx come into being in the 19th Dynasty, ca. 1200 BCE?

With statues of Ramses II, you always have to be suspicious about whether they were carved for that pharaoh initially, or whether they were appropriated by him from some

earlier king. Ramses II is well known as ancient Egypt's greatest temple builder. He deserves that reputation and he got it not just by building many temples, but also by taking over his predecessors' monuments. An outstanding example of this reuse of earlier statues is the other big Ramses statue in the Penn Museum: a seated figure of Ramses from the city of Herakleopolis. Today it sits upstairs from the Sphinx, in the Upper Egyptian Hall of the Museum's Coxe Wing.

The seated Ramses II is somewhat strange to look at. He has solid, massive-looking legs and a robust, muscular torso. However, his head is much too small for his body. Although you might think the ancient stone carvers made a mistake (perhaps accidentally chipping the head) and had to make the head smaller than they wanted, in fact, there is a better reason the head is so small. This statue originally belonged to an earlier pharaoh, one of the kings of the Middle Kingdom (ca. 2050–1750 BCE), and Ramses II had his sculptors recarve it. They shaved the sides of the throne away (removing earlier inscriptions) and added the titulary of Ramses II. They reworked the head, making it fit the style of Ramses II's official sculptures, but also reducing the head's size relative to its body. This statue was set up in the temple of the local god Herishef at Herakleopolis, which Ramses substantially rebuilt using recycled masonry.

Also in the Penn Museum is another reused part of that same temple: a red granite palmiform column (the capital of the column mimics the appearance of

8.35a, b. Statue of Ramses II (reused from another, earlier pharaoh) came from the city of Herakleopolis. [UPM object # E635]

8.36. This palmiform column (originally dating to the Old Kingdom) was reused by Ramses II at Herakleopolis, in the same temple as the seated statue above. Ramses II's successor, Merenptah, also added his titulary. [UPM object # E636]

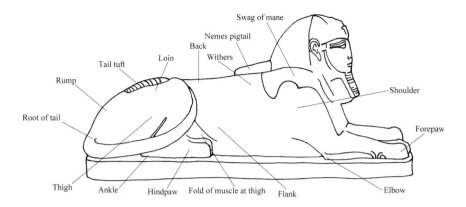

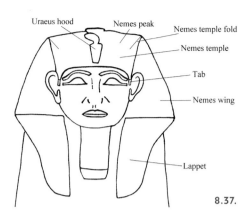

8.37.

8.37. The anatomy of a sphinx. Variations in style and treatment of these various elements can be chronologically important since sculptural style evolved over time. [After Biri Fay, *The Louvre Sphinx* (1996), Figs. 5 and 6]

8.38. A palimpsest inscription: the name of Merenptah inscribed over an earlier pharaoh's name (Amenemhat II) on the chest of the Louvre colossal sphinx.

a palm tree). It has inscriptions of Ramses II and Merenptah but it was originally a column from a temple of the late Old Kingdom (5th–6th Dynasties, ca. 2300–2200 BCE), a thousand years before Ramses II.

Could the Penn Museum Sphinx also have been recarved for Ramses II from a preexisting statue of an earlier pharaoh? Colossal sphinxes were statues ripe for reuse. Sphinxes could easily stand for many centuries in front of temple gateways. But sooner or later a temple would fall into disrepair, or some later king would decide it was time to rebuild or improve a temple's pylon. As a result, what happened was recarving. We see this process very well on the Louvre colossal sphinx, which has been studied in detail by the Egyptologist Biri Fay. The Louvre sphinx, which was found at the site of Tanis in the Nile Delta, had been reused first by king Apophis of the 15th Dynasty (ca. 1600 BCE). Later on Merenptah (ca. 1150 BCE) in the 19th Dynasty took it over, and then Sheshonq I (ca. 950 BCE) of the 22nd Dynasty appropriated it as his own. However, the king that originally carved it was Amenemhat II (ca. 1900 BCE) of the 12th Dynasty. The "lifespan" of the Louvre colossal sphinx extends more than a thousand years and the statue bears the name of four different pharaohs.

In order to determine if a statue is reused we may look for obvious signs of recarving. The clearest indication occurs where there are later inscriptions that were added over the top of earlier ones. This creates a "palimpsest" or series of superimposed inscriptions. That is how we know the Louvre colossal sphinx belonged originally to Amenemhat II, but was reused by three later pharaohs. If, however, the recarving is well done there may be no obvious palimpsest inscriptions. Then we have to look at elements of style—the way the figure is portrayed, or other indicators that reflect sculpture from a certain time period.

The most helpful element for dating royal statues, including sphinxes, is the head since these have the pharaoh's image and reflect sculptural styles of a given time period or reign. For

8.38.

sphinxes, a good indicator is the stripes on the *nemes* crown. In earlier periods (going back to the Great Sphinx at Giza in the 4th Dynasty), the stripes consist of one wide stripe flanked by two thinner stripes. This was the common style through the Middle Kingdom. Then in the New Kingdom they changed to a simpler pattern of stripes of the same width. Unfortunately, in the case of the Philadelphia Sphinx, the face is quite eroded and the upper part of the *nemes* crown preserves no stripes that might indicate a date of carving. It is really difficult to say whether the head, like that of the Herakleopolis statue, might be recarved. Can we look at some other clues to see if Ramses II carved this Sphinx or took it over from an earlier king?

Masters of Disguise

If Ramses II's sculptors recarved the Sphinx, removing the original name of an earlier pharaoh, they certainly did a good job. The inscriptions on the base and chest are well cut. Nowhere is there evidence of any earlier king's inscription that was erased or covered over. Unlike the Louvre colossal sphinx there is no obvious palimpsest inscription where a new name was inscribed over an older one leaving traces of the original hieroglyphs. Seemingly, this sphinx DID belong to Ramses II...except for one thing.

8.43.

8.42.

8.44.

8.42. The raised carving of the swag of the mane on the sphinx's shoulder.

8.43. The flat front of the mane with shallow incised lines.

8.44. The mane of a semi-maned sphinx includes the swag that hangs behind the shoulders, and the front part covering the chest and extending down to the front legs. These should be raised as in this sphinx of Senwosret III in the Metropolitan Museum, New York. [17.9.2, Gift of Edward S. Harkness, 1917. Image courtesy of The Metropolitan Museum of Art, www.metmuseum.org]

If you spend a little time getting to know the statue you will notice something quite strange. This is a magnificently carved statue. The musculature of the Sphinx's legs glisten, its ribs are delineated with care, its elbows and paws are carved with fine anatomical details and smoothly polished to perfection. Despite the damage to its head, the body of the Sphinx is a real masterpiece of ancient Egyptian sphinx carving.

But then look at the Sphinx's mane. This is the "pin-striped" area on the chest and shoulders. It is quite glaring how the workmanship there really does not match the quality of the carving you see in the rest of the statue. The lines are just lightly incised (and not even parallel to each other). Why would the sculptors have lavished so much effort on the rest of the Sphinx's body, then been careless about the appearance of the Sphinx's front—the very part that would be most visible to the viewer?

Once you notice that particular anomaly, there is something else that does not make sense. If you look up on the Sphinx's back, you will see the rear part of the mane—the swag—where it hangs down behind the Sphinx's shoulders. Here the mane is carved in *raised* relief so that it projects out from the main surface of the body. Look back now at the edge of the mane on the Sphinx's chest and in a few spots you will see that, once upon a time, the front of the mane was *also raised*. Someone carefully carved away the original mane on the front and redecorated the chest of this Sphinx, giving it a flat mane. The work is quite well done and fools

8.46.

8.45.

8.45. View of the mane on the Louvre "Lesser Sphinx." [Image courtesy of Matteo Giovanni Colnago]

8.46. Part of the titulary of Ramses II carved on the Sphinx's chest. It reads, "Lord of the Two-Lands (User-maat-Re-Setep-en-Re), Lord of Appearances (Ramses-Mery-Amun), given life eternally."

the eye, until you start wondering why the mane is raised on the shoulders and back, but flat on the front.

Like other sphinxes, the Philadelphia Sphinx would originally have had a more prominent, projecting mane. We call this form a "semi-maned" sphinx; there are also fully "maned-sphinxes" where the king's crown is replaced by a full lion's mane on the head. You see the appearance of this feature (which resembles a child's bib) on sphinxes of all periods of ancient Egyptian history. Good indications of what the Penn Museum Sphinx would originally have looked like are the two illustrated here: a small sphinx of Senwosret III (12th Dynasty) in the Metropolitan Museum (Fig. 8.44), and the "Lesser Sphinx" in the Louvre (Fig. 8.45).

So, why go to all of the effort to shave off the mane on the front and redecorate the Sphinx's chest? Originally, the mane in the front probably extended across the entire chest of the Sphinx. In the center would have been the name of the pharaoh for whom this Sphinx was first carved. Ramses II's sculptors wanted to repurpose the whole center of the chest for the titulary of Ramses II, including the king's nomen and prenomen (in cartouches). To do this they shaved away the projecting mane with its original inscription and smooth dressed the front again. Then they added the lightly incised lines giving the Sphinx back his mane and cut in the name of Ramses the Great. These were no second-rate sculptors doing a slapdash job. They were masters of granite carving and their goal was to completely appropriate the Sphinx on behalf of Ramses II. Their work simply does not quite match up to the outstanding quality of the carving of the rest of the Sphinx.

It's a Mystery: Whose Sphinx Originally?

By looking carefully at details of the carving of the Philadelphia Sphinx we see that this statue is another example of Ramses' sculptors reworking the monument of an earlier pharaoh. They did so in a masterful way that was only appropriate given the Sphinx's location in the great temple of Ptah at Memphis, one of Egypt's grand state temples. Having determined that the Sphinx was "recycled," can we make any further headway in identifying which pharaoh originally commissioned the Sphinx? Unfortunately, the Philadelphia Sphinx does not retain any vestigial inscriptions as sometimes occurs on reused statues (for instance on the Louvre colossal sphinx). The original king's name is entirely eradicated. That makes it unlikely that we can ever know for certain which pre-Ramesside pharaoh this Sphinx represents. However, we can make some suggestions about the *period* to which the Sphinx may have belonged.

Two major phases of sphinx carving in ancient Egypt are the Middle Kingdom (11th–13th Dynasties, ca. 2050–1750 BCE) and the New Kingdom (18th–20th Dynasties, ca. 1550–1050 BCE). Both of these periods represent eras of great wealth and power in Egypt. The pharaohs during these periods controlled vast resources. The royal government was very stable and able to invest funds in temple construction. This included commissioning the great stone sculptures of gods and royalty that adorned the temples. Although it is true that practically every pharaoh of ancient Egypt would have had sphinxes, the really great ones— like the Penn Museum's colossal Sphinx—primarily date to these periods when Egypt was at its peak of economic and political power.

Particularly notable monument builders were the pharaohs of the 12th Dynasty, the longest lasting and wealthiest dynasty of the Middle Kingdom. These kings built extensively and are known for having transformed many of Egypt's temples with the addition of stone pylons, gateways, and stone statuary. They had an interest in both scale and permanence. After the decline of the Middle Kingdom, however, many of the Middle Kingdom temples fared badly during a phase of political fragmentation and economic decline that we call the Second Intermediate Period. When kings of Thebes reunited Egypt, ca. 1550 BCE, and founded the New Kingdom, they began substantial reconstruction of the centuries-old temples of the Middle Kingdom. So, that is how statues of earlier pharaohs were now up for reclamation by kings such as Ramses II.

So did Ramses II recarve this Sphinx from one of his immediate predecessors, one of the kings of the earlier 18th Dynasty? Or, is it possible the statue originally dates to an even earlier age, perhaps the Middle Kingdom? Although Ramses' sculptors are unlikely to have recarved a sphinx of one of the great pharaohs of the 18th Dynasty, we do know that there are a few "discredited" pharaohs of that period whose monuments were ripe for reuse by the likes of Ramses II. One example is the female pharaoh Hatshepsut whose reign coincided with that of her nephew, Thutmose III. Although she was a great builder of monuments including sphinxes (the famous Alabaster Sphinx at Memphis might belong to her), after she died her successors removed her name from the kinglists and her monuments were either destroyed or recarved. Another example is the heretic pharaoh Akhenaten and his immediate successors of the Amarna Period, including Tutankhamun. During the time of Ramses the Great, these kings had been erased from the royal kinglists in order to expunge their memory. Similarly, their monuments were dismantled and the stone put to use elsewhere.

In the Penn Museum's Egyptian galleries, another monument illustrates this reuse of stonework belonging to Akhenaten. It too belongs to a sphinx. The object is a huge quartzite slab that is decorated on one side with scenes of Akhenaten and his eldest daughter, princess Meretaten (see Fig. 8.70). Originally, this was part of a chapel called a "Sunshade" dedicated to Meretaten. After Akhenaten's death, the chapel was vandalized and at some point, it was taken down. During the reign of Merenptah, Ramses II's son and successor, this particular block was recarved with a flat front and rounded back to form the base for a sphinx. We know from the inscriptions that the sphinx stood at a temple in the city of Heliopolis. The sphinx itself is gone (it was a separate sculpture mounted on the base), but the titulary of Merenptah wraps around the edges showing its use as a sphinx base.

During the 19th Dynasty when Ramses II ruled, the monuments of the 18th Dynasty were still largely standing and functioning. Ramses added to, and aggrandized, temples to suit his own interests but aside from the discredited Amarna Period kings, he did not engage in the extensive reappropriation of the sculptures of his immediate predecessors. The Middle Kingdom, on the other

8.47.

hand, was a far more ancient time, an era of legendary kings whose monuments had largely become defunct, abandoned, or replaced by new ones. They were a suitable target for reuse.

Because of a common pattern of the Ramesside kings reusing Middle Kingdom monuments, sphinxes, and other statues, there is a good possibility that the Penn Museum Sphinx originally belonged to one of the kings of that earlier period. The amazing carving quality of the Sphinx's granite body is on a par with the fine workmanship we see during the 12th Dynasty, for example on the Louvre colossal sphinx. The fine treatment of musculature and leonine anatomy is comparable to that we see on other Middle Kingdom sphinxes reused at the Ramessside capital city, *Per-Ramses,* and other sites.

We have already seen that Ramses II was an active builder at Memphis, substantially adding to the Ptah Temple—the *Hut-Ka-Ptah*—with huge stone portals adorned with colossal figures of the king. We have discussed how Ramses II expanded and aggrandized the temple, giving it a new name: *Glorious-is-Ramses-in-the-Domain-of-Ptah.* Consider also that the Ptah Temple was a place with a long history and major buildings nearby dating to the Middle Kingdom. What happened to sculptures such as sphinxes of that earlier era that had lost the connection to their original buildings? Reuse may have been not so much

8.47. This grainy photograph shows the quartzite gateway lintel of Amenemhat III found near the Sphinx in the area of the North Gate. The huge block measures 13 feet (3.96 m) in length and 4 feet (1.2 m) in height. This convinced Petrie of the veracity of Herodotus' account of king Moeris as the builder of the North Gate. (After Petrie, *Memphis* V, pl. lxxvii)

8.48.

a theft of earlier kings' monuments as a dutiful reworking of them (although now with the name of Ramses II being the only king's name on them).

Let us recall the legends recounted in the writings of Herodotus: that the North Gateway of the Ptah Temple was renowned for having been built by a pharaoh Moeris. Moeris is the Greek version of the name of a king of Egypt's 12th Dynasty, usually identified with Amenemhat III. Flinders Petrie, in fact, found a tremendous doorway lintel, 13 feet wide and over 4 feet high, with the name of Amenemhat III in the area of the North Gateway. He also found a huge jamb belonging to the same gateway of Amenemhat III. Petrie was convinced of the accuracy of Herodotus. If those old legends are true, could Ramses II have rebuilt the North Gateway, as he did other areas of the Ptah Temple, and had his sculptors repurpose some of the existing architecture and statues in that area? Possibly the Penn Museum's Sphinx could have originated as a sculpture of Amenemhat III that had already stood nearby for over 500 years by the time of Ramses II.

Based on everything we have seen to this point, we can propose a theory about the possible reuse of the Sphinx

8.48. An over life-size statue of Amenemhat III from the Temple of Ptah at Memphis that was reused by Merenptah, son of Ramses II. [In the Neues Museum, Berlin, ÄM 1121]

and who originally owned it. It would have been far easier for Ramses II's builders to reuse a colossal statue close to its original location. It might have originally stood in part of the temple complex constructed during the Middle Kingdom. Like the reused North Gate blocks of Amenemhat III, perhaps when Ramses II constructed his new enclosure dedicated to Ptah-Tatenen, he repurposed an existing Middle Kingdom sphinx. Could this Sphinx have belonged originally to a pharaoh such as Amenemhat III?

This theory is hard to prove or refute but, apart from Herodotus, we know that Amenemhat III was a great builder at Memphis. There is a fine example in Berlin of a statue of Amenemhat III that was reused, not by Ramses II but rather his son, Merenptah. The statue was discovered in the ruins of the Ptah Temple. Its face was left intact and bears the style of Amenemhat III. The original inscriptions, however, were removed in the 19th Dynasty and we find only Merenptah's name on the back pillar of the statue. Perhaps both Ramses II and his son were in the business of recarving existing statues of the Middle Kingdom and using them for their own purposes in the great temple enclosure of *Hut-Ka-Ptah* at Memphis.

Was the Sphinx Painted?

Just because the Sphinx looks the way it does today does not mean it always appeared that way. Apart from the recarving and new inscriptions added by successive pharaohs, three thousand years can do a lot of damage to a sphinx. Of course, its head is severely eroded, testifying to the ravages of time, but there is something else interesting about the Sphinx's original appearance: it probably was painted. Although the texture of polished granite is beautiful, we know that the Ancient Egyptians regularly painted their stone statues. For them a hard stone like granite was not just pleasing to the eye, it was first and foremost a material of enduring strength. Paint added the necessary touch of human vitality to what was otherwise just a stone image.

If it was painted why there is no paint remaining anywhere on the Sphinx? To answer that consider not only that the Sphinx is over 3,000 years old, but also that it spent much of its time before its excavation in 1912 buried in mud below the water table of the Nile floodplain. Over thousands of years, the city of Memphis has gradually been claimed by the growing height of the Nile alluvium, as well as the height of the water table, which has risen a lot since ancient times. Flinders Petrie and Ernest Mackay literally dredged this statue out of the watery muck that is the remains of the Ptah temple. (See the photographs of its excavation in Figs. 2.17a, b) In that kind of environment, the painted decoration has simply dissolved and washed away. If the Sphinx was originally painted, what did it look like? Was it entirely painted or only selective parts? What colors were used?

One way to approach these questions is to look for sphinxes from drier environments where paint has been preserved. The colossal sphinxes from Hatshepsut's mortuary temple at Deir el-Bahri provide some evidence. Like the Penn Museum's Sphinx, these are made of granite. We know there were originally six sphinxes that faced each other. They were smashed to fragments in ancient times but have been reassembled by archaeologists. Most fragments preserve

8.50.

remains of paint; the best example is the sphinx of Hatshepsut now in Berlin. The Berlin sphinx has yellow and blue stripes on its *nemes* headdress. Yellow was used for Hatshepsut's cartouche. A reddish brown was used for the skin tone. We see the same color arrangement, though not so well preserved, on the sphinx of Hatshepsut in the Metropolitan Museum.

Some good examples of the kind of painted decoration that once existed on the Penn Museum's Sphinx can be seen on other objects from the reign of Ramses II in the Penn Museum. One example of a painted colossal statue can be seen in the upper part of a mummiform figure of Ramses II from a temple at Abydos (Fig. 8.50). This statue was originally one of a series of Osiride figures (statues depicting the king in the guise of the god of the netherworld, Osiris). Only the upper part of this figure is preserved but we see here the use of red, yellow, blue, and black to highlight the collar, scepters, uraeus, and eyes of the figure. Ramses II's artisans would have applied this same basic color palette to the sphinx.

How would these colors look applied to red Aswan granite? Another artifact, not a statue but a granite sarcophagus, gives a feel of painted decoration on the same stone as the Philadelphia Sphinx. This object is the sarcophagus of a woman named Nofretmut in the Penn Museum (Fig. 8.51). This particular lady was the wife of one of Ramses II's highest governmental officials, a man named Setau who was "viceroy of Kush." Setau was the governor in charge of the land of Nubia during this time period. It was Setau who built many of Ramses II's famous temples in Nubia. Although it has not been conclusively proven, Nofretmut herself was probably a sister of Ramses II.

8.51. The painted granite sarcophagus of Nofretmut. This image shows the ibis-headed god Thoth. [UPM object # 29-87-633]

Clarence Fisher, director of the Museum's Coxe Egyptian Expedition, excavated the granite sarcophagus of Nofretmut in the necropolis of Dra Abu el-Naga at Thebes in the 1920s. The tomb of Setau and Nofretmut was severely plundered in ancient times. It was part of a large necropolis used by many of the highest officials of southern Egypt: the Viceroys of Kush, various military officials in charge of this part of the empire, as well as priests of Amun who worked in the great temple of Karnak on the east bank of Thebes. Because it comes from a dry tomb in the desert hills of western Thebes, the sarcophagus of Nofretmut, like the sphinxes of Hatshepsut, preserves its painted decoration very well. Here the background of the sarcophagus is not painted but the head—like a royal *nemes*—is decorated with stripes of yellow and black. The hieroglyphs are filled in with red. Figures of the gods have their hair, skin, and garments painted.

We can conclude that the Penn Museum Sphinx, like other colossal statues, was certainly once painted. Like the Hatshepsut sphinxes, it would have had a *nemes* of alternating yellow and blue stripes. Its uraeus may have resembled that of the Osiride Ramses from Abydos. The Sphinx's body and face were probably a reddish brown color, and perhaps the mane was highlighted in yellow. The primary area of exposed granite was probably the base. There the inscriptions were probably illuminated like on the sarcophagus of Nofretmut to make them stand out, in either yellow or blue against the bare granite background. Although it seems a shame to cover most of the beautiful granite with paint, it would have been an impressive statue to behold!

Did the Sphinx Have a Crown?

In addition to its paint, there is something else the Penn Museum Sphinx might once have had that he lost long ago: the rest of his crown. Here we are talking not about the eroded head, but some actual missing components. As we have seen, this is a "semi-maned" sphinx. The head is that of the pharaoh wearing the *nemes* headdress. A sphinx with the *nemes* alone is perfectly acceptable as a complete sphinx. In earlier periods like the Old and Middle Kingdoms, they may have stopped with the *nemes* alone. However, during the New Kingdom there is a strong preference for an additional piece of headgear on large sphinxes. If we look again at the sphinxes of Ramses II in front of the Wadi el-Sebua temple in Nubia (we saw these in the last chapter), each of these has a combination crown with the *nemes* surmounted by the Double Crown. The Double Crown is the combination of the Red Crown of Lower Egypt and the White Crown of Upper Egypt forming a single crown that symbolized the pharaoh as ruler of a united country. The pharaoh can wear these elements singly or together, or in combination with the *nemes*: a composite crown. It is quite likely that a colossal sphinx of Ramses II decorating the entrance to a temple as important as that of Ptah at Memphis would have been given a Double Crown atop the *nemes*. Since the Sphinx, as we have seen, was altered—a statue usurped from an earlier pharaoh—it probably did not come with a Double Crown, but could easily have had this element added. Of course, a tall projecting crown like this would be the first element to break off and would have vanished long ago.

Ramses II was a master of the gargantuan guardian statues. His colossi at Memphis are all toppled but in many other locations they are still standing: temples like Luxor or Abu Simbel with its four massive figures of the king carved in stone. We see these figures of the king in seated and standing pose, as well as rendered in the form of sphinxes. One thing that is quite consistent in the guardian statues of Ramses II is the preference for the full statement of royal power: the combination of crown with *nemes*, and Double Crown. This bears a symbolic message to the viewers because it emphasizes the power of the king as pharaoh of a unified and stable Egypt. Geometrically, too, the use of the combination crown adds an extra visual punch to a guardian image. It makes the statue taller and just a bit more imposing. Like a top hat or fez worn by men a century ago, this headgear added stature and authority. That is why Ramses II favored it and that is why the Philadelphia Sphinx might have lost part of his crown.

8.52. Sphinx with a double crown at the temple of Wadi el-Sebua in Nubia. [Photo by Mike Gadd]

8.52.

8.53.

8.55.

8.54.

8.53. Temple statues of Ramses II with the *nemes* and double crown at Abu Simbel. [Image courtesy of Mike Gadd]

8.54. Temple statues of Ramses II with the *nemes* and double crown at Luxor Temple. [Image courtesy of Michael Tinkler]

8.55. A close-up of one of the Luxor statues. [Image courtesy of John and Linda McMackin]

8.56. The St. Petersburg sphinxes from the temple of Amenhotep III have the double crown atop the *nemes*. [Image courtesy of Konstantin M. Koryakoff]

8.57. The block in the Penn Museum from Amenhotep III's mortuary temple shows the same or a similar sphinx pair with the double crown. [UPM object # E2096]

8.57.

8.56.

8.58.

8.58. The Penn Museum Sphinx seen from above. There is no clear evidence of a double crown. Since the top of the head is eroded, the Sphinx may have lost its crown and evidence for its attachment to the head long ago.

Before Ramses II, sphinxes with double crowns had become very prominent during the reign of pharaoh Amenhotep III in Egypt's 18th Dynasty. We see this form in the two colossal sphinxes from Amenhotep III's mortuary temple at Thebes (modern Luxor) now in St. Petersburg, Russia. The double crown appears also on the decorated block from Amenhotep III's mortuary temple in the Penn Museum. In fact, from the late 18th Dynasty onwards there are so few sphinxes without double crowns that it seems the Egyptians began to regard this as an indispensible element for a royal sphinx. Since the sphinx is a manifestation of the King-of-Upper-and-Lower-Egypt in leonine form, the double crown—which shows the pharaoh as ruler of the Two Lands—was a natural way to show this.

As we see on the St. Petersburg colossal sphinxes, for big statues these crowns were composed of separately carved elements cemented directly atop the *nemes* crown. Although the sculptors might have used a small pin or dowel to center the double crown, there was really no need for any separate element to hold it on. The base of the crown was carved so that it cups over the rounded top of the sphinx's head. The combination of a layer of gypsum mortar and gravity would have been enough to 'glue' the crown to the sphinx's head and hold it securely on.

Is there any indication on the Penn Museum Sphinx that it once sported a double crown? Here we are frustrated by the severe erosion of the head. We have already seen that this has erased clear evidence for the stripe pattern of the Sphinx's *nemes* headdress. If we look at the top of the Sphinx's head, there is no remnant of a hole for a centering pin or dowel. Nor are there any patches of mortar proving that a double crown was once affixed to the head.

However, if the Sphinx lost his double crown long ago and any sign of attachment was subsequently eroded (during a period of time when just his head was poking above ground), then it would actually be surprising to find evidence for the crown preserved on the statue. It remains an unproven but distinct possibility that the Penn Museum Sphinx—like other colossal sphinxes and guardian statues of Ramses II—was adorned with the double crown. It might be a little unsettling to picture the Sphinx with this extra appendage, but it was considered an important part of sphinxes of Ramses II.

What Did the Sphinx Originally Look Like?

Part of the charm of the granite Sphinx of Ramses II in Philadelphia is undoubtedly its time-ravaged, eroded face. The sense of mystery and antiquity behind its veiled eyes makes it a quintessential sphinx, "gazing out over the Ocean of Time" as Mark Twain said 150 years ago.

Despite this, it is entertaining to consider what the Sphinx's head originally looked like. When the Sphinx first came to the Museum in 1913, Director Gordon and Flinders Petrie corresponded over the possibility of making a cast of another statue of Ramses II in order to restore the head. Fortunately, they never did that. It would have marred the timeworn beauty of the head, and would have been essentially guesswork as to what it had looked like.

A century later, with the advantage of modern computer technology and imaging software, we can actually experiment with different possible reconstructions of the way the Sphinx might have looked. Based on what we have examined so far, we can speculate about the Sphinx's face, the use of paint, and possible addition of a double crown to try to visualize its original appearance when it stood at Memphis during the reign of Ramses II.

One of the key questions is what kind of face to restore to the statue. If it was a recarved sphinx like the Louvre colossal sphinx it may be that the statue was given new inscriptions but the face was left intact. In that case, the head could easily have still borne the face of some earlier king. On the other hand, Ramses II's sculptors often reworked the heads of statues to give them an image of Ramses II. We have

8.59. A selection of renditions of Ramses II's face on colossal and life-size statues.

Colossal seated statues, Abu Simbel

Seated colossus, Luxor Temple

Fallen colossus, Luxor Temple

Osirid colossus from Abydos, Penn Museum

Seated statue from Tanis Louvre

Seated statue from Herakleopolis Penn Museum

"Ozymandius" from the Ramesseum at Thebes, British Museum

Seated statue Museo Egizio, Turin

8.59.

seen that in the example of the seated statue of Ramses II from Herakleopolis in the Penn Museum. Let us assume that the statue had a face of Ramses II.

Over the course of Ramses II's 67-year reign, there was considerable evolution in the king's sculptural style. Nevertheless, Ramses II's sculptors developed a distinctive model, which we see on a range of statues, from statuettes to the large, colossal figures like those at Abu Simbel or on the colossi at Memphis. Faces of Ramses II differ depending on the size of the statue and type of stone used. Large figures like the seated figures of the king at Abu Simbel tend to be idealized and blocky-looking with squarish-looking cheeks and nose. Smaller-scale statues, particularly those in softer stones, have a more refined style. Perhaps the most famous image of the king (thought to be close to his actual appearance) is the diorite seated statue of the king in the Turin Museum.

The hard granite of the Penn colossal Sphinx would tend towards the more blocky appearance we see in the larger, hard-stone statuary. Probably the best indication for the style of the Sphinx is to be found in the granite dyad of Ramses II and Ptah-Tatenen. Since the Copenhagen dyad came from the very same area of the Ptah Temple at Memphis and is also carved in granite, let us adopt the face of the Copenhagen dyad as a good model for the face on the Sphinx.

If we add a face based on the Copenhagen statue we can restore the Sphinx's head to something like this:

8.60. *A restoration of the Sphinx's face.*

8.60.

But, this Sphinx was probably painted. Let us add some color to the headdress and the inscriptions to give a sense of what that might have looked like:

8.61.

8.61. A restoration with painted details.

8.62. A restoration with a double crown.

8.62.

Finally, there is a good possibility that when it stood at Memphis the Sphinx was completed with a Double Crown atop the *nemes* headdress. If we add this element, then the Sphinx comes out looking like the image to the left:

These reconstructions are, of course, based on some educated guesses about what its face might once have looked like. We cannot know for certain so it is just fun to squint at it and envision in your mind's eye what this Sphinx looked like thousands of years ago before he ever traveled to what Ramses II would have considered a remote outpost— Philadelphia.

8.63.

8.63. An assortment of Penn Museum scarabs with sphinx iconography. [UPM object #s from top left: E11506; 86-35-219; E12859 (criosphinx); E13042 (winged hieracosphinx); E13812; 55-35-2 (seated androsphinx); E11675 (seated androsphinx); 48-10-13; E12832; E15281E; E13057 (striding hieracosphinx); E13771; E12824 (recumbent hieracosphinx); E11049 (striding androsphinx atop bound enemies); E13070 (striding androsphinx); E11047]

The Museum's Many Sphinxes

While the granite Sphinx from Memphis is the largest and most impressive sphinx in the Penn Museum, it is not the only one in our Egyptian collection. The Museum houses a number of other sphinxes from different time periods and different geographical locations created in a variety of materials. How do these sphinxes compare with the red granite Sphinx?

Sphinxes were popular decorative elements for the bases of scarabs. A number of scarabs in our collection feature sphinx motifs.

Our collection also includes a number of small sphinx statuettes. Some are very fragmentary. Some are very poorly executed. Not all sphinxes are as large (or as noble looking) as the red granite Sphinx of Ramses II that resides in our Lower Egyptian gallery.

Terracotta figurines were mass-produced in molds. Most artifacts of this type date to the Ptolemaic and Roman Periods and classical or hybrid motifs are quite common. However, there are examples of terracottas with purely Egyptian iconography such as sphinxes.

The Penn Museum houses many stone architectural elements from the ceremonial palace of Merenptah at Memphis. Windows such as this limestone example served functional, decorative, and protective purposes. Placed high on the wall, the relatively small openings would allow light in, but perhaps minimize the amount of heat and dust that would enter the building. The windows are decorated with an array of religious imagery including two seated sphinxes facing

8.64.

8.65.

8.66.

8.67.

8.68.

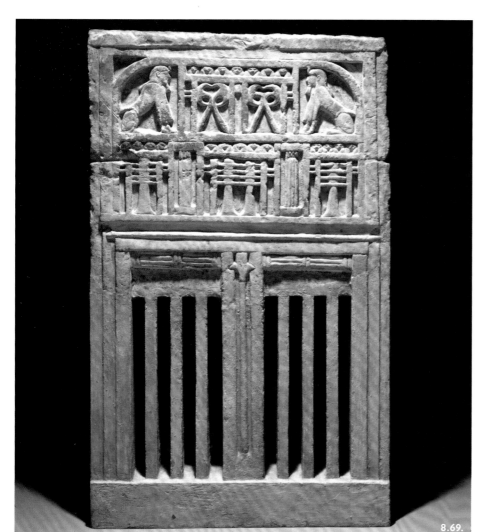

8.69.

8.64. One of the smallest and lightest of our sphinxes is a tiny electrum bead that was part of a necklace or bracelet. This sphinx dates to the Middle Kingdom and is very similar to examples in the British Museum. [UPM object #E3314]

8.65. The humble limestone sphinx is from Memphis; it was obviously not carved by a master sculptor. [UPM object # 29-75-422. Photo by Steve Minicola, University Communications]

8.66. Paw from a statue of a sphinx (or lion). The base is inscribed in both Greek and Demotic. [UPM object # E2499]

8.67. A cluster of mold-made terracotta sphinxes. All of these sphinxes were excavated at the site of Memphis by the Coxe Expedition.

8.68. Limestone window from the place of Merenptah excavated by the Coxe Expedition in 1915. [UPM object # E13564]

8.69. A close-up of one of the seated sphinxes on the window, wearing a *khat* headdress with a uraeus and a false beard.

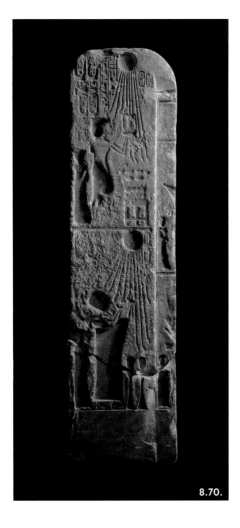

8.70.

8.71.

8.70. This quartzite relief of Akhenaten and his daughter, Meretaten, was reused as the base of a sphinx by a later king. We have no idea where this sphinx may be. [UPM object # E16230]

8.71. Sphinx on a base.

8.72. Reconstructed ebony box decorated with ivory inlays, including sphinxes, from a tomb at Karanog, Nubia. [UPM object # E7519]

towards the center of the window, many falcon heads perhaps representing the sun god Re, bound lotus flowers, and *djed* pillars. Above the vertical slits in the window the artists imitated the rolled-up reed blinds in stone.

We do have an object in our collection related to a fairly large sphinx. However, it no longer bears any sign of the sphinx with which it was once associated. The so-called Amarna Stela was originally part of a wall from a type of small religious structure known as a "Sunshade." This "Sunshade" temple was dedicated to Meretaten, the eldest daughter of King Akhenaten. The scenes on the stela show King Akhenaten with the princess Meretaten offering to the Aten. The deeply carved bodies of the royal figures, as well as the disk of the Aten once contained inlay, probably in multi-colored faience.

After the Amarna Period, artisans cut the original relief to its present size and shape, placed it face down to hide the images of Akhenaten, and reused the stone as the base for a sphinx of Pharaoh Merenptah of the 18th Dynasty. There are hieroglyphs along the sides that contain the names of this later king, the same one who added his name to our red granite Sphinx. Looking at the measurement of the base, this sphinx would have been almost 8 feet (2.5 m) long from paws to rump!

During the Meroitic Period (100 BCE–300 CE), artisans in Nubia combined Egyptian, classical motifs, and native Nubian iconography. This ebony box (Fig. 8.72) is inlaid with ivory decorations that show the variety of cultural influences. The front-facing human figures wear draped clothing in a classical style. Sphinxes and lotus flowers reflect Egyptian influence. The lion heads may represent the Nubian deity Apademak.

Boxes like this held items such as toiletry implements and jewelry. These items were used in life, but also would be desired in the afterlife and so were buried with their owners.

8.72.

8.73.

The Sphinx's Life in the Gallery Today

The Penn Museum Sphinx is today a very visible, unofficial mascot of the Museum. Since the opening day of the Egyptian gallery in 1926, countless visitors of all ages from schoolchildren to retirees have stood near his paws to listen to guides and docents tell our Sphinx's story.

Our Sphinx has been a very large guest at every event that has taken place in our Lower Egyptian gallery. From lectures to luncheons, weddings to memorial services, the Sphinx has silently stood watch for almost a century and with all of the events happening in the Museum, he is hardly ever alone.

In the spring of 2013, the Penn Museum introduced new "touch tours" for blind and visually impaired guests. The Sphinx is one of the stops on the tour. Visitors on these special tours have a chance to interact with the Sphinx in a unique way. After some light precautions (removing large rings and bracelets, using oil-removing hand wipes), guests are introduced to objects in the galleries and explore the details of scale, texture, and temperature with their hands, which gives participants a very intimate experience.

8.74.

8.73. Visitors to the Penn Museum explore the Lower Egyptian (Sphinx) Gallery and its centerpiece, the Sphinx of Ramses II from Memphis, Egypt. [Image courtesy of Jim Graham]

8.74. Jessica and Victor were married in the Lower Egyptian Gallery before the Sphinx in 2010. [Image courtesy of Robert Korb, Jr.]

8.75. The Sphinx gets into the party mood. The Penn Museum's Sphinx is probably the only ancient Egyptian sphinx that is the proud owner of a very large bespoke Santa hat made by one of the Egyptian Section's associate curators.

8.75.

A very popular program that our Sphinx is very much a part of is "40 Winks with the Sphinx," the Penn Museum's sleepover where guests get to have an overnight "expedition" at the Museum. The night's activities give young explorers a chance to discover more about ancient Egyptian history and culture. The children and their adult chaperones get to spend the night in the Museum and can set up their sleeping bags around the base of the Sphinx—a very modern version of the story we find recorded on the Dream Stele of Tuthmosis IV.

Our Sphinx inspires artists of all kinds. The Lower Egyptian gallery is often the setting for multicultural performances in music, drama, and dance. Dancing in front of the Sphinx was probably not something that often occurred at Memphis during the time of Ramses II!

The Sphinx is not shy about posing for pictures, or paintings. Bucks County artist Robert Beck visited the Penn Museum with easel, brushes, panel, and a general plan—to find the one inspirational "spot" where he could experience a "moment of discovery." He chose the Sphinx as his inspiration and created a beautiful painting of the statue.

The thousands of schoolchildren who visit the Egyptian galleries each year learn a great deal about the history, religion, culture, and art of Ancient Egypt, but it seems that on some recent gallery tours, the Penn Museum Sphinx has even helped to make math fun. One of the Penn Museum's docents, Dr. Ben Ashcom,

8.76. Singer, songwriter, and pianist Blessing Offor explores the hieroglyphs on the base of the Sphinx during a Touch Tour.

8.77. "Forty Winks with the Sphinx" advertisement.

8.78. Young explorers (in their pajamas) get ready to spend a fun night with the Sphinx during a Museum sleepover.

8.79. The local Philadelphia ensemble Magdaliz and Her Trio Crisol perform acoustic Latin music in the Lower Egyptian gallery. [Image courtesy of Tom Stanley]

8.80. Bucks County artist Robert Beck at work on his painting of the Sphinx in the Lower Egyptian Gallery.

8.81. Robert Beck's painting of the Sphinx done at the Penn Museum. The painting was shown at the Rosenfeld Gallery in Philadelphia, part of an exhibition titled "Philadelphia Heartbeat." [Image courtesy of Robert Beck]

8.82. A group of Penn Museum summer campers hears a lecture in front of the sphinx.

devised a tour of the galleries using objects on display to teach lessons in math, architecture, and engineering to students. The Sphinx was part of the tour and the kids had great fun measuring the Sphinx to try to estimate its volume and weight.

Every summer, the Penn Museum runs a summer camp called "Anthropologists in the Making." During the eight-week run of the camp, campers learn about a variety of ancient and modern cultures through scavenger hunts, art activities, games, and special guest performances. Gallery tours are a daily event and the Lower Egyptian gallery and the Sphinx are often a focus.

As part of the Penn Museum's 2013 centennial celebration of the Sphinx's arrival in Philadelphia, people were invited to pose with images of the Sphinx and send those photos to the Museum for display in the gallery and online at the Museum's website. This way, the Sphinx, which has "lived" in Philadelphia for over 100 years, gets a chance to make new friends, see the sights of his adopted city, and visit parts of the country in which he now resides.

Looking towards the future, in coming years, the Sphinx will preside over exciting new changes at the Penn Museum as the Museum embarks on a plan to renovate and reinstall the Egyptian galleries that the Sphinx now calls home. The Museum is currently examining ways to finally display the palace of Merenptah in its intended location in the Upper Egyptian hall. The vision in this redesign is to use the architectural elements of this unique palace to re-create aspects of the original appearance of the palace at Memphis. When this happens, the Sphinx will remain downstairs in the Lower Egyptian gallery. It will continue to be an ambassador from the days of Ramses the Great—greeting every visitor and presiding over every event that takes place in the expanded galleries that house the Penn Museum's remarkable Egyptian collection.

8.87.

8.83. The Phillie Phanatic, another beloved Philadelphia icon, takes a moment to pose with a "portable" version of the Penn Sphinx at Citizens Bank Park in Philadelphia. This visit to the baseball stadium was particularly nice for the Penn Sphinx, given the delays caused by the baseball World Series of 1913!

8.84. The President of the University of Pennsylvania, Dr. Amy Gutman, poses with the "portable sphinx" in her office at Penn.

8.85. Penn Museum Egyptian Section Curators, Dr. David P. Silverman, Dr. Jen Wegner, and Dr. Joe Wegner, took the portable sphinx to visit some friends in the Egyptian galleries at the Brooklyn Museum in New York.

8.86. The "portable sphinx" visits the grave of Eckley B. Coxe, Jr., in The Woodlands Cemetery in West Philadelphia.

8.87. Close-up of the "portable sphinx."

That is the story of
one artifact in the
Penn Museum . . .

...imagine how many
other stories there are!

The End

SELECT BIBLIOGRAPHY

For a general history of the University of Pennsylvania Museum of Archaeology and Anthropology, its expeditions, and collections, see:

Madeira, Percy Chester. 1964. *Men in Search of Man; The First Seventy-five Years of the University Museum of the University of Pennsylvania.* Philadelphia: University of Pennsylvania Press.

Winegrad, Dilys Pegler. 1993. *Through Time, Across Continents: A Hundred Years of Archaeology and Anthropology at the University Museum.* Philadelphia: University Museum, University of Pennsylvania.

For information about the ancient city of Memphis, see:

Anthes, Rudolf. 1965. *Mit Rahineh 1956.* Philadelphia: The University Museum, University of Pennsylvania.

Fisher, Clarence. S. 1915. "The Eckley B. Coxe, Jr. Egyptian Expedition." *The Museum Journal* (University of Pennsylvania) 6.2: 63–84.

—— 1917. "The Eckley B. Coxe Jr. Egyptian Expedition." *The Museum Journal* (University of Pennsylvania) 8.4: 211–237

—— 1921. "The Throne Room of Merenptah." *The Museum Journal* (University of Pennsylvania) 12.1: 30–34.

Harvey, Stephen P., and Melinda K. Hartwig. 2001. *Gods of Ancient Memphis.* Memphis: University of Memphis Institute of Egyptian Art & Archaeology.

O'Connor, David. 1991. "Mirror of the Cosmos: The Palace of Merenptah." In *Fragments of a Shattered Visage: The Proceedings of the International Symposium of Ramesses the Great,* ed. Edward Bleiberg and Rita Freed, pp. 167–198. Memphis, TN: Memphis State University.

The Penn Museum's Egyptian collection is world-renowned and it houses over 45,000 objects from the Predynastic period through the Pharaonic period into Greco-Roman and Coptic periods, covering the full geographical span of ancient Egypt from the Delta south to the second cataract of the Nile. For overviews of the collection, see:

Amarillo Art Center. 1983. *Archaeological Treasures of Ancient Egypt: An Exhibition Organized by the Amarillo Art Center and the University Museum, University of Pennsylvania, Philadelphia.* Amarillo, TX: The Amarillo Art Center.

Fleming, Stuart, et al. 1980. *The Egyptian Mummy: Secrets and Science.* Philadelphia: University Museum.

Milde, H. 1991. *The Vignettes in the Book of the Dead of Neferrenpet.* Leiden: Nederlands Instituut voor het Nabije Oosten.

O'Connor, David. 1993. *Ancient Nubia: Egypt's Rival in Africa.* Philadelphia: University Museum of Archaeology and Anthropology.

—— 1969. "Abydos and the University Museum: 1898–1969." *Expedition* 12.1: 28–39.

O'Connor, David, and David Silverman. 1979a. "The University Museum in Egypt: The Past. Introduction." *Expedition* 21.2: 4–8.

—— 1979b. "The University, the Museum, and the Study of Ancient Egypt." *Expedition* 21.2: 9–12.

—— 1979c. "The Egyptian Collection." *Expedition* 21.2: 13–32.

Ranke, Hermann. 1950. "The Egyptian Collections of the University Museum." *University Museum Bulletin* 15.2-3. Philadelphia: University of Pennsylvania.

Silverman, David P., ed. 1997. *Searching for Ancient Egypt: Art, Architecture, and Artifacts from the University of Pennsylvania Museum of Archaeology and Anthropology.* Ithaca, NY: Cornell University Press.

For general works on the history, literature, and culture of ancient Egypt, see:

Clayton, Peter A. 1994. *Chronicle of the Pharaohs.* London: Thames and Hudson Ltd.

Houlihan, Patrick F. 1996. *The Animal World of the Pharaohs.* Cairo: The American University in Cairo Press.

Lehner, Mark. 1997. *The Complete Pyramids.* New York: Thames and Hudson.

Lichtheim, Miriam. 1973–1980. *Ancient Egyptian Literature; A Book of Readings.* 3 vols. Berkeley: University of California Press.

Redford, Donald B., ed. 2001. *The Oxford Encyclopedia of Ancient Egypt.* 3 vols. Oxford: Oxford University Press.

Silverman, David P., ed. 1997. *Ancient Egypt.* New York: Oxford University Press.

Simpson, William Kelly, ed. 2001. *The Literature of Ancient Egypt: An Anthology of Stories, Instructions, Stelae, Autobiographies, and Poetry.* New Haven, CT: Yale University Press.

Wilkinson, Richard H. 2003. *The Complete Gods and Goddesses of Ancient Egypt.* New York: Thames & Hudson.

Discussions on the form and iconography of sphinxes can be found in:

Fay, Biri. 1996. *The Louvre Sphinx and Royal Sculpture from the Reign of Amenemhat II.* Mainz: Verlag Philipp von Zabern.

Hall, E.H. 1914. "A Granite Sphinx from Memphis." *The Museum Journal* (University of Pennsylvania) 5.2: 49–54.

Hawass, Zahi A. 1998. *The Secrets of the Sphinx: Restoration Past and Present.* Cairo: American University in Cairo Press.

Lehner, Mark. 1991. Archaeology of an Image: The Great Sphinx of Giza. Ph.D. thesis, Yale University.

Schweitzer, Ursula. 1948. *Löwe und Sphinx im alten Ägypten.* Glückstadt: J.J. Augustin.

Zivie-Coche, Christiane. 2002. *Sphinx: History of a Monument.* Ithaca, NY: Cornell University Press.

For children, there is a wonderfully illustrated storybook that tells the story of a traveling sphinx, very similar to ours:

Hartland, Jessie. 2010. *How the Sphinx Got to the Museum.* Maplewood, NJ: Blue Apple Books.